INTIMATE TIES,
BITTER STRUGGLES

Issues in the History of American Foreign Relations

Series Editor: Robert J. McMahon, The Ohio State University

In this series

*Crisis and Crossfire: The United States and the
Middle East Since 1945*
Peter L. Hahn

*Intimate Ties, Bitter Struggles:
The United States and Latin America Since 1945*
Alan McPherson

Forthcoming

*Franklin D. Roosevelt and the
International Crisis of the 1930s*
David F. Schmitz

*The Color of Empire: Race
and American Foreign Relations*
Michael L. Krenn

INTIMATE TIES, BITTER STRUGGLES

The United States and Latin America Since 1945

Alan McPherson

Potomac Books, Inc.
Washington, D.C.

Library of Congress Cataloging-in-Publication Data

McPherson, Alan L.
Intimate ties, bitter struggles : the United States and Latin America since 1945/Alan McPherson.--1st ed.
p. cm. – (Issues in the history of American foreign relations)
Includes bibliographical references and index
ISBN 1-57488-875-7 (alk. paper) -- ISBN 1-57488-876-5 (pbk. : alk. paper)
1. Latin America--Foreign relations--United States. 2. United States--Foreign Relations--Latin America. 3. Latin America--Foreign relations--1948-1980. 4. Latin America--Foreign relations--1980- 5. United States--Foreign relations--1945-1989. 6. United States--Foreign relations--1989- I. Title. II. Series.

F1418.M3728 2005
327.7308--dc22

2005054954

Potomac Books, Inc.
22841 Quicksilver Drive
Dulles, Virginia 20166

First Edition

10 9 8 7 6 5 4 3 2 1

To John Charles Chasteen, Louis A. Pèrez, Jr., and Lars Schoultz, superb Latin Americanists all.

Contents

ILLUSTRATIONS

Maps

Photographs and Drawings

SERIES EDITOR'S NOTE

FROM THE BIRTH OF THE AMERICAN REPUBLIC in the late eighteenth century to the emergence of the United States as a fledgling world power at the end of the nineteenth century, the place of the United States within the broader international system of nation-states posed fundamental challenges to American and foreign statesmen alike. What role would—and could—a non-European power play in a Eurocentric world order? The combination of America's stunning economic transformation and two devastating world wars helped shatter the old European order, catapulting the United States into a position of global preeminence by the middle decades of the twentieth century. Since the mid-1940s, it has become common to refer to the United States as a superpower. Since the collapse of the Soviet Union, America's only serious rival, and the concomitant end of the Cold War, it has become common to label the United States as the world's lone superpower, or "hyperpower," as a French diplomat labeled it in the late-1990s.

By any standard of measurement, the United States has long been, as it remains today, the dominant force in world affairs—economically, politically, militarily, and culturally.

The United States has placed, and continues to place, its own indelible stamp on the international system while shaping the aspirations, mores, tastes, living standards, and sometimes resentments and hatreds of hundreds of millions of ordinary people across the globe. Few subjects, consequently, loom larger in the history of the modern world than the often uneasy encounter between the United States and the nations and peoples beyond its shores.

This series, *Issues in the History of American Foreign Relations,* aims to provide students and general readers alike with a wide range of books, written by some of the outstanding scholarly experts of this generation, that elucidate key issues, themes, topics, and individuals in the nearly 250-year history of U.S. foreign relations. The series covers an array of diverse subjects spanning from the era of the founding fathers to the present. Each book offers a concise, accessible narrative, based upon the latest scholarship, followed by a careful selection of relevant primary documents. Primary sources enable readers to immerse themselves in the raw material of history, thereby facilitating the formation of informed, independent judgments about the subject at hand. To capitalize upon the unprecedented amount of non-American archival sources and materials currently available, most books feature foreign as well as American material in the documentary section. A broad, international perspective on the external behavior of the United States, one of the major trends of recent scholarship, is a prominent feature of the books in this series.

It is my fondest hope that this series will contribute to a greater engagement with and understanding of the complexities of this fascinating—and critical—subject.

Robert J. McMahon
Ohio State University

ACKNOWLEDGMENTS

FIRST, I WISH TO THANK HOWARD UNIVERSITY'S New Faculty Research Grant for allowing me the resources to see this project through to completion. The History Department and the College of Arts and Sciences at Howard were also supportive. Robert McMahon, the editor of this series, took a chance that a young author could pull off a survey of this type; I hope he feels the gamble paid off. At Potomac Books, Don Jacobs was an encouraging, available, and generous presence throughout the writing, and Lisa Camner and Julie Kimmel helped soften the edges of the manuscript enormously. Two outside readers gave me some of the most helpful advice I have ever received. Finally, I want to thank my wife and best friend, Cindy. We met, fell in love, and married while I wrote this book. Through it all, she proved a welcome distraction and a constant source of support, and as a therapist-in-training, she got a lot of practice nursing the anxieties of a scribbling husband.

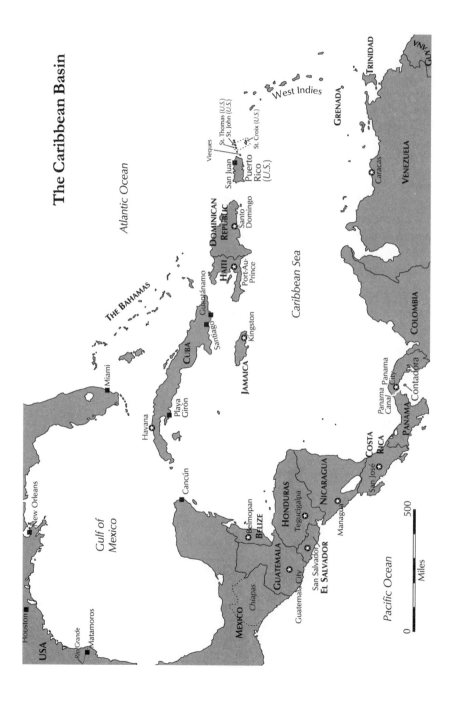

The Caribbean Basin

Caribbean Sea

GRENADA

PANAMA

TRINIDAD

South America

Caracas

Orinoco

Medellín

VENEZUELA

Georgetown

Paramaribo

Panama
Canal

Bogotá

Cayenne

COLOMBIA

FRENCH GUIANA

Quito

GUYANA

SURINAME

ECUADOR

Amazon

PERU

BRAZIL

Lima

La Paz

Brasília

BOLIVIA

Cochabamba

South
Pacific
Ocean

PARAGUAY

Asunción

Rio de Janeiro

CHILE

Pôrto Alegre

Viña del Mar

ARGENTINA

URUGUAY

Santiago

Buenos
Aires

Punta del Este

Montevideo

South
Atlantic
Ocean

0   500

Miles

Strait of
Magellan

Falkland
Islands
(administered by U.K.
claimed by Argentina)

Tierra del
Fuego

South Georgia

Introduction:
Unequal Interdependence

THE MOST IMPORTANT ASPECT OF U.S. RELATIONS with Latin America since the end of World War II has been how these two great masses of humanity from the Western Hemisphere, north and south, grew more involved in each other's existence in every way—economically, politically, militarily, socially, and culturally. Whatever the name it took—integration, interconnectedness, transnationalism, symbiosis, or intimacy—that interdependence is this book's main theme.

Interdependence became more obvious after the Cold War. The fear and drama of the U.S.-Soviet conflict from 1945 to 1991 tended to overshadow all other international relationships. When that conflict evaporated, issues that spoke to the interweaving of the two entities of the hemisphere took center stage. These issues ranged from trade liberalization to drug trafficking to immigration.

In truth, these "new" issues were quite old by 1991. The end of the Cold War did not create interdependence—it revealed it. Latin Americans had long been dependent on the United States for investment capital, technology, security, jobs, finished goods, and popular culture. U.S. citizens, meanwhile, had long looked to Latin America for fertile lands, military allies, raw materials, low-wage labor, immigrants—and yes, popular culture. After 1991 the volume of trade between the United States and Latin America continued to increase while barriers to that trade declined further still. More Latinos lived in the United States than ever, and one of every five Latin Americans was a Protestant—a major development in a traditionally Catholic region.

The argument of this book is that the intertwining of the two regions of the Western Hemisphere has been a critical feature of U.S.–Latin American relations not only since the end of the Cold War but during the Cold War as well. While many U.S. officials and observers were distracted by other areas of the world, Latin America became essential to the United

1

States and vice versa. North-South intimacies grew in size and seriousness while the East-West struggle with the Soviets raged.

Some may think that Latin America has ceased to be important to the United States in the early twenty-first century. They may observe that the U.S. government is redirecting many resources toward terrorism, the Middle East, and Asia. And this is partly true. Yet the increased focus on terrorism has also directed much high-level U.S. attention to Latin America—especially to guerrilla-ridden Colombia; to Venezuela, where, Washington suspects, President Hugo Chávez supports terrorist training; and to the always-sensitive Panama Canal region.

The United States has maintained interest in Latin America for an even more fundamental reason. In 1945 the United States and Latin America had roughly the same population—about 140 million people each. But by 2005 Latin America held almost twice the U.S. population—546 million to about 295 million. These 546 million in 2005 did not even include the roughly 40 million Latin Americans living in the United States legally and the additional 5 million or so living there illegally. As those numbers kept increasing (the Latin American population was projected to reach over 800 million by 2050), Latin America loomed ever larger in the U.S. consciousness, both as a region of 20 republics and as a cultural presence.[1] So, in an era marked by talk of globalization, anti-Americanism, and unilateral militarism, the conflation of the United States and Latin America is more relevant than ever.

Intimacy but also Struggle

This book does *not* make the case that interdependence has been either overwhelmingly good or bad for the United States or for Latin America, but it seeks to weave the theme of intimacy together with the stories of struggles for equality and dignity in Latin America. Few would deny that interdependence has been an unequal phenomenon or that many Latin Americans aimed for independence from the United States somewhat like colonies fought for separation from their imperialist centers. However, Latin America's struggles over the sixty years following World War II were not primarily about cutting off ties with the United States. They were about making the independence that already existed fairer, safer, more humane, and more respectful. U.S.–Latin American relationships were asymmetrical, hegemonic, and unfairly dominated by the United States, but they were nevertheless relationships, complex interactions between a multitude of actors at various levels. They were also relationships that deepened with time.

To be sure, this book is not free of value judgments. But a goal more useful than merely judging interdependence is to describe the *types* of interdependence that evolved since 1945, the *impact* of interdependence on governments and ordinary people, and the *resistance* to it inside and outside of Latin America. A major aspect of this book, for instance, is the continuing debate between "diffusion" and "dependency" theories, between those who argue that economic integration has meant a healthy transfer of productivity from the United States to Latin America (the diffusion model) and those who see instead a draining of resources from Latin America to the United States (the dependency model). This debate is important, first, because it has never been resolved and, second, because it can be extended beyond the economy to ask whether interdependence has been good or bad in matters ranging from security against terrorism to civil-military relations to what ends up on the dinner table. Both sides of the debate have disagreed on much, but they have generally agreed that the North and South have interwoven their societies for decades, even centuries.

Unequal interdependence hinged not only on U.S. "hard" power in Latin America, whether military or economic. It also rested on a bedrock of long expressed, deeply held, and widely shared cultural assumptions among U.S. citizens that together branded Latin American culture as inherently inferior. This cultural "branding" was the result of three levels of U.S. beliefs.

At the first level were general U.S. cultural beliefs: anti-Spanish sentiment, anti-Catholicism, and antimonarchy; antiblack racism and white supremacy; paternalism, patriarchy, and sexism; the sanctity of private property; and the fear of revolution and the belief that the Anglo-Saxon "rule of law" was the superior social order. At the second level, these general beliefs shaped more specific U.S. stereotypes about Latin American behavior—that Latin Americans were unable to govern themselves, inherently violent, economically unproductive, and easily seduced by foreign ideas. At the final level, these stereotypes helped justify U.S. policies that promoted unequal interdependence: military intervention and occupation, covert operations, support for dictators, economic domination, diplomatic arm twisting, anticommunist pressure, and cultural infiltration. Negative stereotypes, finally, made it easier for U.S. citizens to absolve themselves of any responsibility for the troubles of Latin America. Since Latin America was so inferior, how could the United States be to blame?

From Independence to Interdependence, 1783–1944

Forging links of interdependence was a long, fitful process of trial and error that was nowhere near completion in 1944. Through trade, treaties, travel, territorial expansion, and war, U.S. and Latin American citizens grew to know each other from the last of the battles pitting the British North American colonies against England in 1783 to the end of the worldwide struggle between the Allies and the Axis a century and a half later. Cultural perceptions sharpened during these encounters, and they justified or reinforced policies and passions. The process was neither planned nor smooth, but the integration of the two halves of the Western Hemisphere grew to affect every aspect of North-South relations. U.S.–Latin American interactions before 1945 can be grouped into four distinct periods: 1783–1830, 1831–97, 1898–1933, and 1934–44.

1783–1830

During the first period, 1783–1830, the hemisphere's independence from European colonialism introduced Latin America to a republic recently baptized as the United States of America, but the political and cultural distance between the two was daunting.

Colonial legacies had already set the hemisphere's two groups of Founding Fathers on different paths. British North America's rebel leaders cherished local political autonomy, individual property rights, free labor for white citizens, and the right of religious dissent. Meanwhile, Latin American "Creoles"—a term for the children of European colonists born in the New World—were far more rigorously administered by central authorities, mired in semifeudal landowning and labor systems, and uniformly Catholic. Perhaps the most telling common feature of the North American and Latin American movements for independence from Europe was that they were both headed by small, native-born social and political elites who sought to exclude women and people of color from the full rights of citizenship.

Both groups of Founders were also more concerned with strengthening their own governments than with reaching out to the rest of the hemisphere. As a result, the first decades of U.S.–Latin American relations witnessed some interaction but little integration. The new "states" in former British North America sought commerce with each other more than with foreign countries. Politically, they wanted to centralize their power against internal mob rule and against external threats from Britain, France, and Spain.

From about 1810 to 1830, therefore, when the U.S. Founding Fathers addressed the independence struggles of Latin America, they offered kind words but largely declined to put their money or their guns where their mouths were. The U.S. government did send agents to South America when the first revolutionary sparks flew, and in 1811 Congress expressed its agreement with the goals of Latin American Creoles and its readiness to establish relations once full independence was achieved. And, although distracted by war against Britain in 1812–14, President James Madison kept trading with Latin Americans rebelling against Spain. Between 1816 and 1821, the value of U.S. exports to Latin America increased by one-fifth.[2] Even the Monroe Doctrine in 1823, which stated that the United States would brook no further European colonies in the Americas, was meant partly to encourage Latin American independence.

Yet the disdain of the U.S. Founding Fathers toward Latin Americans contradicted these friendly overtures. In 1821 Secretary of State John Quincy Adams listed what he thought were unchanging faults in Latin America's own Founding Fathers:

> I wish well to their cause; but I have not yet seen and do not now see any prospect that they will establish free or liberal institutions of government. . . . Arbitrary power, military and ecclesiastical, is stamped upon their education, upon their habits, and upon all their institu-

tions. Civil dissension is infused into all their seminal principles. War and mutual destruction are in every member of their organization, moral, political, and physical. I have little expectation of any beneficial result to this country from any future connection with them, political or commercial.[3]

The same year as Adams's comment, only about 2 percent of U.S. exports were sent to Latin America.[4] Most U.S. observers shared Adams's cultural distrust of Latin Americans' alleged fatal flaws: their inability for self-rule, their undeveloped economy, and their "priest-ridden" religion that kept them mired in ignorance and subservience.[5] The elder John Adams, John Q.'s father and a former president, wrote to Thomas Jefferson in his old age that "a free government and the Roman Catholick religion can never exist together in any nation or Country. . . . I have seen such a prostration and prostitution of Human Nature to the Priesthood in old Spain as settled my judgment long ago, and I understand that in new Spain it is still worse, if that is possible."[6]

As Adams's comments suggested, anti-Spanish stereotyping accounted for part of the distrust the United States now extended to Latin America. An exaggerated "black legend" of Spain's abuses in the New World was common in the nineteenth-century United States. This legend characterized Spanish civilization as lazy and immoral and as having unleashed a cruel conquest of the New World. "Naturally weak and effeminate," U.S. students learned in school, Spaniards "dedicate the greatest part of their lives to loitering and inactive pleasures. Luxurious without variety or elegance, and expensive with great parade and little convenience, their character is nothing more than a grave and specious insignificance."[7]

In 1822, the U.S. government recognized the independence of Spanish America—three years before any European government—yet, as a result of its disregard for its southern neighbors, little followed from that recognition. All loans, grants, and military expeditions headed to Latin America had already come to an end.

Venezuela's own hero of independence, Simón Bolívar, grew disenchanted by what he perceived to be U.S. hypocrisy. In 1806, when Bolívar's compatriot Francisco Miranda organized raids against the Spanish, Madison, who was then Secretary of State, failed to provide the support that Miranda had been given to believe was coming. In 1810, when the Venezuelan elite declared the nation's independence, again the U.S. government refused to support it. One Venezuelan diplomat expressed the bitter lesson learned: "Every day I am more persuaded that it is necessary for each country to rely on its own resources; foreign aid always depends upon the rewards that are expected."[8]

Partly in self-defense, therefore, Bolívar kept the United States at arm's length of the inter-American conference of 1826. "The North Americans . . . are foreigners to us," he grumbled. He feared that, for "selfish" reasons, U.S. citizens would be his "greatest opponents."[9] "There is at the head of this great continent," he warned in 1822, "a very powerful country, very rich, very warlike, and capable of anything."[10] Latin American elites expressed shock at the bluntness of U.S. racism and the overt embrace of slavery in the former British colonies. Any friendly alliance with the United States would have to wait. Besides, for the moment, the foreigners who mattered to Creoles far more than U.S. citizens were the financiers, merchants, and intellectuals of Madrid, Paris, and London.

1831–1897

The second period in U.S.–Latin American relations began in the 1830s, when Latin American independence was secure but the twin U.S. anxieties over slavery and territorial expansion began to collide in a fatal run-up to the U.S. Civil War of 1861–65. Until 1897, this period distinguished itself from the one previous by its aggressive U.S. land expansion and from the one following by the largely continental limits of that expansion. This period also witnessed increased interactions between U.S. citizens and Latin Americans, both in and out of government. Shared trade and land began to cement long-standing ties. Yet violent clashes and cultural disdain equally led to abiding resentments on both sides.

In 1836, when settlers in Texas declared themselves independent from Mexico, the first sustained interaction between the United States and Latin America occurred. The United States swallowed up a population of about eighty thousand Spanish-speaking Mexicans in Texas and the surroundings territories. The encounter between these *tejanos* and white U.S. citizens set several precedents.

First, it revealed to Latin Americans the white settlers' hunger for land. The Louisiana Purchase of 1803 and the wresting of Florida in 1819 had already shown settlers that French- and Spanish-speaking territories could be severed from their empires with relative ease. The momentum set by these acquisitions contributed to what became known as "Manifest Destiny" in the 1840s, a nationalist zeal to turn the United States into a landmass stretching from the Atlantic to the Pacific, dominated by white Protestants.

Second, the Mexican War of 1846–48 established long-lasting stereotypes of Latin Americans in U.S. minds. It introduced ambitious, racist, often volunteer U.S. soldiers and settlers to a particularly rough type of frontier society in Mexico—populated disproportionately by subsistence farmers, bandits, prostitutes, and *vaqueros* (cowboys).[11] The new U.S. arrivals imagined that the "wild west" reality of this encounter justified war and plunder. In 1835 one U.S. Army officer in New Mexico thought he recognized something in those who spoke Spanish around him. They were "the meanest looking race of people I ever saw, [and] don't appear more civilized than our Indians generally. Dirty, filthy looking creatures." One Californian described Spanish Americans in his state as "an essentially amoral and childlike people."

These stereotypes soon included not only all Mexicans but all Latin Americans. One U.S. woman traveling through the Isthmus of Panama described the "natives" there as "impetuous and excitable." Their "tempestuousness," she added, "was further aggravated by their tendency to drink, gamble, and fight." For many, the best political regime for such a civilization was an authoritarian one. As another traveler to Central America and Mexico reasoned, "[Dictatorship] is a form of government not entirely unfitted to a people in the bulk utterly indifferent as to who or what rules them so [long as] they are left to loaf in their hammocks in peace."[12]

Third, once Mexico lost the war in 1848, the United States established a key precedent: only lands where a European-American majority could exist would become U.S. territory. U.S. lawmakers clearly saw Mexicans—and again, most Latin Americans—as a "mongrel" race that the United States must avoid becoming. One U.S. proconsul to Mexico, who called his hosts "an ignorant and immoral race," was of the opinion that miscegenation between Spaniards and indigenous people "contributed to render the Mexicans a more ignorant and debauched people than their ancestors had been."[13] And again, cultural stereotyping came with a policy consequence: the refusal to annex all of Mexico. As one senator explained in 1847, "Mexico and the United States are peopled by two distinct and utterly unhomogenous races. In no reasonable period could we amalgamate."[14] The famous "color line" thus hugged the shores of the Rio Grande.

Before the Civil War, the Caribbean and Central America, too, were sites of military struggle and cultural stereotyping. Starting in 1831, when the Nat Turner slave rebellion scared Southern slaveholders into an archconservative defense of slavery, only additional lands seemed capable of safeguarding the "peculiar institution" from "Northern aggression." Many slaveholders therefore looked not only west for those lands but also south, to the Caribbean area, where there lay militarily weak nations with a climate perhaps suitable for plantation agriculture and a population in some cases already coerced into bound labor. Expanding slavery would not only enrich the South, but it would increase the power of slave states in Washington, D.C., by adding senators and representatives to Congress.

And so, with the often-open blessing of Southern politicians and other patrons, modern pirates took off to conquer foreign lands with a fervor worthy of Manifest Destiny. In the 1850s several "filibusterers"—the word came from the Dutch *vrijbuiter* or "freebooter," denoting pirates who plundered the Spanish West Indies—plotted raids on Cuba and other Latin American lands in the hopes of annexing them as slave states. All failed.

The most notorious—and temporarily successful—filibusterer was William Walker. Known as the "Grey-Eyed Man of Destiny," Walker was a Tennessean who, leading only fifty-eight men, seized and held Nicaragua from 1855 to 1857. At various times during those two years, he drew on support from U.S. entrepreneurs, U.S. politicians, and the Nicaraguan Liberal Party. He got himself elected president of Nicaragua, and then he declared the country open to slavery. He wanted to save Nicaragua from itself. He called it "a country for which nature has done so much and man little; and the effect of even what little man had done was marred by the constant signs of revolutionary violence."[15] After wreaking violence of his own, in mid-1857 Walker was forced to abandon Nicaragua. In 1860 the British captured him and handed him over to the Hondurans. The Hondurans shot him. In response to the adventurism of Walker and others, Latin American delegates held a conference to insist on their territorial integrity.

Between the Civil War and the War of 1898, U.S.–Latin American relations were more peaceful. U.S. imports from Latin America remained steady while U.S. exports heading southward doubled.[16] Land grabs in these years were more focused on Alaska and the Pacific Islands. Yet in the lands taken by the U.S. after the Mexican War, tejanos and Native Americans, both previously majorities in wide-open spaces, soon found themselves minorities surrounded by white settlers who took up all the best lands. Among former Mexicans, many families lost their fortunes while some prospered in distinctly Mexican towns. From 1870 to 1912, Mexico attracted more U.S. direct investment than any other country in the world.[17]

From 1831 to 1897, Latin American elites increasingly expressed their fear of U.S. expansion and their cultural disdain for U.S. civilization. In 1856 Francisco Bilbao of Chile analyzed the South-North relationship as having a distinctly "we" and "they" tone: "We prefer the social to the individual, beauty to wealth, justice to power, art to commerce, poetry to industry, philosophy to textbooks, pure spirit to calculation, duty to self-interest."[18] By the end of the century, Latin American intellectuals developed a full-blown movement based on these differences. Called "Arielism" after Uruguayan José Enrique Rodó's 1900 essay "Ariel," the movement held that Latin America harbored a more genteel, sophisticated, and "spiritual" culture than did the money-driven, materialist, crude United States. Countless poems, novels, songs, journals, and organizations expressed this sense of superiority. This school of thought was a reaction partly to the particular savagery of U.S. capitalism in the Gilded Age and partly to the fact that Latin American elites identified more with European than with U.S. standards of culture. This identification eventually changed as more Latin Americans studied in U.S. schools and learned from U.S. publications and practices.

Without paying much attention to the opinions of elite Latin Americans, in the 1890s the U.S. government prepared to assert its predominance over Latin America. Several factors drove U.S. policymakers south. First, they lived in an era of global imperial competition, when great powers carved up pieces of Asia, the Near East, and Africa. Second, economic depression in the 1890s moved Congress and corporations to crave expansion southward to provide a market for U.S. goods and cheap lands for U.S. investors. Secretary of State James Blaine explained in 1890, "we have developed a volume of manufactures which . . . overruns the demands of the home market. . . . Our great demand is expansion. I mean expansion of trade with countries where we can find profitable exchanges. We are not seeking annexation of territory. At the same time I think we should be unwisely content if we did not seek to engage in what the younger Pitt so well termed the annexation of trade."[19]

Third, U.S. citizens had already been long involved in Latin America. Plenty of U.S. missionaries were slowly converting Catholics to Protestantism, and U.S. trade and investment there had existed for at least a century. Finally, Latin America remained, in the U.S. imagination, a passive land of dark-skinned natives and corrupt Creoles who were of little threat to the outside world but were perpetually unable to achieve stability and prosperity without the help of a "higher" civilization such as that of the United States.

In July 1895 Secretary of State Richard Olney sent a message to London that signaled U.S. intervention in a boundary dispute between Venezuela and Great Britain. London had long refused U.S. requests for arbitration, and now Olney demanded it outright. Olney stated first that no European power should subjugate any American state to its whims. Then he plainly stated that the United States was now making the rules in the hemisphere: "To-day the United States is practically sovereign on this continent, and its fiat is law upon the subject to which it confines its interposition."[20] The secretary threatened U.S. intervention, and the confrontation might have prompted a war with Britain if Britain had not accepted a compromise. The Olney Declaration, as this episode came to be called, proved a major step in the transition from European—and specifically British—imperialism to U.S. predominance in the Americas.

1898–1933

The third period in pre-1945 U.S.–Latin American relations extended from the War of 1898 to the development of the Good Neighbor Policy in 1933. This period established the pattern of informal control—called hegemony—that marked the biggest step in creating unequal interdependence for the rest of the twentieth century. It began with a bang—literally—when the USS *Maine* blew up in Havana harbor on February 15, 1898, killing 266 U.S. sailors on board. The sinking of the *Maine*—it may or may not have been a Spanish attack, and the matter has never been settled—offered a golden opportunity to those who wanted to pull the United States into the ongoing anticolonial war that Cuban rebels had fought for years against Spain. The clash that followed in the spring was, as Secretary of State John Hay said, a "splendid little war" for the United States. In a few short months, the industrial juggernaut of the United States easily defeated the waning navy of the Spanish. The victory gave the United States control over the fate not only of Cuba but also of Puerto Rico, Guam, and the Philippines, all possessions lost by the Spanish. The United States was now a global power.

Shortly after its victory in the Caribbean, which soon became known as the "American lake," the U.S. government moved to secure the area's key ports and sea-lanes. Bases rose on many islands, perhaps the most important being in Guantánamo Bay, Cuba. And most important, in 1903 the Theodore Roosevelt administration fomented a revolution of Panamanian patriots against Colombia. The successful outcome of this revolution made Panama a republic and secured for the United States the right to occupy a ten-mile-wide slice of land in that tiny isthmus of Central America. There, engineers from the United States and laborers from all over Latin America and the West Indies proceeded with the greatest engineering feat in history up to that point: the Panama Canal. The canal opened in 1914, by which time the United States had overtaken not only Spain but also England as the primary foreign power in Latin America. In 1904 Roosevelt moved beyond Panama to the Dominican Republic, where he established U.S. control over the country's customs receipts in order to, as he said, "show those Dagos that they will have to behave decently."[21]

The increased importance of the Caribbean area to the United States became clearer still once World War I began in 1914. President Woodrow Wilson feared that a hostile power such as Germany would take the war to the Caribbean. To combat the possible threat, Wilson reneged on his promise not to occupy any more land in Latin America and ordered the navy to take over Haiti (1915–34) and the Dominican Republic (1916–24).

Cultural and racial disdain again reinforced these decisions. U.S. attitudes toward Haiti's black population, for instance, had long been negative. Before the Civil War, this white bias was based on the fear among Southern planters that the example set by Haiti, whose slaves had successfully revolted against their French masters, might spark a similar revolution in the United States. For that reason, the U.S. government did not recognize Haiti until more than half a century after its independence, in 1862, and U.S. policymakers continued to keep the Caribbean nation isolated from world commerce. During the occupation begun in 1915, U.S. racism toward Haiti again was again conditioned by racism at home. U.S. colonial leaders enforced Jim Crow in Haiti, where they also revived outdated laws forcing Haitians to build roads without pay. When Wilson's secretary of state William Jennings Bryan was informed of the situation in Haiti, he exclaimed, "Dear me, think of it—niggers speaking French!"[22]

Such sentiments were not limited to lands that were home to blacks. In 1927 former Secretary of War Henry Stimson observed, for instance, that U.S. intervention in Nicaragua was necessary because Nicaraguans "were not fitted for the responsibilities that go with independence and still less fitted for popular self-government."[23] The years 1898 to 1933 witnessed over thirty-five armed U.S. interventions not only in Cuba, Haiti, and the Dominican Republic but also in Costa Rica (1921), Guatemala (1920), Honduras (1903, 1907, 1911, 1912, 1917–22), Panama (1903–14, 1921, and 1925), Mexico (1913, 1914, 1916–17, 1918–19), and Nicaragua (1909–10, 1912–25, and 1926–33).

Between 1898 and 1933, the question was not would the United States penetrate further into Latin America (and vice versa), but how. Historians have called the U.S. pattern of expansion a "new empire," mostly because it did not call for annexation of new lands. What it *did* call for, first, were arrangements that gave U.S. officials significant control over Latin American foreign relations. The cleverest embodiment of this informal imperialism was the Platt Amendment, muscled into the Cuban Constitution in 1901. The Platt Amendment allowed the United States to build naval bases in Cuba, oversee its foreign debts, approve its treaties, and intervene to restore "stability" in its internal politics. As a result, interventions in Cuba followed frequently: 1898–1902, 1906–1909, and 1917–22. Platt-like arrangements—formalized or not—became the norm in most of Central America and the Caribbean through 1933.

Also typical in this period was the southward expansion of U.S. business. From 1900 to 1929, U.S. exports to Latin America grew by 750 percent and ran the gamut of consumer goods, from electric irons to radios to automobiles. In roughly the same period, U.S. private investment catapulted 1,200 percent, mostly in sugar, copper, oil, bananas, and coffee.[24] This expansion was so ambitious and almost religious in tone that one historian called it "the revolutionary mission."[25] Entrepreneurs such as Minor Keith and Sam "the Banana Man" Zemurray, who both developed giant fruit plantations in Central America, not only shipped fruit back home but aimed to change the very culture of Latin American economic life. They wanted it to be more productive, consumerist, and responsive to private enterprise. They and U.S. government officials shared a sincere belief that they improved Latin America by increasing material wealth, work discipline, individual achievement, and social justice. Washington collaborated with these capitalists by encouraging concessions of government land to corporations, the loosening of land-ownership laws, and the signing of "reciprocity" treaties that reduced tariffs on agricultural goods going to the United States and finished products going to Latin America.

Neither the diplomatic, military, nor business integrations of the hemisphere went unanswered by Latin Americans. At every turn, they fought not to cut off all ties with the United States but to alter what they perceived to be unequal terms of interdependence. When the United States defeated Spain in Cuba, for instance, Cuban patriots resented how their newfound "independence" left them with little actual freedom. When the marines occupied Haiti, Nicaragua, and the Dominican Republic, peasants rose up in violent guerrilla struggles to fight back Yankee troops or to put an end to forced labor. In the cities, meanwhile, journalists and politicians wrote antioccupation pamphlets, organized street protests, and pushed Washington for the withdrawal of the marines. And finally, the growth of U.S. business in Latin America, while often welcome by those who enjoyed its steady wages and consumer goods, also met resistance. Land squatters, for instance, petitioned local governments and courts to gain the right to own the plots they had always worked rather than hand them over to already large U.S. interests.

These upheavals against the most offensive aspects of U.S. expansion helped convince U.S. presidents Herbert Hoover (1929–33) and Franklin Roosevelt (1933–45) to find a different path of interdependence. "Never before in our history have we had fewer friends in the Western Hemisphere than we have today," observed Roosevelt when he was still governor of New York in 1928.[26] Hoover agreed. While president, he began to articulate a noninterventionist model of U.S.–Latin American relations and pushed to withdraw troops from the Caribbean. When Roosevelt became president in 1933, this model became widely known as the Good Neighbor Policy. The clearest manifestations of this policy were the rescinding of the Platt Amendment, the withdrawal of U.S. troops from the circum-Caribbean, and the forswearing of any further armed intervention in the hemisphere. As intended, those steps created an enormous reservoir of good will toward the United States and specifically toward Roosevelt.

1934–1944

The goal of the Good Neighbor Policy was never to leave Latin America entirely. The Roosevelt administration in fact increased the interdependence of the United States and Latin America from 1934 to 1944. It placed great emphasis on treaties increasing two-way commerce and developed closer ties to rulers who, thanks to U.S. interventions, enjoyed apparatuses that both united their nations under a central state and integrated that state more closely into U.S. plans for the hemisphere. New paved roads, telegraph wires, and especially well-trained and well-supplied armies were now in place to allow local leaders to do the job that the marines traditionally did—to ensure political and financial "stability." Indirectly out of the Good Neighbor Policy, therefore, rose cruel and corrupt dictators such as Anastasio Somoza in Nicaragua and Rafael Trujillo in the Dominican Republic. In Cuba, the State Department withheld recognition of a reformist government in 1933 and 1934, in effect pressuring Cuban reformists to yield to a more hard-line regime under the control of future dictator Fulgencio Batista.

Roosevelt's timing in securing the pacification and collaboration of Latin American governments was impeccable. He needed them when war erupted in Europe in late 1939. Soon, the Axis powers—Germany, Japan, and Italy—launched aggressions in much of the world. This included warfare in the Caribbean, which began in mid-February 1942 when a German U-boat sank five oil tankers near Aruba. With so few allies left in Europe and Asia, one congressman argued that "the future of the United States lies to the south, and if we bend our efforts to effecting closer relationships with Latin America we will never worry about getting entangled with the petty quarrels of old Europe."[27] Thankfully for the United States, as a show of solidarity, nine Central American and Caribbean governments declared war on Japan within days of the attack on Pearl Harbor. All others, except Argentina, soon broke relations with the Axis.

Latin American leaders also allowed military integration with the United

States during the war. Cuba, Nicaragua, Panama, Mexico, Puerto Rico, and Brazil were particularly crucial partners in letting the U.S. military build airfields and naval bases on their territory and use their ports as stopovers on their way across the Atlantic. The United States also acquired from the British a string of Caribbean island bases in exchange for destroyers. Brazil and Mexico even sent troops to the war. A quarter million Mexicans served, and over a thousand died in combat.[28]

War fever spread. In Costa Rica, crowds damaged German-owned property, carrying signs that read, "Now it's not just Hitler, it's all Germans."[29] And the United States collaborated with Latin American governments to deport over four thousand Germans living in Latin America (along with Japanese and Italians) into prison camps in the United States. (In a strange twist, this effort threw together innocent German Jews with anti-Semitic Nazis!)[30]

During the war, the United States also needed Latin America for economic reasons. The region was both a seller of crucial foodstuffs and raw materials and one of the only consumers of U.S. finished goods left in the world. Inter-American relations were not without their tensions during World War II—especially as the United States kept the prices of raw materials artificially low and displaced many peasants with its new military installations. But overall the Western Hemisphere stood together against totalitarianism.

The U.S. government increased its cultural links to Latin America with equal vigor during the war, especially through the newly created Office of the Coordinator of Inter-American Affairs. Headed by Nelson Rockefeller, the office notably opened a Motion Picture Section, which recruited Walt Disney into making films that would encourage cooperation against the Axis. *Saludos Amigos!* (1943) and *The Three Caballeros* (1945) were its most famous cartoons, which featured Donald Duck and his friend, a green parrot called José Carioca, who taught Donald all about his neighbors to the south.

Finally, during World War II, another kind of integration accelerated— Latin American immigration to the United States. With it came both opportunities and problems. On one hand, Mexican workers saw the chance for a better material life in the Bracero Program. Launched in 1942 by an agreement between Washington and Mexico City, the Bracero Program recruited mainly unskilled young males to cross the border on temporary work permits in railroad construction and agriculture. With so many U.S. men at war, the demand for this temporary labor was high. The supply was there, too. During the first year of the program, Mexicans crossing northward increased from 4,142 to 75,923. In all, 4.5 million *braceros* found their way north before the end of the program in 1964.[31]

On the other hand, with immigration came conflicts. First, migration across the Rio Grande had never been severely regulated before. Now that it was, a new category of "illegal aliens" from Latin America appeared, since many temporary workers overstayed their permits and settled in the United

States. Second, in the middle of World War II, some groups of white U.S. citizens saw immigrants, especially those of mixed race, as less than patriotic or even treasonous. Suspicion turned violent in June 1943, when U.S. sailors in Los Angeles attacked Mexican American youths wearing "zoot suits." Even though Mexican-Americans were overrepresented in the war effort, their insistence upon distinguishing themselves met with a xenophobic, often racist, reaction.

The so-called Zoot-Suit Riots illustrated larger dynamics that continued after the Allied victories in Europe and Asia. After World War II Latin Americans pursued broad economic and social goals that were similar to those of U.S. citizens—peace, prosperity, democracy, and equal rights under the law.

At the end of World War II, U.S.–Latin American relations operated on a fairer, more hopeful footing than perhaps they ever had. The democratic impulse was growing throughout the Americas. Dictators fell, labor unions demanded better working conditions, and new middle classes took shape in the cities. A long-term movement—what one historian called "the Western Hemisphere Idea"—seemed to be culminating. This "anti-European idea" imagined a growing solidarity among the nations of the hemisphere based on distinct shared commitments to republican government and political freedoms.[32] U.S. Secretary of Agriculture Henry Wallace described such an idea in 1939.

> We are challenged to build here in this hemisphere a new culture which is neither Latin American nor North American but genuinely inter-American. Undoubtedly it is possible to build an inter-American consciousness and an inter-American culture which will transcend both its Anglo-Saxon and its Iberian origins.[33]

What happened next—the U.S. adoption of a Cold War lens that distorted events in Latin America—was not inevitable. It was a choice pursued by Washington and its allies in Latin American governments. The failure to sustain the Good Neighbor spirit in the postwar era was a result of the continuing sense of cultural superiority toward Latin Americans that U.S. observers had expressed at mid-century.

About This Book

This book pursues the theme of unequal interdependence and uses a chronological approach to the major trends and events of the post–World War II era. It includes in its definition of Latin America all the Spanish-speaking republics of the Western Hemisphere, plus two other countries speaking Latin-based languages, Brazil and Haiti. Its focus is not only on state-to-state relations but also on any other relations between U.S. citizens and Latin Americans that became larger issues in these societies. It begins with this short introduction to U.S.–Latin American relations before 1945. Its five main chapters then coalesce loosely around decades but also around major turns in U.S.–Latin American relations—a new president, a revolution, a change of tack in the Cold War, and so on. To help show how historians write history, it reproduces illustrations and documents that convey themes discussed in its chapters. This book is informed by the best secondary literature on U.S.–Latin American relations available today and on the latest declassifications of historical documents and the freshest news stories as of mid-2005. It is aimed at students and at a general public who wish to understand the importance of those relations, and, hopefully, to move the inevitable growth of hemispheric interdependence in a more positive direction.

CHAPTER 1

CHILLS

Cold War, Dictatorship, and Rising Expectations,
1945–1958

I N **FEBRUARY 1947 THE OPENING** of the first Sears department
store in Mexico was a hit; shoppers mobbed the store. In the first two
weeks alone, they bought more than $1 million worth of cheap yet
well-made consumer goods, from dolls to toasters to ready-to-wear shirts.
The Sears opening marked a milestone of sorts for U.S. relations with Latin
America, indicating that U.S. influence could be accepted south of the Rio
Grande if that influence adapted to local conditions. U.S. managers successfully transferred their business model. They offered a great variety on their
shelves, restocked goods quickly, and did it all with a small markup. The
promise of "democratization" through consumption had arrived. At the
same time, Sears bowed to Mexico's national and religious identities, hiring
Mexicans to work its store and marketing slyly to Mexican men and women.
Knowing the populace would react with less suspicion to a *gringo* store if it
were approved by the highest spiritual authority in the 95-percent-Catholic
country, Sears sealed the deal by inviting the Mexican archbishop to the
grand opening festivities. The archbishop showed up, blessed the store, and
set it on its way.[1]

The Mexican embrace of Sears reflected the growth of interdependence amid conflict that characterized U.S.–Latin American relations in the
decade or so after World War II. The war sparked great changes in inter-
American affairs as the Western Hemisphere largely united to fight what it
considered the evil of fascism. A coming together of this kind intensified
integration and made Latin Americans hungry for a higher standard of
living and more democracy.

But the war also created a new split in world politics. In one direction
went the countries led by the United States; in the other, those under the
control of the Soviet Union. The Cold War reduced the influence of Latin
America in the world. It also boosted dictators, who sought military integration at the expense of social integration. The tension between potential

prosperity and the spread of fear made 1945–58 a disappointing period for Latin Americans, who saw the lofty promises of World War II go unfulfilled. The disillusion exploded in anti-U.S. anger and foretold the coming to power of a new generation.

From World War Cooperation to Cold War Bipolarity

As the Cold War settled on the North Atlantic from 1945 to 1948, it rippled through inter-American relations. Arrangements between U.S. and Latin American diplomats that in 1945 had focused on strengthening hemispheric unity suddenly became far more about addressing U.S. concerns about Soviet advances. While Latin America's middle-class reformers felt both betrayed and neglected by their northern neighbors, U.S. policymakers rationalized their chummy relations with ruthless dictators by resurrecting traditional images of Latin Americans as unfit for self-government.

As World War II ended, two conferences convened that promised to promote Latin American interests not just within the hemisphere but also throughout a newly integrated world. The consensus on extending antifascist cooperation was broad because both North and South needed each other. After the war, one-quarter of U.S. exports were destined for Latin America, as were more than one-third of U.S. foreign investments.[2]

Standard Oil drilling rigs along the shoreline of Lake Maracaibo, Venezuela, 1944. During World War II, one of the principal U.S. interests in Latin America, and the principal interest in Venezuela, was the extraction of petroleum. The Venezuelan government by and large enjoyed the taxes it generated, but not the pollution or the perceived loss of sovereignty. Photo by John Vachon.

The World War II Conferences:
Chapultepec and San Francisco, 1945

The first inter-American conference brought delegates to the ancient Aztec palace of Chapultepec, in Mexico City, from February 21 to March 8, 1945. As its name implied, the Inter-American Conference on the Problems of War and Peace bridged the war and postwar periods. The Act of Chapultepec that resulted applied to the Western Hemisphere the principle of collective security: an attack on one country should be considered an attack on all. Thus, the biggest country in the hemisphere would have to defend the smallest from outside attack no matter the circumstances. For Latin American delegates, so far so good. This made official the end of U.S. military intervention in their countries, a commitment that the Good Neighbor Policy had made unofficial. Conference attendees also vowed to refuse refuge to officials from the Axis powers and continued anti-Axis sanctions. To top off the spirit of cooperation, all declared a "fervent adherence to democratic principles." No quarter of the Western Hemisphere would be given to fascism. The Act of Chapultepec was the crowning achievement of President Franklin Roosevelt in Latin American affairs.

It was also his last. One month after the meeting in Mexico, Roosevelt suffered a fatal brain hemorrhage as the founding conference of the United Nations (UN) convened in April 1945 in San Francisco. Latin Americans saw this second conference as a confirmation of their newly expanded role in world diplomacy. Compared to African and Asian peoples, who still largely lived under colonialism and could not send delegates, Latin Americans participated fully. They made up two-fifths of the votes at the UN General Assembly. They notably helped pass Articles 51 and 52 of the UN Charter, which allowed for regional UN-type organizations.

These achievements on the world stage reflected a broader optimism about democracy and unity among U.S. citizens and Latin Americans. Idealistic U.S. citizens, called "One Worlders," dreamed of a soon-to-be global government under which all societies would respect political freedoms and adopt free markets. Latin Americans expressed this optimism by pushing their governments to be more open and fair, and as a result, democratic regimes suddenly took hold in Latin America. In 1944, of the twenty Latin American republics, only Uruguay, Chile, Costa Rica, and Colombia could call themselves representative democracies—societies ruled by elected civilians who respected basic liberties. Two years later, only five—Paraguay, El Salvador, Honduras, Nicaragua, and the Dominican Republic—could *not*.

What happened? Local struggles and global trends complemented each other to the benefit of democracy. Urbanization and literacy made inroads, and the middle classes and organized workers took down dictatorships one at a time. The worldwide victory of democracy over fascism helped. The U.S. government played little direct role in the rise of these democracies, but it did encourage them through propaganda and the extension of recognition and aid. The new Latin American democracies were so open that communist parties operated legally—as the U.S. Communist Party did throughout the Cold War—and even spearheaded some antidictatorial movements. As a result, several of these new regimes operated from the left of the political center. Most powerful among these were those of Democratic Action in Venezuela, the American Popular Revolutionary Alliance in Peru, and the Auténticos in Cuba. These parties had charismatic civilian leaders as well as broad support among the middle classes, workers, and some peasants. They were also wise enough to be friendly with Washington.

Cold War and U.S. Paternalism

Soon however, U.S.–Latin American relations felt the chill of the Cold War. U.S. officials and their Western European allies accused Soviet leader Joseph Stalin of going back on the promises he had made during World War II to evacuate his Red Army from Eastern Europe and the Middle East and to allow local populations to choose their own governments. In early 1946 former British prime minister Winston Churchill declared gravely that an "iron curtain" was falling between Eastern and Western Europe. In addition, in the wrecked cities and countrysides of France, Italy, and elsewhere on the western side of the curtain, socialist and communist parties rose in popularity. When insurgencies threatened the pro-Western dictatorships of Greece and Turkey in 1947, the U.S. government took over from the British the protector's role and pledged to repel communist aggression there— and anywhere else. In the summer, President Harry Truman followed up with the Marshall Plan, a multibillion-dollar aid program to rebuild Europe, convince it not to turn communist, and conveniently provide a market for a thriving U.S. economy. As Western and Soviet soldiers aimed rifles at each other in the streets of Berlin, this "cold" confrontation sent shivers throughout the world.

Latin America was one of the regions of the globe where the confrontation between capitalist and communist visions took shape. Amid the good cheer at the end of the war, there were already signs of conflict between Latin American and U.S. interests. The United States seemed to ignore Latin America's demands for increased economic aid that would give a backbone to middle-class democracy. During World War II, for instance, 70 percent of U.S. Lend-Lease aid headed south had gone to only one country, Brazil—then under a dictatorship. To other Latin Americans, this seemed to contradict Roosevelt's talk of defending the "four freedoms"— of religion and of speech, from want and from fear—throughout the world.

At Chapultepec and San Francisco, U.S. officials brushed off talk of economic aid. Many saw Latin American nations as subordinates in the coming confrontation with the Soviets at the UN. As one senator told Nelson Rockefeller, who headed U.S. diplomacy for the "American Republics," "Your God-damned peanut nations aren't voting right. Go line them up."[3] "Lining them up" meant arm-twisting of every kind: holding back or promising aid and recognizing or not recognizing new regimes. The 1945 conferences, it turned out, had not been giveaways to Latin America. U.S. delegates in Mexico had agreed to the Act of Chapultepec because for them, it kept Great Britain and the Soviet Union out of Latin American affairs. To Arthur Vandenberg, a senator and delegate, the act "preserved the Monroe Doctrine and the Inter-American system."[4] Vandenberg exulted that collective security served U.S. purposes well: "We have retained a complete veto—exclusive in our own hands—over any decisions involving external activities." It was brilliant. The U.S. preserved their power over Latin America despite renouncing military intervention.

"I think that it's not asking too much to have our little region over here which never has bothered anybody."[5] With this statement, Secretary of War Henry Stimson, like many others, justified his desire for U.S. domination with traditional paternalistic images of Latin Americans as immature and unfit for self-government. As the Cold War breathed new life into U.S. support for trustworthy dictatorships rather than the sometimes-messy insecurity of democracy, U.S. officials turned to these images. Louis Halle, in an article approved by the State Department and titled "On a Certain Impatience with Latin America," elaborated. Using the pseudonym "Y," Halle argued that "democracy is not an absolute condition, to be assumed by a people as one puts on an overcoat. It is political maturity." When Latin American graffiti expressed the desire for "death" to opposition candidates during elections, for instance, Halle saw this as "not the behavior of mature men and women. It resembles, rather, the conduct of schoolboy gangs."[6] Secretary of State John Foster Dulles in 1953 echoed this disdain for Latin Americans. He counseled a colleague that, to make Latin Americans cooperate, "you have to pat them a little bit and make them think you are fond of them."[7]

In a deeper sense, as one historian explained, the impact of the Cold War on Latin America took the shape of both a "revolution" and a "counterrevolution." The revolution was the spread of the democratic promise. The defeat of totalitarianism during World War II and U.S.-led integration of the hemisphere after the war loudly proclaimed the superiority of fair elections, personal liberty, press freedoms, and other mainstays of U.S.-style democracy over any other system. Such ideas ignited the passions of ordinary Latin Americans and helped them organize into labor unions, peasant cooperatives, and democratic parties to protest long-time dictatorships. The counterrevolution, however, was the simultaneous spread, again facilitated by the United States, of not only anticommunist paranoia but also improved tools and techniques for stamping out insurgents: surveillance, modern weaponry and training, and if necessary, mass executions. This tended to help dictators *stay* in power. These two influences contradicted each other: one encouraged democracy while the other repressed it. The result was the narrowing of allowed political options. In the Cold War "democracy" no longer meant advocating equality, solidarity, and social security, as poor and indigenous Latin Americans had long done. The new U.S. definition limited itself to a few political and personal freedoms for the individual and it separated individuals from traditional societies so as to thrust them into new, highly bureaucratic and commercialized societies.[8]

The Cold War Conferences: Rio and Bogotá, 1947–48

Cold War insecurity framed the next round of inter-American conferences in 1948. At this point, lamented long-time specialist on Latin America Adolf Berle, the Washington "men who know the hemisphere and love it are few, and those who are known by the hemisphere and loved by it are fewer still."[9] At the 1945 conferences, delegates had tabled most resolutions for collective security until the next meeting. That meeting took place in fall 1947, when delegates hammered out the Inter-American Treaty of Reciprocal Assistance in Rio de Janeiro, Brazil. The Rio Pact, as it was known, reasserted that an attack on one was an attack on all, pledged members to seek peace within the Americas before going to the UN, and specified that any collective action must garner a two-thirds majority and that no state could be forced to use force against another. In essence, Latin Americans exchanged the U.S. promise of nonintervention for a regional organization dominated by Washington instead of an international organization, like the UN, in which Washington had to contend with the Soviet veto. As a sign of how U.S. lawmakers looked fondly on the Rio Pact, it passed the Senate 72 to 1.

Latin American delegates at Rio expected U.S. economic aid to be their reward. Truman stoked these expectations with his dramatic arrival in the Brazilian city aboard the USS *Missouri,* the battleship on which the Japanese had surrendered in 1945. Yet the U.S. president sorely disappointed his Latin American audience. At the closing ceremonies, he declared, "the problems of countries in this hemisphere are different in nature and cannot be relieved by the same means and the same approaches which are in contemplation in Europe."[10] Latin Americans listened in disbelief as Truman said there would be no Marshall Plan for Latin America, even though Europe, still devastated, was yet better off economically. The reason for this disparity was plain: the Soviets posed no direct threat to Latin America in 1947. They had no atom bomb, no long-range air force, and an ineffective navy. Latin Americans finally understood why the U.S. delegates had been so reluctant to discuss economic aid in 1945, the year Truman approved drafts of the Rio Pact: they had had no intention of giving it.

The Truman administration even refused to support an inter-American development bank. Instead of borrowing public U.S. funds from such a bank, Truman argued, why didn't Latin Americans encourage private investment? Why didn't they get in on the lucrative European rebuilding? During his time in office, Truman's purse strings remained tight. Only slightly more than $400 million went to all twenty countries of Latin America, less than U.S. aid to tiny Belgium and Luxembourg combined.[11]

The Truman approach to Latin America was not merely one of "neglect." After the Rio conference came another meeting—in Bogotá, the capital of Colombia, from March 30 to May 2, 1948. The Bogotá conference mission was to charter a regional UN for Latin America known as the Organization of American States (OAS), which would update the inter-American system heretofore embodied by the Pan-American Union. The OAS charter again broadened the principle of collective security to cover not only armed attacks on Latin American countries but also "any other form of interference or attempted threat."[12] This language smacked of anticommunist paranoia. On the eve of the conference, the U.S. National Security Council had approved NSC 7, a document which warned that "the ultimate objective of Soviet-directed world communism is the domination of the world." NSC 7 ordered a "world-wide counter-offensive." The same day, so that no one would miss the point, a State Department paper extended that claim to Latin America, though qualifying it by saying that communism was "a potential danger, but . . . not seriously dangerous."[13]

As if on cue, chaos helped scare delegates into clamping down on left-leaning democracies. Right in the middle of the conference, on the streets of Bogotá, an assassin took the life of Colombian Liberal Party leader Jorge Eliecer Gaitán. Riots ensued. The seat of the conference, the Capitolio, suffered severe damage, and delegates suspended their work until they could reconvene in a schoolhouse. Secretary of State George Marshall, who headed the delegation, pointed out that some communists participated in the riots, using this argument to push through an anticommunist resolution. The Latin American delegates went home shaken and disappointed. For Colombia, the assassination's aftermath was much worse. The riots led to a decade of internecine warfare known as La Violencia.

Anticommunism and Its Relation to Military Might

In summer 1949 the Soviets developed an atom bomb. Later that year the Chinese Revolution added several hundred million more human beings to the communist ledger. Six months after that, in mid-1950, communist North Korea attacked South Korea, prompting a U.S.-led UN intervention called the Korean War. With this globalization of the communist threat, Washington perceived communism to be, more than ever, "seriously dangerous" in Latin America.

Cultural commentary was particularly useful to Americans arguing during this period that Latin America could not resist the lure of communism. President Truman, for one, found Latin Americans to be "very emotional" and difficult to deal with. His secretary of state, Dean Acheson, believed that Latin America's woes could be blamed on "Hispano-Indian culture—or the lack of it." The region, to Acheson, combined "an explosive population, stagnant economy, archaic society, primitive politics, massive ignorance, illiteracy, and poverty."[14]

In 1950 George Kennan, one of the architects of U.S. "containment" of the Soviet Union, traveled to Latin America for the first and only time in his life. He suffered a bad case of culture shock. The noise, congestion, and climate appalled him, as did the contrast between the "inordinate splendor and pretense" of the cities and the "wretchedness and squalor of the hinterlands."[15] He blamed geography, history, and race—all things about which nothing could be done—for Latin American shortcomings. Kennan's reception in the South no doubt also shaped his judgment. Demonstrations and riots met him in several stops, and in Brazil and Peru crowds burned him in effigy and yelled at him to "go home."

When Kennan did go home, he wrote up a report so scathing that his superiors locked it up. In it, he admitted not knowing the number of communists in Latin America or the threat they posed, but nevertheless he recommended support for dictators. Since children could not be trusted to resist the ever-wily communists, he concluded, "we cannot be too dogmatic about the methods by which local communists can be dealt with." "The final answer might be an unpleasant one, but . . . we should not hesitate before police repression by the local government. . . . It is better to have a strong regime in power than a liberal government if it is indulgent and penetrated by Communists."[16]

Another policymaker arrived at similar conclusions. "The attainment of a stable constitutional democracy [in Latin America]," said Assistant Secretary of State for Inter-American Affairs Edward Miller, "cannot be achieved overnight." Miller recommended a "long period of education and political development, particularly in the case of those nations that are less advanced." The United States should expect, he added, "revolutions, coups d'état and local dictatorships," and should "exercise patience and tolerance toward these regrettable but inevitable manifestations as long as they do not involve Western Hemisphere security . . . or totalitarian infiltration."[17] Miller was more knowledgeable about Latin America and more careful with his words than Kennan, but the policies he advocated also emerged from the mutual reinforcement between paternalism and anticommunism.

One of these policies was a program of military aid, which filled a void left by the Rio Pact—a set of principles and mechanisms for self-defense, not an aid plan—and a 1949 congressional act that provided for $1.3 billion in military aid to much of the world except Latin America. Not until 1951—after the Soviet bomb, the Chinese Revolution, and the North Korean attack—did Congress pass the Military Defense Assistance Act. This one *was* for Latin America. Its logic was this: Latin America could not deter a nuclear or conventional attack from the Soviets; the United States would have to do that. But strong military regimes in Latin America *could* defeat local leftist insurgencies if properly equipped and trained. Embodying that logic, the act provided $38.5 million in weapons and training for Latin American counterinsurgency, not conventional warfare. U.S. officers would train Latin Americans in the Panama Canal Zone and at an institution that in 1963 came to be known as the School of the Americas.[18]

Soon enough the political algebra of U.S.-defined anticommunism became clear. No matter how many communists a Latin American leader actually had in his country, he could pretend to have more by "red-baiting" his political opponents—accusing them of sympathizing with communism. This would get him more U.S. aid to strengthen his military. U.S. fear of communism made it easier for dictators to take and keep power by any means necessary. As a result, by 1954 several of the democratizing regimes of the mid-1940s had reverted. Now, thirteen of twenty Latin American nations were dictatorships tied closely to Washington. This was not the integration many had wished for in 1945.

The Rise of the Third Way: Diffusion, Dependency, and Negotiating With U.S. Power

The replacement of World War II collaboration with Cold War bipolarity took place alongside another evolving schism that estranged U.S. citizens from Latin Americans and Latin Americans from one another. In the 1950s two schools of thought arose, and by the 1960s they were in full conflict. These schools disagreed over not political but *economic* questions. Why did the U.S. economy out-produce Latin America's nine times over when the populations of both regions were roughly equal?[19] Was economic integration—mainly the increased flow of capital and finished goods from the United States in exchange for more labor and raw materials from Latin America—good or bad for Latin America? Those who argued that integration was good were the advocates of "modernization" theory, otherwise known as the "diffusionists." Those who argued that it was bad espoused the "dependency" theory. To many Latin Americans, this economic schism was more important than debates over communism because it influenced political economies and led to confrontations with U.S. policymakers. The debate between diffusion and dependency also helped shape a Latin American alternative to both communism and capitalism that was called the "third way."

Diffusionism

The dominant view in the United States was modernization, or the diffusion theory, which was in vogue around 1950 but was explained best by Walt Rostow in *The Process of Economic Growth* in 1953 and *The Stages of Economic Growth: A Non-Communist Manifesto* in 1960. Rostow and others argued that all nations' economies could develop in a more or less similar way toward full, "modern" industrialization. Once countries had mechanized their agriculture and produced enough food to avoid famines and export surpluses, they accumulated capital to build factories and sustain workers in cities. With enough investment, economies would then enter a "take-off" stage of accelerated growth. And capital was certainly available: from 1950 to 1961 U.S. direct investments in Latin America doubled, reaching over $9 billion.[20]

What this meant for U.S.–Latin American relations was that the more "advanced" economies, such as U.S. industrial capitalism, would eventually help "backward" Latin American economies along through "diffusion," or the transfer of technology, knowledge, and capital from north to south.

Diffusionists stressed that the problem was not imperialism but "internal colonialism"—Latin Americans in the cities and rich landholders in the countryside exploiting the poor and holding back their productivity. The major Truman-era aid program for Latin America, Point Four, reflected modernization theory. It provided a small amount—$25 million per year—for the mechanization of agriculture.[21]

One assumption of diffusionists was that the U.S. and Latin American economies were compatible—not the same, of course, but mutually beneficial. Another assumption was that obstacles to development were mainly cultural and psychological—i.e., Latin Americans should break free of feudal ways of thinking and embrace free market principles of trust, equality of opportunity, and limited government intervention. Greater contact between the two economies, therefore, would lead to a more stable and more pluralistic Latin America. In many respects the modernization theory implied that those who opposed U.S. influence were wrong. As Roy Rubottom, the head of Latin American affairs in the State Department in the late 1950s, concluded, sincere anti-Americanism was a result of miscommunication, not divergent interest. "I am convinced that the true basis of any unfriendliness toward the United States finds its roots in misunderstandings." Others who criticized U.S.–Latin American ties, it further followed, must be communists, "those in the Americas whose single purpose is to create ill will and thwart all efforts to reach understanding."[22]

Dependency Theory

Advocates of dependency theory—*dependencistas*—answered that "ill will" had nothing to do with it. Thinkers such as Fernando Henrique Cardoso and Enzo Faletto of Brazil and especially Argentine economist Raúl Prebisch of the UN's Economic Commission for Latin America championed a view diametrically opposed to modernization. They held that the movement of capital and ideas to the South, when it came from a North hungry for cheap raw materials, resulted in a net loss to the South. U.S. investors provided capital only if they could recoup a hefty profit, which they then spent in their own country.

Moreover, the *kind* of investments they made encouraged not diversification but the hardening of economies around one or two low-priced crops. Prebisch presented historical statistics that showed a consistent decrease in the prices paid for agricultural goods—the more cotton was produced, the cheaper it became—while the prices of finished goods, manufactured in the North, increased. André Gunder Frank, another dependency theorist, called this "the development of underdevelopment." Mechanizing sugar mills in Cuba, for instance, forced peasants off their land and into a cash economy where their welfare depended on the ups and downs of the global price of sugar. And politically, foreign investors had little interest in providing living wages or the right to unionize to Latin American workers. The several hundred thousand rural workers of Latin America who had lost their jobs or seen their wages decimated by the Great Depression understood this inequality without much effort.

The dependencistas' beliefs and prescriptions were opposite those of diffusionists. They reversed the assumption that U.S. and Latin American contacts were mutually beneficial and argued that trade harmed the South. Colonialism was not internal, but external: the most "backward" regions of Latin America were not isolated from the world economy but were that way *because* of it. Wealth gaps were not the result of culture, but economic structure. What the dependencistas recommended, it followed, was not less government control but more. Prebisch argued for greater protection of trade and higher subsidies to domestic industry, a combination called import-substitution industrialization (ISI). For many Latin American leaders, ISI was attractive because it seemed to follow a moderate third way between capitalism and communism. Others went further. They argued for full socialist revolution to eliminate the elite that allegedly acted as puppets of U.S. investors before Latin American laborers.

Both sets of arguments appeared to have empirical grounding; this explains why they persisted for decades. On the dependency side, Prebisch showed that for a decade after 1952, the combined price index of coffee, wheat, corn, tin, cotton, sisal, lead, zinc, nitrates, and sugar—all major exports of Latin America—had declined in every year except one.[23] U.S. official Adolf Berle, who had spent a life working to expand U.S. influence in Latin America, admitted toward the end of his career that "when Latin Americans insist that private investment costs them more in foreign exchange through remittance of profit than it brings in through inflowing investment of capital, they are frequently right."[24] One U.S. government report, for instance, found a net *outflow* of profits of $4 billion back to the United States from 1961 to 1968.[25]

On the diffusion side, many U.S. officials and business representatives answered that dependencistas only looked at prices of exports and not at the benefits of investment, such as salaries, wages, materials, tax revenues, and transfers of technology from the United States to Latin America. When those were counted, one report tallied, the net flow southward was not negative $4 billion but rather a very positive $8.55 billion per year.[26]

Appearances deceived. There existed few solid studies of dependency or diffusion, especially long-term ones. The appeal of the two theories was in the comfort they provided, not the numbers. Diffusionism and dependency reached a peak of influence on political leaders in the 1950s and 1960s because they offered an intelligent way to debate the grey areas amid increasingly black and white Cold War politics. ISI, for instance, fueled the policies of moderate democratic leaders such as Juscelino Kubitschek of Brazil, Eduardo Frei of Chile, and Arturo Frondizi of Argentina. Many observers commented on the "rising expectations" of Latin American working and middle classes and predicted that Latin America was perched on the brink of *some* kind of revolution—a "take off," socialism, even anarchy.

Table 1. Diffusionism and Dependency Contrasted

	Diffusionism/Modernization Theory	*Dependency Theory*
Major conclusion	All countries can achieve modernization	Wealthy countries do not let poor countries modernize
Key concept	The "take off" stage	The "development of underdevelopment"
Secondary assertions	Colonialism is internal: rich Latin Americans dominate through corruption and tradition	Colonialism is external: wealthy countries built poor ones into single-crop economies dependent on world prices
	Transfers of technology, knowledge, and capital occur naturally	Poor countries cannot compete with wealthy ones in industrial production
Suggested remedies	Less government interference in business	Government protection of infant industries
	Poor countries must change their attitudes toward work, business, and consumption	Wealthy countries must reassess their racism, greed, and fear of insecurity

Third Way I: Juan Perón and "Justicialism" in Argentina

Because of the enormous political consequences of any economic path in the Cold War, the "third way" came to be defined in two ways: economically, as a mix of socialism and capitalism and, politically, as a "neutral" stance in the U.S.-Soviet struggle or at least as a stance more independent from the United States. The first Latin American to seriously espouse a third way was Col. Juan Domingo Perón of Argentina, who came to power in 1946, but Perón's way did not resonate for long because of its association with World War II fascism.

On one hand, Perón adopted an attractive neutralism toward the Cold War. He declared his enemies to be both "communism" and "Yankee imperialism." His alternative, sometimes called "justicialism," proposed that the Argentine state should run the country in a close partnership with the workers. It would nationalize major industries, provide benefits to workers, and organize sectors of society to advise the state. There would be no "dictatorship of the proletariat" the way Marxism preached, but foreign investors would lose much of their influence.

On the other hand, Perón's sympathies were often holdovers from close relations with Nazi Germany. During World War II, Argentina stood out in the hemisphere for refusing to break diplomatic relations with the Axis. It finally did so in 1944, but without declaring war on Germany. Franklin Roosevelt remained hostile—and paternalistic—toward Argentina, telling his secretary of state to "make a face to the Argentineans once a week. You have to treat them like children."[27] Only after the Act of Chapultepec, which gave UN membership only to those American republics that cooperated in the war, did Argentina declare war on Germany and Japan. Ironically, this strengthened the role of the military in Buenos Aires politics and boosted Perón's stature. Once firmly in power in the late 1940s, Perón's methods reflected his early sympathies. He ensured Argentines' loyalty to him with an intrusive secret police and brutal crackdowns on his opponents.

Many in Washington considered Argentina's embrace of hemispheric unity too little, too late. They disliked Perón's past and his style of leadership, and they suspected that he harbored former Nazis. One man, especially, promoted U.S.-style democracy in Argentina through unconventional means. As a career diplomat, Spruille Braden believed that sovereignty lay not in governments but in the people whom those governments claimed to rule. If he could use U.S. power to bring forth that true sovereign, he figured, it was his duty to do so. Braden saw his chance when he became ambassador to Argentina in May 1945 and rose to assistant secretary of state for American republic affairs in September of that same year. His time in Buenos Aires convinced him that "so long as Perón and his military remain in control of this country we are faced with a fundamental policy issue, [the] importance of which cannot be exaggerated. Appeasement will be fatal and we must rigidly stand on our principles."[28] As ambassador, Braden encouraged U.S. companies to give Argentine workers time off to join anti-Perón demonstrations. He reversed the decision to relax the war-time arms embargo against Argentina. And he helped postpone the signing of the Rio Pact to keep Perón out of it.

Already, Braden's interference was bold, but he was not done. In February 1946, two weeks before elections in which Perón ran for president, Braden published the so-called Blue Book, a set of documents—bound in a blue cover—that accused the Argentine government of partnering with Nazis (document 1). In response to Braden's publication, Perón seized on the image of campaigning against Yankee imperialism: he presented the choice to voters as "Perón or Braden." Perón won a resounding victory.

In the months that followed, Perón and his wife Eva remained popular at home, but what they called the "Third Position" won few adherents abroad. Some ISI schemes worked, but others failed miserably. When Perón offered food aid to poorer neighbors Peru and Bolivia, he could not compete against the deep pockets of the Truman administration and so was never able to break South America's dependence on the United States. By 1947 he was once again importing U.S. weapons, with diplomatic relations fully reestablished; he even pledged to side with the United States in any war with the Soviets. Just as neutralism had not worked for Perón, other than to get him elected, by that year, too, prodemocracy idealism was fading fast in Washington. U.S. diplomats received an order to stay away from Latin American political campaigns.[29]

Third Way II: Puerto Rico and Commonwealth Prosperity

A far more diffusionist pattern took shape in Puerto Rico in the postwar years, yet Puerto Ricans opted for enough political independence to merit inclusion in the third way. Since the War of 1898, Puerto Ricans, fewer in number and closer to the United States than Argentines, had steadily integrated into the U.S. economy. Compared to its neighbors in the Caribbean and Central America, Puerto Rico had suffered less military intervention and civil unrest, so the process of integration was smoother. Moreover, Puerto Ricans migrated en masse to the United States and became the first important "Latino" community on the East Coast.

Integration of Puerto Rico was also U.S. policy. Education specialists targeted the island for transformation into an English-speaking, Protestant land of promise. During World War II, especially, the U.S. government infused the small island with military dollars and U.S. corporations attracted Puerto Rican workers to the mainland. When peace returned, Puerto Rican and U.S. leaders began Operation Bootstrap, a classic diffusionist program that encouraged the transfer of U.S. investment and technology to Puerto Rico through lower wages, no taxes, and duty-free exports to the mainland. This often meant a growing gap between rich and poor and more emigration to the United States—in 1946 alone, more than forty thousand Puerto Ricans landed in New York City.[30] Overall, on the eve of the Cuban Revolution in 1958, Puerto Ricans enjoyed the highest per capita income in Latin America.

However, the fear of being swallowed by both U.S. capitalism and U.S. culture prompted political movements for more autonomy, if not full independence. Integration cost Puerto Rico much of its pride as other Latin Americans mocked its supposed servility to U.S. desires. As one Venezuelan remarked, "The worst thing that could happen to us would be to transform ourselves into second-class Yankees or to have their culture imposed upon us or to suffer an adulteration of native spiritual values, like that which a badly organized North American education has produced in Puerto Rico."[31] Puerto Ricans were U.S. citizens who neither were represented in Congress nor paid federal taxes—they were "foreign in a domestic sense," as the U.S. Supreme Court put it.

To recoup lost pride, former pro-independence leader Luis Muñoz Marín and his supporters relinquished their quest for total independence but sought more control over their destiny. In 1947 Muñoz Marín encouraged Congress to pass the Elective Governor Act, under which he became the first elected governor of Puerto Rico in 1948. The independence movement remained strong, however, and two Puerto Rican nationalists even tried to assassinate President Truman on November 1, 1950, in a gunfight that left one of the assassins with a bullet in his head. That same year Congress validated the new status of the island as a commonwealth. In 1952 Puerto Rican voters approved commonwealth status, and they did so again in plebiscites in the decades that followed.

Puerto Rico was poised to live out the rest of the twentieth century in a middle state—not rich but less poor than its neighbors, not sovereign but distinct from the U.S. mainland. Puerto Rican women especially became experts at resisting U.S. influence expressed in subtle ways, including U.S. efforts to limit the size of families through birth control. When women saw in these policies a way to eradicate poverty, they went along, but when they perceived "cultural imperialism," they held on to their traditional embrace of large families.[32]

Third Way III: The Bolivian Revolution, 1952

The Bolivian Revolution of 1952 indicated a *third* third way. In contrast to both the hostility of Argentina and the collaboration of Puerto Rico, the Bolivian way showed an understanding of limited shared interest with the United States. During World War II, the Nationalist Revolutionary Movement (MNR) rose to prominence in Bolivia by opposing concessions to foreign companies that wanted to extract Bolivia's resources, such as Standard Oil. The shadow of Perón loomed as the U.S. government associated the MNR with the Nazis and withheld recognition of a Bolivian regime until it purged itself of MNR ministers. In 1951, however, the MNR returned. Víctor Paz Estenssoro—who had returned from Perón's Argentina—easily won election to the presidency with MNR support. When the Bolivian army opposed the new regime, workers in the tin industry—Bolivia's most important—took to the streets, and they ensured Paz's ascendance in

April 1952. Paz rewarded them by expropriating the three largest tin companies, pushing through land reforms, promising universal suffrage, and stripping the army of its power.

The U.S. government and the tin companies were in a bind. They felt that foreign companies should operate free from government intrusion in Bolivia and that such freedom was ultimately good for workers, who would get higher wages. This system was also good for the Bolivian government, they argued, which would get higher taxes from higher profits. But the U.S. ability to reverse Paz's reforms was limited. The army was weak, as were political parties who could be potential allies. And Bolivia had its share of communists but not enough to create a panic in the United States. So the State Department decided that the Bolivian revolution was, as it said, not "communist orientated."[33]

Both sides reached a compromise. Paz compensated the companies at a reasonable rate, which was better than plain expropriation. In return, Washington bought all Bolivia's available tin and President Truman recognized the new government on June 2, 1952. The government of Dwight Eisenhower continued Truman's policy, purchasing more tin than it needed until 1957. The United States had decided to buy the MNR's sympathies rather than see Bolivia fall to chaos and communism. Soon aid money joined tin money. In the 1950s Bolivia received more U.S. aid per capita than any other country in the world.

Cultural and Social Integration

As political regimes negotiated semiautonomous status in the early Cold War, the decade after World War II saw increasing cultural and social contacts and exchanges between the United States and Latin America. These interactions were complex: sometimes harmonious, other times acrimonious; sometimes two-way streets, other times symptomatic of "cultural imperialism." But always, they grew.

U.S. tourists, for instance, increasingly saw Latin America, and especially Mexico and the Caribbean, not as a land of revolution and disease but as a hospitable, affordable nearby tropical paradise of sandy beaches, ancient ruins, and legalized gambling. As a 1946 song extolled,

> Managua, Nicaragua, is a beautiful town,
> You buy a hacienda for a few dollars down. . . .
> Managua, Nicaragua, what a wonderful spot!
> There's coffee and bananas and a temp'rature hot,
> So take a trip and on a ship go sailing away—
> Across the *agua* to Managua, Nicaragua. Olé![34]

Mexico was always popular: from 1945 to 1960 U.S. tourists there increased from 165,988 to 719,138.[35] Mexico along with Cuba and Puerto Rico specialized in resorts that catered to the *anglo-sajones*, who wanted high-quality accommodations, friendly service, and guilt-free drinking, gambling, and prostitution. Airlines such as PanAm also now offered affordable air travel: a one-way ticket to Puerto Rico in the late 1940s was less than $50—about a week's average wage—bringing the fantasy of a pleasure island closer to reality for a middle class family.

Each year, also, thousands of U.S. and Latin American students sojourned in one another's countries. This led to one interesting set of interviews of Mexican students temporarily studying at the University of California in Los Angeles in 1954. The students, both men and women, were impressed with the widespread material wealth of U.S citizens. "All [Americans], or at least most of them," said one, "have a high standard for living well. . . . The worker of a factory has his own car and his refrigerator . . . all the things that make for a comfortable living which in Mexico our laborers don't have." Many of these Mexican students had also changed their minds about the United States. "The impression we had [in Mexico]," explained one, "was that the United States didn't care very much about art or people who really counted. I believed Americans did not teach anything about living; being phlegmatic, practical, not sentimental, not having poetry. . . . This changed when I began reading other things." Some things still shocked them: the informality in social relations, especially between men and women, and the impression—both good and bad—that "all American girls are easy." Overall, they appreciated education in the United States and were more willing to undertake practical professions such as business and engineering.[36]

By the 1950s, finally, popular culture brought Latin America and the United States closer together. As the opening of Sears in Mexico indicated, U.S. consumer goods were more and more in circulation in Latin America. They ranged from Coca-Cola's soft drinks to Singer's sewing machines to the many household products made by Bristol-Myers. U.S. newspaper correspondents now resided permanently in Latin America's big cites, and books and magazines such as *Life en español* and *Selecciones (Readers Digest)* presented similar content to both regions. At the end of the 1950s some of the nationalities most infused with U.S. culture—Cuban, Mexican, and Venezuelan—went to the movies almost as often as U.S. citizens did.[37]

Some U.S. cultural products, to be sure, still distorted Latin America into simplistic images. Peggy Lee's song "Mañana (Is Soon Enough for Me)" crudely perpetuated the caricature of Latin Americans as laid-back buffoons. Desi Arnaz, comedian Lucille Ball's husband on and off the immensely popular situation comedy *I Love Lucy,* was often reduced to a bumbling, hysterical Cuban-American stereotype. In 1957 *West Side Story* was a Broadway hit musical whose composer, Leonard Bernstein, interpreted for mainstream audiences the experiences of Puerto Rican youth in New York City. In 1961 the musical became a hit movie, which, along with *Cry Tough* (1959) and *Young Savages* (1961), tended to reinforce the stereotype of Puerto Ricans as knife-wielding criminals.

Other productions, while still entertaining, spoke of the already ingrained Latin American influence on U.S. culture. Among the thousands of U.S. songs influenced by Latin music, one of the best, rhythm and blues singer Ray Charles's 1959 "What'd I Say," rolled along to a rumba beat, unbeknownst to most who danced to it. Even Hollywood went through a Latin phase: *The Ox-Bow Incident* (1943), *Border Incident* (1949), *High Noon* (1952), and *Salt of the Earth* (1953) all portrayed strong Latin American characters.

As U.S.–Latin American relations demonstrated again and again after 1945, a rapprochement of two cultures—through music, film, or consumption—did not necessarily translate into improved relations between governments. From Guatemala to Venezuela, the 1950s demonstrated the dangers of a third way when the U.S. government considered itself in a worldwide struggle with only two ways—the U.S.-led "free world" or Soviet communism.

Fall of the Third Way: Arbenz, Guerrillas, and a Vice President Stoned

The experiences of the administration of former World War II general Dwight Eisenhower with Latin America from 1953 to 1958 integrated the hemisphere more and more into a global anticommunist strategy. This new state of things sparked much self-congratulation on the U.S. mainland. But while Latin American governments remained securely within the U.S. sphere of influence on the surface, rising anger in the new urban populations seethed in the background.

Fear of "Third World" Neutralism

Around the time Eisenhower and the Republicans took control of the White House, African and Asian countries from Ghana to India to Vietnam emerged as free nations and inspired poor people around the world to seek their own path beyond superpower rivalry. The term "Third World" emerged in the 1950s to describe these nations that could go either way in the East-West divide. These changes induced the Cold War race for cheap raw materials, which intensified as Washington and Moscow saw themselves in a zero-sum game: if one got access to an African country's cobalt, for instance, the other would have access to that much less.

In March 1953 NSC 144/1 laid out the Eisenhower vision of what all this meant for Latin America. Washington's polls in Latin America had not been encouraging. One in Mexico, for instance, revealed that 71 percent of Mexicans wanted to be on "neither side" of the communist-anticommunist divide.[38] NSC 144/1 pledged to do explicitly what Truman had done de facto and defeat this kind of neutralism. Picking up on U.S. disdain for Latin America, it described the region as disunited, undemocratic, mired in social injustice, and led by "immature and impractical idealists."[39] Latin America could be useful to the United States almost uniquely as a regional bulwark against world communism. Ike and his influential secretary of state John Foster Dulles wanted four things from Latin America: support at the

UN (for instance in the Korean War—which they got); eradication of communism in the hemisphere; access to strategic raw materials; and military cooperation (document 2).

The U.S. government partly pursed these goals through "soft power," or persuasion. In 1953 the Eisenhower government gave birth to the U.S. Information Agency (USIA), whose mission was to "sell" U.S. foreign policy objectives to the rest of the world. The agency did some of this openly, for instance by building libraries where Latin Americans could come to read English-language books, magazines, and newspapers. But it also ran a covert program of "grey propaganda," named so because it was not as invasive as the "black propaganda" of the CIA, which planted anticommunist articles in the foreign press, subsidized books in foreign languages, and jammed radio programs of groups opposed to U.S. allies. The USIA, by contrast, encouraged the dissemination of "soft" positive news about the United States—the peaceful use of atomic energy, progress in the space race, the visit of Mexican little league champions to the White House. In Mexico, the USIA's "Project Pedro" hired a Hollywood executive who in turn paid Mexican businessmen to act as fronts for Mexican companies whose U.S. managers covertly produced newsreels for almost four hundred movie theaters. These newsreels mixed pro-U.S. news with advertising for Goodyear, Kodak, and Pepsi and with stories on boxing and bullfighting, which made the pill of Cold War propaganda easier to swallow. By involving Mexicans and Mexico in the making of these newsreels, the cultural Cold War in Latin America became increasingly transnational.[40]

The Eisenhower administration also intensified its military training programs, which further internalized the Cold War for Latin Americans. The easiest way to secure anticommunism was to support dictators. After all, they had an interest in stomping on their critics and were only too happy to label them communists. "Do nothing to offend the dictators," Dulles ordered his diplomats.[41] Eisenhower did more than "nothing." Not only did he recognize two dictators—Manuel Odría in Peru and Marcos Pérez Jiménez in Venezuela—who overthrew popularly elected regimes, but he awarded both men the Legion of Merit, the highest U.S. award for foreigners. In 1952 an elected government also fell to Fulgencio Batista in Cuba. In 1955 Vice President Richard Nixon visited the island and toasted the dictator as a man comparable to Abraham Lincoln. Rafael Trujillo in the Dominican Republic, firmly in power since 1930, also solidified his stock with Eisenhower by allowing the U.S. Air Force to operate a guided missile tracking station on his territory. By 1954 only four democracies remained in Latin America—Uruguay, Costa Rica, Chile, and Brazil. To reinforce their military relationships, the Republicans signed mutual defense pacts with twelve Latin American nations and established military missions in every nation except Mexico.[42]

NSC 144/1 did not ignore the desire for development in Latin America. "There is an increasing popular demand for immediate improvement in the low living standards of the masses," it explained, "with the result that most Latin American governments are under intense domestic political pressures to increase production and to diversify their economies." The president's own brother, Milton, took a much-publicized trip to Latin America in 1953 and came back with a similar message of urgency: "They want greater production and higher standards of living, and they want them *now*."[43]

Ike, Dulles, and others, however, continued the Truman practice of seeking development and diversification only through *private* initiatives. There still would be no Marshall Plan for Latin America. Instead, recommended NSC 144/1, Latin Americans needed "to recognize that . . . their own self-interest requires the creation of a climate which will attract private investment."

Working-Class Anticommunism: The AFL-CIO
in Latin America

The climate to attract private investment included "responsible" unions. In the United States, the leaders of the American Federation of Labor, which after 1955 joined with the Congress of Industrial Organizations to form the AFL-CIO, wholeheartedly joined in the anticommunist crusade. That alliance between labor and political leaders reproduced itself in Latin America, where the AFL sent "ambassadors" to convince Latin American unions to disaffiliate from the procommunist Confederation of Latin American Workers (CTAL). By 1951 the AFL helped establish the Inter-American Regional Organization of Workers (ORIT), whose goal was to whittle away adherents to CTAL. Argentine workers, being close to presidential power in their country, were of course offended by this U.S. effort to take over hemispheric unionizing. They shot back, accusing ORIT of being "State Department-dominated" and organizing their own umbrella union. Their protest was in vain. ORIT prevailed by training over forty thousand labor leaders, spreading literature, and helping in some antidictatorial struggles. ORIT's overall message to unions under its umbrella was to partner with corporations and abandon any unionization that smacked of communism. By the mid-1960s, the AFL-CIO through ORIT reached twenty-eight million workers in fifty-two affiliated organizations in thirty-nine republics, territories, and possessions of the hemisphere.[44] Its work likely prevented the labor movement in Latin American from being far more radical.

The Guatemala Coup, 1954

Two main concerns of Eisenhower and Dulles—defending private enterprise and fighting the Cold War—came together most notoriously in the overthrow of Guatemalan president Jacobo Arbenz Guzmán in June 1954. Guatemala was one of the poorest countries in the hemisphere. In its classically dependent economy, bananas and coffee made up $42 million of a total $50 million in exports in 1948. That same year the United States supplied 82 percent of imports to Guatemala. The fact that about half the population consisted of non-Spanish speaking indigenous peoples only widened the gap between the few rich and the many poor. And that gap was tremendous: 2 percent owned 72 percent of the land, while half were confined to 4 percent of the land.[45]

Guatemalans aimed to end dependence when they overthrew dictator Jorge Ubico in 1944. The freely elected president who followed Ubico, Juan José Arévalo, began a public works program and a reform of the feudal labor laws. But the real promise of an overhaul came with the election of Jacobo Arbenz in 1951. A military man, President Arbenz applied discipline and will to reforms. A leftist labor union helped him design an agrarian reform, and for the first time in Guatemalan history, indigenous peasants administered the new program at the local level. By 1954 one hundred thousand families received land as well as bank credit and technical aid so they could turn Guatemala into what Arbenz described as a "modern capitalist state."[46]

Before 1954 much of this land belonged to the Boston-based United Fruit Company (UFCO), which transformed it into huge plantations primarily for growing bananas. At the end of World War II UFCO owned 566,000 acres and employed fifteen thousand Guatemalans, making it the largest landowner (owning 40 percent of the land) and employer in the nation.[47] UFCO also owned the railroad, which was the second-largest employer and which brought the bananas to the shore and controlled the telephone and telegraph that ran alongside the railroad. UFCO owned the port facilities that helped heave the bananas onto ships, and it owned fifty freighters that carried the bananas to their final destination. In short, UFCO well deserved the nickname Latin Americans gave it: El Pulpo (The Octopus). In its defense, UFCO claimed—truthfully—that its employees enjoyed quality housing, schooling, and hospital care and better salaries than anyone else in Guatemala. But it neglected to note that many had owned their own land until UFCO forced them out of the market.

El Pulpo's tentacles also reached deep into Washington. UFCO's president was the brother of President Eisenhower's first assistant secretary of state for Latin America, John Moors Cabot. UN Ambassador Henry Cabot Lodge owned stock in UFCO. The company had been a client of John Foster Dulles and his brother Allen, director of the CIA, when they worked for the law firm of Sullivan and Cromwell. And finally, UFCO's principal lobbyist, Ed Whitman, was none other than the husband of Ike's personal secretary, Ann.

In 1953 Arbenz announced that his government would seize 234,000 acres of uncultivated UFCO land (85 percent of UFCO's land in Guatemala was an undeveloped reserve).[48] The Guatemalans would compensate UFCO at the declared value of the land. The problem was UFCO had been falsely declaring that its acreage was worth a fraction of its actual value so that it would owe fewer taxes. Not surprisingly, UFCO suddenly changed its numbers, and in April 1953 the Department of State—not UFCO—demanded twenty times more than Arbenz offered. Guatemalan Foreign Minister Guillermo Toriello called State Department efforts "a pretext for intervention in our internal affairs. . . . They wanted to find a ready expedient to maintain the economic dependence of the American Republics and suppress the legitimate desires of their peoples."[49]

When negotiations failed, Eisenhower and Secretary Dulles began secretly to pursue the overthrow of Arbenz while publicly claiming that he was a communist sympathizer. Many have been suspicious of this assertion. Arbenz himself claimed that the CIA and others "have used the pretext of anticommunism. The truth is very different. The truth is to be found in the financial interests of the fruit company and the other U.S. monopolies which have invested great amounts of money in Latin America and fear that the example of Guatemala would be followed by other Latin American countries."[50]

However, this choice between pro-UFCO and anticommunist intervention is a false dichotomy—a choice that doesn't need to be made. To Eisenhower, the Dulleses, and UFCO, communism and land reform were almost indistinguishable. Arbenz's expropriation was *in itself* evidence of control from Moscow. Policymakers on both sides remarked on this conflation. Secretary Dulles explained in a news conference in mid-1954: "If the United Fruit matter were settled," he said, "if they gave a gold piece for every banana, the problem would remain just as it is today as far as the presence of communist infiltration in Guatemala is concerned. That is the problem, not United Fruit." José Manuel Fortuny, former general secretary of the labor union in Guatemala, a committed socialist and a friend of Arbenz, said much the same thing. "They would have overthrown us even if we had grown no bananas," declared Fortuny years after the affair.[51] For many Guatemalans, the question of whether Arbenz was a communist was irrelevant for other reasons. "Maybe he was," reflected one working-class activist, "but look what he did for Guatemala, the labor code, the Agrarian Reform, the Institute of Social Security, the Atlantic highway. I have my pension because of him."[52]

The obstacle preventing Washington from overthrowing Arbenz outright was that collective defense principles protected against U.S. intervention. The only way around that obstacle was to demonstrate outside influence in Guatemala. UFCO's lobbyists and publicists, therefore, did their best to paint Arbenz as Moscow-controlled, for instance by publishing full-page ads in the *New York Times* that explained "Why the Kremlin Hates Bananas." The Guatemalan Congress also shot itself in the foot by marking a minute of silence when Stalin died in 1953. And the pro-Moscow leanings of Arbenz's wife and his allies in the labor unions did not help. As U.S. Ambassador John Peurifoy said after he first met Arbenz, "if the President is not a Communist he will certainly do until one comes along."[53]

Secretary Dulles admitted it was "impossible to produce evidence clearly tying the Guatemalan government to Moscow."[54] Yet he soldiered on. In Caracas, Venezuela, in March 1954, the secretary got the other American republics to support an amendment that legitimated collective action to defend against "dangers originating outside this hemisphere." It was a vague formulation. To Dulles, it meant that even holding an outside *ideology* such as communism warranted an overthrow. In mid-1954, when a ship carrying weapons from behind the Iron Curtain docked in Guatemala, the U.S. government made its move.

The overthrow itself, like successful surgery, was quick and relatively painless. In late 1953 Eisenhower had authorized an operation, and the CIA started turning members of Arbenz's military, headed by Col. Carlos Castillo Armas, against him. On June 18, 1954, from neighboring Honduras, Castillo Armas and 150 Guatemalans and mercenaries moved six miles into Guatemala, just enough to create rumors of an invasion. To amplify those rumors, CIA-trained pilots flew clunky planes from Nicaragua into Guatemala and unleashed "psychological warfare" on Arbenz. They dropped small sticks of dynamite—sometimes only Coke bottles—on the presidential palace while the CIA jammed radio transmissions and announced over loudspeakers that a huge army was marching toward Guatemala City.[55] Arbenz feared defections in his own air force, so he grounded it. The army also stayed in its barracks. Foreign Minister Toriello denounced this "criminal invasion" at the UN, but Washington denied any involvement.[56] After a bit more than a week, Arbenz fled into exile. Back in Washington, the CIA celebrated a cheap and easy coup. Eisenhower held a White House reception, and John Foster Dulles celebrated what had been the "biggest success in the last five years against communism."[57]

While largely bloodless at the time, the Eisenhower coup against Arbenz eventually cost great bloodshed and treasure. Castillo Armas took over provisionally on July 7, 1954, and secured his hold with an election that he won with almost miraculous numbers: 486,000 votes for, 400 against. With massive U.S. economic aid, Castillo Armas outlawed more than five hundred unions, returned more than 1.5 million acres to UFCO and other big landowners, and began a violent regime of terror. Civil wars and dictatorships killed over two hundred thousand Guatemalans in the following four decades.[58]

From Guatemala to Cuba

One young Argentine in Guatemala at the time witnessed the downfall first hand, and he promised not to repeat Arbenz's mistakes. Ernesto "Che" Guevara, a physician and adventurer, faulted the Guatemalan for being not too bold but too cautious. Arbenz should have secured the military and the borders, Che thought, and taken not only the land but also the utilities and the ports. Soon after, Che was in Mexico, where he met another brilliant, ambitious revolutionary: Fidel Castro.

Castro was already semifamous. The son of a comfortable landowner in Cuba, he earned a law degree but then revolted against the lack of social justice and sovereignty in Cuba. He cut his teeth in sometimes violent—and always bold—exploits in the service of prominent Cuban nationalists. Most famously, on July 26, 1953, Castro led a failed raid on the Moncada army barracks in Santiago. During the trial that followed his capture, he gave an unapologetic defense called "History Will Absolve Me." After more than a year in prison with his brother Raúl and others, he was released into exile. From Mexico, the Castros continued the search for money and men—men like Guevara, idealistic and ready to sacrifice. They plotted to invade Cuba and wrest it from the clutches of Batista and his Yankee supporters. In 1956, along with eighty others, the Castros and Che climbed aboard the creaky vessel *Granma* and sailed into Oriente province in Cuba. There they were met by an ambush that sank their ship. But eighteen from the *Granma* survived, fled to the wilderness of the Sierra Maestra, and began a years-long effort to unseat Batista.

In the late 1950s Cuba was not necessarily ripe for revolution because life there was relatively good. Its income per person was almost $400, second highest among Latin American nations (but far behind $2,000 in the United States). Cuba was first in per capita television sets, newspapers, telephones, and private motor vehicles, and in rail mileage per square miles.[59] U.S. investments were significant, but not as monopolistic as they once had been. Finally, rural workers, small farmers, and landless peasants, by far the poorest Cubans, had rarely engaged in revolutionary activities, nor did they do much to support Castro's struggle from 1956 to 1958.

So why Cuba? Why were guerrillas so successful against a dictatorship there while they failed elsewhere? First, Batista was weak and barely held together an unmotivated military and government. Second, Castro was a charismatic leader who convinced men and women to follow him in a long-shot struggle and garnered sympathy from the media, even in the United States. Third, the island had an urban underground consisting of thousands of Cubans who largely evaded the henchmen of Batista and helped prepare a Castro victory. Fourth, U.S. investments *did* account for much of Cuba's treasure: 36 of 161 sugar mills, 2 of 3 oil refineries, 90 percent of public utilities, and half the railroads and mines.[60]

Fifth and finally, ordinary Cubans rejected the U.S. presence in Cuba precisely because it was so successful. U.S. dollars had transformed Cuba into what many considered a den of sin and crime. Future presidential adviser Arthur Schlesinger Jr. recalled visiting Havana in 1950. "I was enchanted by Havana—and appalled by the way that lovely city was being debased into a giant casino and brothel for American businessmen over for a weekend from Miami. My fellow countrymen reeled through the streets, picking up fourteen-year-old Cuban girls and tossing coins to make men scramble in the gutter. One wondered how any Cuban—on the basis of this evidence—could regard the United States with anything but hatred."[61] In this atmosphere great value is placed on material luxury, and $400 per year bought little of it. What Castro called for as a corrective appeared U.S.-

inspired: a New Deal–type redistribution of income, a more representative political system, and an end to the Jim Crow racism that Batista enforced largely for the sake of his U.S. patrons.

For all these reasons, Guevara and Castro saw Cuba as the next logical place for a revolution that would radically free Latin Americans from the control of U.S. imperialism while avoiding the missteps of the reformist Arbenz. "Cuba will not be Guatemala," Guevara vowed.[62]

The Caribbean Legion and Tumbling Dictators

Castro remained off the U.S. radar screen in postwar Latin America partly because he remained a small player in a much larger game of attempting to unseat dictators. José Figueres in Costa Rica, Ramón Grau San Martín in Cuba, Rómulo Betancourt in Venezuela, and Juan José Arévalo in Guatemala were democratically elected leaders who had gained office promising third-way reforms. In the late 1940s, calling themselves the Caribbean Legion, these men banded together to raise insurrections against the fiercest dictatorships in Latin America. Chief among their targets was Trujillo in the Dominican Republic, who ruled his island with an iron fist and hypnotized it with a cult of personality, but they were never able to unseat him because he always uncovered their plots. As much as Trujillo's militarism and extravagance displeased Washington, Assistant Secretary Rubottom explained how such crusading third-way democrats were even more dangerous. "We cannot allow individual groups of 'liberators' to pass judgment on the governments of particular countries and to undertake from bases in other countries to launch attacks aiming to oust violently the governments they dislike. That would be anarchy."[63] In the wake of the Arbenz overthrow, such statements sounded hypocritical to many in Latin America.

And "anarchy" did prevail in the late 1950s as one dictator after another fell to representative regimes: Perón in Argentina in 1955, Odría in Peru in 1956, and Gustavo Rojas Pinilla in Colombia in 1957. Once this phenomenon was under way, President Eisenhower in 1958 again sent his brother Milton to Latin America. Milton reported back an even greater urgency than he had six years previous. "There is absolutely no doubt in my mind that revolution is inevitable in Latin America," he wrote to his brother.[64] Adding to the rising anxiety, a recession hit the United States in 1957–58. It sent shock waves through Latin America, where foreign investment fell along with the prices paid for raw materials. The State Department now thought seriously about abandoning its bias against public financing and considered a Development Loan Fund and an Inter-American Development Bank that would stabilize local economies and export prices.

Richard Nixon's Goodwill Disaster, 1958

In May 1958 relief had not yet come to Venezuela, where Vice President Richard Nixon visited during his goodwill tour of Latin America. Venezuela verged on instability. The previous January, a military junta had taken power after the overthrow of yet another dictator, Marcos Pérez Jiménez, and a legitimate government had yet to be elected in place of the junta. Moreover, the U.S. government had imposed restrictions on crude oil imports, a move that, Venezuelans argued, contradicted Washington's free-trade ideology and crippled Venezuela's comparative trade advantage. Finally, several small communist groups operated freely while security forces felt restrained in their use of force lest they be accused of trying to return the country to a brutal dictatorship. Despite the danger—and the many warnings the CIA gave him—Nixon insisted on riding from the airport into Caracas, the capital, and even asked for an open car. "Are you people out of your minds?" said the Caracans.[65]

Maybe not, but Nixon almost lost his head. By the time he got to Caracas, the trip through South America had already been perilous. There were demonstrations at almost every stop. Nixon engaged in a finger-wagging and shouting match in Lima, Peru, where students stoned him. Even the *New York Times* blamed the hostility on communism. "Nixon Stoned by Red Mob," read its headline.

Caracas was worse. Hundreds of booing Venezuelans met Nixon and his wife Pat at the airport. They spat on the dignitaries, who quickly jumped into cars. Along the road leading downtown, mobs surged around the cars, rocked them up and down and smashed windows with steel bars and sticks. Nixon restrained security guards who whipped out their guns, but he shared their shock and fear before this hatred from the crowd. "Those who had no weapons used their feet and bare fists to beat upon the car," he recalled. "The spit was flying so fast that the driver turned on his windshield wipers."[66] Suddenly, Nixon's driver saw an opening and gunned the car out of the crowd and straight to the U.S. embassy. The torment had lasted fourteen minutes.

The Caracas riot and Nixon's return accelerated the reconsideration of how Washington helped create instability in Latin America. Certainly, violence such as this was partly due to local, temporary factors, including a breakdown in security. But Nixon and others recognized the larger relationships between U.S. encouragement for development or the lack of that encouragement, dismay at the lack of social justice and democracy in Latin America, and resulting Latin American attitudes toward the United States. Back in 1956 President Juscelino Kubitschek of Brazil had unsuccessfully argued to Eisenhower that the "way to defeat leftist totalitarianism" was "to combat poverty wherever it may be encountered."[67] In June 1958, seizing on the new openness in Washington, Kubitschek and Alberto Lleras Camargo of Colombia sent a formal proposal for a massive public aid program. This would become "Operation Pan America," the inspiration for the Alliance for Progress under President John Kennedy (document 3).

For the moment, the U.S. government agreed only to discuss new price-support agreements, to increase loans to Latin America in already-existing programs, and to support new public-loan agencies such as the

Inter-American Development Bank in 1959 and the Social Progress Trust Fund in 1960. The Washington bureaucracy could not respond fast enough to mushrooming problems, and many within it felt that giving too much would simply encourage communists to riot more. This was not enough for many in Latin America. Figueres of Costa Rica assessed the situation thus: "What we have today, instead of a desired hemispheric unity, is an utter indifference in the United States, and a bitter resentment in Latin America. Both indifference and resentment are so generalized, so rooted, so extended to all branches of our respective societies, that the remedies, though easy to prescribe, are enormously difficult to apply."[68]

Caracas was a sped up replay of the previous fifteen years. Amid increasing contacts between Latin Americans and U.S. citizens in diplomacy, business, travel, and military cooperation, hopes for democracy burgeoned, but so did anti-Americanism. U.S. policymakers split over whether this anti-Americanism reflected genuine public opinion or another communist trick. While some wanted to limit U.S. interventions to the Guatemalan overthrow and support for dictators, others urged more. The more aggressive policymakers' only solutions, however, were tepid reforms that did not address deeper inequalities in U.S.–Latin American relations. The Cuban Revolution, coming on the heels of the Caracas riots, pulled those inequalities up by their roots. It was the first in a series of blowbacks against U.S. Cold War hegemony.

CHAPTER 2

Anti-U.S. Sentiment, Socialism, and U.S. Gunboats,
1959–69

I
N MARCH 1959 A MINOR COMMENT set off a major anti-U.S. protest in Bolivia. Talking to a reporter from the Latin American
edition of *Time,* a U.S. embassy official made the inappropriate remark
that landlocked, impoverished Bolivia would not be worse off if it were
split in two and handed to its neighbors, Peru and Chile. Bolivians often
made this wry joke, but others were not to utter it. The Bolivians struck
back. When the plane carrying copies of *Time* landed in La Paz, President
Hernán Siles Zuazo ordered them seized, and a government paper called
Time "The Fingernail of Imperialism's Vile Claw." For the next two days,
students burned U.S. flags, smashed windows at the U.S. Information Service (USIS) library, and stoned U.S. aid offices. The U.S. secretary of state,
Christian Herter, was furious. He railed against his official's "wise crack"
and evacuated the embassy.[1]

This incident in Bolivia was a portent of the decade to come in U.S.–
Latin American affairs. In the Western Hemisphere, like almost everywhere
else in the world, the 1960s was a decade of upheavals. From Cuba to Peru,
Latin America's upheavals were "blowbacks," defined here as dramatic political events stemming from unequal interdependence and challenging it in
fundamental ways. Different analysts characterized blowbacks differently.
On the far left of the political spectrum, blowbacks were considered to be
for the good. They aimed to break the Southern Hemisphere's dependency
on the Northern, an evil led by Wall Street and Yankee imperialists. In the
middle, where many moderate yet still nationalist Latin Americans and their
U.S. sympathizers stood, blowbacks promised to increase local control over
the economy and establish democracy more firmly. On the right, finally,
U.S. policymakers and Latin American elites saw blowbacks as a symptom
of youthful foolishness and of the seductive power of radical socialism.
They also saw them as opportunities to *increase* interdependence by bringing

45

Latin America closer to the United States through new political, economic, and military schemes, including the return of "gunboat diplomacy."

No matter the vision, most agreed that pivotal change could come at any moment: President John F. Kennedy called Latin America "the most dangerous area in the world," while his political nemesis, Nikita Khrushchev of the Soviet Union, said, "Latin America reminds one of an active volcano." Many Latin Americans expressed frustration not with their own supposedly fiery politics, but with how the East-West Cold War distorted North-South problems.[2]

The Cuban Crucible

The importance of the Cuban Revolution, triumphant on January 1, 1959, and still going as of 2005, is that it presented a workable—not smashingly successful, but workable—model of development independent of U.S. influence. Fidel Castro would not have survived long had he not been able to bring at least some gains to the Cuban people: better health and education for the masses, a decent standard of living for rural peasants and workers, and pride in achieving independence from the United States. To be sure, the revolution had a price. Political freedoms evaporated, many suffered exile or a lowered standard of living, and Cuba soon depended on a new outside power, the Soviet Union. Through time, some of these conditions changed. But in the 1960s Cuba was such a radical break from the norm that it became a crucible for U.S.–Latin American relations as a whole and allowed both U.S. citizens and Latin Americans to experiment with different combinations of responses and reforms.

The first year or so of the Cuban Revolution tells parallel stories of public and private events. Publicly, there was some civility. Castro was courteous because he still had many domestic opponents and feared Washington's anticommunism. Eisenhower's aides, meanwhile, were paralyzed into inaction because Castro could not credibly be accused of being a communist. Privately, however, both sides were deeply suspicious, assuming the worst and planning to undermine one another.

On New Year's Eve 1958, in the middle of the night, dictator Fulgencio Batista sensed the noose of the Castro-led rebellion tightening around him. He hopped on a plane and left the island. In the days that followed, Castro, his *barbudo* (bearded) rebels, and the urban underground that supported them marched through the land triumphantly, winning the hearts and minds of most Cubans. It was a time of breathless enthusiasm, during which Castro solidified his position as preeminent leader of the revolution and the barbudos prepared for a new society "of the poor, by the poor, and for the poor."[3]

The Anti-Americanization of Cuba

Shortly after taking power, Castro's group, the 26th of July Movement, and many of its moderate partners switched focus from an anti-Batista to an anti-U.S. struggle. Castro vowed to finish the job started by the Cuban patriots before the War of 1898, in which, they claimed, the United States had freed Cuba from Spanish colonialism only to hijack the island's independence with the Platt Amendment (see introduction). In the first nine months after January 1, 1959, therefore, the Cuban revolutionaries passed roughly fifteen hundred decrees, many undermining U.S. influence on their island. They slashed the rates of the U.S.-affiliated power company, increased sugar-cane cutters' wages by 15 percent, and restricted the importation of over two hundred luxury goods.[4]

Castro also made quick political moves. In January 1959 he legalized the Communist Party, and in February he declared himself premier of Cuba and postponed elections for two years. In those first few months, the barbudos held public show trials for Batista's supporters and then executed about 550 of them. All the while, Castro strongly denied being a communist and suggested he might take economic aid from Washington or other Latin American nations. He had clearly learned from Jacobo Arbenz of Guatemala that he had to move fast to inoculate himself against political enemies and economic dependence (see chapter 1).

Once his economic and political authority was more secure, Castro moved on to longer-lasting reforms. In March the Urban Reform Law passed. It reduced rents by as much as half, grabbed vacant lots for public housing, and abolished legal racial discrimination from beaches to restaurants. The Agrarian Reform, the most important law of the Cuban Revolution, followed in May. It restricted all real estate to 1,000 acres at most, raising that allowance to 3,333 acres on lands used for sugar, rice, and livestock. The Cubans would compensate expropriated landowners with bonds of twenty years at 4.5 percent, which, Havana said, was better than the U.S. government had allowed Japan after World War II. These lands would become government-owned farms, cooperatives, or small individual holdings. As 1959 went on, however, expropriations moved faster than the law allowed. Rebels on horseback often showed up waving papers at plantation doors and claiming the land for the revolution. Few owners believed they would ever be compensated for their losses, and they never were.

With the roots of U.S. economic power pulled out of Cuba, Castro locked down his political power. In April 1959 he postponed elections indefinitely. In October he put hard-liners in charge of important portfolios: for example, Che Guevara became president of the National Bank, although he knew little about finance or budgets. Castro also accused a fellow revolutionary who was having doubts, Húber Matos, of being a traitor and jailed him for twenty years. This sent a message to all others who might be tempted: toe the revolutionary line or leave Cuba. In each of the three years after 1959, over sixty thousand Cubans—most of them from the upper and middle classes—moved permanently to places such as Miami, New York City, and New Jersey.[5] In early 1960, finally, Castro shut down independent news organizations.

U.S. Paralysis

Throughout 1959 the U.S. government did little in public response to Castro's sweeping moves. At first the embassy in Havana counseled caution, fearing that any criticism might move Castro further to the left or even bring the Communist Party to power. Washington even *raised* the amount of sugar it would buy from Cuba as an enticement to moderation. When Castro visited the United States and Canada in April 1959 and made an effort to appear cooperative, crowds of thousands welcomed him as an antidictatorial reformist. He was a hero to many: a hip, anti-establishment model of rebellion for many youths and a rugged cowboy on horseback for many in the U.S. South. Children even dressed up like him and played guerrilla warfare instead of cowboys and Indians. U.S. women, too, found him irresistible. "I don't know if I'm interested or not in the Revolution," one said, "but Fidel Castro is the biggest thing to happen to North American women since Rudolph Valentino."[6] This was not the sort of leader who could be easily overthrown.

When reforms became more serious, however, U.S. ambassadors found themselves unable even to schedule meetings with Cubans. Written protests went unanswered or rejected, and the Cuban government's plans were anyone's guess. There was little that Washington could do. Cuba was a sovereign nation, was not threatening any neighbor, and was not (yet) receiving aid from behind the Iron Curtain. Castro's revolution operated within the postwar framework set up by the nations of the Western Hemisphere.

Castro Turns to the Soviets, 1960

In February 1960, however, Castro broke the postwar framework when he signed a massive trade agreement with the Soviet Union, thus making sure that someone would buy whatever goods—including one hundred million tons of sugar in the next five years—that Cuba would soon no longer sell to U.S. buyers. In return, Cuba would buy its oil from the Soviets.

The rest of the world looked on at the international tennis match unfolding before them, with Castro and Eisenhower hitting harder and harder smashes at each other. When Castro served up the Soviet trade deal, Secretary Herter returned by presenting the U.S. Congress with a plan to reduce the U.S. sugar quota for Cuba, which would either force Cuba to sell at lower prices on the world market or force the Soviets to buy at an inflated price. In June Castro hit back. He ordered U.S. oil companies in Cuba to refine oil that Castro was now buying from the Soviets. They refused, so Castro took them over. In July Eisenhower retaliated by cutting the sugar quota. Four days later the Soviets announced they would buy whatever Washington had just cut. In the coming months Castro nationalized all the banks and extended the land reform.

The Plan to Overthrow Castro

Washington's private response, meanwhile, was slow to come, but when it came, it was radical. In March 1960, one month after the Soviet trade deal, the master strategy crystallized when Eisenhower approved a four-part plan to overthrow Castro. The Central Intelligence Agency (CIA) would recruit Cuban exiles to form the opposition to Castro, conduct propaganda, spy inside Cuba, and train a force for a possible invasion. The administration made no explicit decision to invade—yet. By October of that year, however, the CIA was training four hundred to five hundred exiled Cubans in Guatemala.

In September 1960 Castro's second visit to the United States as the leader of Cuba indicated how tense the match had become. In contrast to his tour the previous year, this time he stayed only in New York City, where he made a speech to the UN in which he sympathized with oppressed peoples around the world. The Cuban delegation especially identified with African Americans, leaving its posh hotel in lower Manhattan for one in black Harlem. There, the Cubans received several guests who opposed U.S. policies, including Khrushchev, India's Jawaharlal Nehru, Egypt's Abdel Gamal Nasser, officials of the National Association for the Advancement of Colored People, baseball race pioneer Jackie Robinson, and Malcolm X, then a rising star in the Nation of Islam.[7]

In October 1960, with Castro back in Cuba, the U.S. government placed an embargo on the island, banning all U.S. exports to it except medicine and food. The same day Cuba nationalized more properties. On January 2, 1961, while he was a lame duck president waiting for the incoming Democratic administration, Eisenhower finally closed the U.S. embassy in Havana after Castro insisted that the staff be reduced to an unworkable number. U.S.-Cuban relations had reached a low unimaginable just a few years prior. John Kennedy, the young senator from Massachusetts who had criticized Eisenhower for being too ignorant and too soft with Castro, was now in the White House.

Kennedy's Activism in Latin America

The events in Cuba determined Kennedy's approach to Latin America. Kennedy was young, but he was from a powerful family of industrialists and statesmen and he had personally fought fascism in World War II. The Castro solution to social injustice—socialism and anti-imperialism—was contrary to Kennedy's upbringing. Fourteen days before Kennedy came into office, Soviet leader Khrushchev, as if to up the ante, pledged support for wars of national liberation anywhere in the world. The outspoken Soviet leader saw the future of communism in Castro-like revolutions that would throw off the shackles of imperialism or at least be a thorn in Washington's side. In response, Kennedy developed a more flexible foreign policy, which relied less on the threat of nuclear weapons and put more resources into conventional warfare and Special Forces units. Kennedy also placed a higher premium on winning "hearts and minds," and in that effort he pushed for more people-to-people contacts and larger aid programs. Kennedy was determined to be more proactive than Eisenhower had been. As he told aide Richard Goodwin, "there's a revolution going on down there [in Latin

America], and I want to be on the right side of it. Hell, we are on the right side. But we have to let them know it, that things have changed."[8]

One way Kennedy changed things in Washington was by promoting Puerto Ricans such as Teodoro Moscoso and others with a more direct understanding of Latin America, including Goodwin and Arthur Schlesinger Jr. These men personally knew moderate democratic reformers in Latin America and were eager to implement reforms that reflected new social science findings. To be sure, modernization was still the name of the game in Washington, and U.S. corporations still wanted access to cheap raw materials. Now, however, modernization benefited from political will: the White House would put its money where its mouth was and not rely just on private investment. Placing these "action intellectuals" in government, Kennedy wanted to co-opt the third way in Latin American politics by demonstrating to potential guerrillas that cooperation with the United States was better for development and democracy than was the Castro option.

The Kennedy officials were serious about changing the dynamics of U.S.–Latin American affairs, starting with the symbols. Young, charming, and Catholic, Kennedy himself was a symbol. His wife, Jackie, spoke Spanish when in Latin America. The president made three visits there, and whenever he interacted with Latin Americans he exhibited sincerity and gentlemanly courtesy. He was loved in Latin America, where his photo hung on

"What's got into you lately?" says the farmer to his nervous cow. This 1960 cartoon by Bill Mauldin expresses the dispute between U.S. investors and Latin Americans over the extraction of primary resources. Just as cows commonly give their milk to farmers without resistance, "outside investors" believe that "Latin America," here "naturalized" as an animal, should therefore give its "milk" to U.S. investors. Copyright ©1960 by Bill Mauldin. Reprinted courtesy of the Mauldin Estate.

many living room walls. In the Dominican Republic his assassination in 1963 set off days of official mourning.[9]

Kennedy's words were also important in U.S.–Latin American affairs. Adviser Adolf Berle called for a "psychological offensive in Latin America," and he got one.[10] Anti-Castro books, magazine articles, and cartoons produced by the U.S. government flooded library shelves and newsstands in Latin America. By early 1963 the radio service Voice of America broadcast 10,110 hours a week on fifteen hundred Latin American radio stations. Kennedy officials also created the Peace Corps as a people-to-people humanitarian program meant to show the underdeveloped world that young U.S. citizens were idealistic and helpful, not degenerate and arrogant. Between its founding in 1961 and 1969, more than nineteen thousand Peace Corps Volunteers served in Latin America.[11]

The Alliance for Progress

Kennedy aides countered blowbacks in Latin American with a boldness of their own—soaring political rhetoric with a massive aid program to back it up. Arthur Schlesinger, clearly influenced by modernization theory, tied the goal of democracy to the means of economic development. He wanted a "*middle-class revolution* where the processes of economic modernization carry the new urban middle class into power and produce, along with it, such necessities of modern technical society as constitutional government, honest public administration, a responsible party system, a rational land system, an efficient system of taxation, mass education, social mobility, etc." [his emphasis].[12] The program that promised to make this a reality, the Alliance for Progress, made its debut at a White House dinner for 250 Latin American dignitaries on March 13, 1961. There, Kennedy promised what the hemisphere had been clamoring for since the 1940s: a Marshall Plan for Latin America (document 4).

Details followed at an August 1961 conference in Punta del Este, Uruguay. The United States pledged $1 billion the first year, and a total of $20 billion over the next ten years, in the hopes of making the 1960s the "decade of development." This was a substantial amount for foreign aid, a budget item for which the U.S. government was notoriously stingy. The alliance set specific goals: a 2.5 percent gross domestic product (GDP) growth per year, a 50 percent rise in the standard of living, and the elimination of adult illiteracy, all by 1970. Then came the reality. The U.S. government would provide only $10 billion of the $20 billion, and private U.S. investors would supposedly put up the other $10 billion. Furthermore, Latin Americans themselves were expected to invest $80 billion of their own funds.[13] Wealthy Latin Americans would also have to curb their own privileges: redistribute land to the poor, pay more taxes (or *some* taxes), diversify trade, increase employment, strengthen democracy, and improve housing, education, and healthcare. Expectations were sky-high.

Observers in North, Central, and South America greeted the Alliance for Progress with great acclaim. But events on the ground quickly showed that few had the ability or even the desire to implement it. During the Punta del Este conference, Che Guevara, accurately reading the alliance as a way to co-opt the promises of the Cuban Revolution, called it unworkable in a capitalist system. Making for strange bedfellows, many conservatives in Washington agreed with Guevara. Both parties suspected that poor farmers who received plots of land would sell them to wealthier neighbors and begin anew the cycle of land concentration, the basis of inequality in Latin America.

Massive aid did flow. Under Kennedy and his successor, Lyndon Johnson, Latin America got twice the slice of U.S. foreign aid that it had received under Eisenhower and six times what Truman served it.[14] The results included improvements in many of the intended areas, and 1 million families received new land.[15]

But the failures were also remarkable. Accountings of the results of the alliance varied, but they generally painted a bleak portrait. The United States came up with maybe three-quarters of what it promised, but the net capital flow was much less because Latin Americans spent the decade re-paying loans.[16] Moreover, UN investigations showed that in the 1960s, out of every $100 increase in wealth, a mere $2 went to the poor; the rest lined the pockets of developers, administrators, and politicians. In the end, only seven countries out of twenty-one reached the growth target of 2.5 per-cent, and when one factors in a population growth of 3 percent, only two did, tiny Panama and Nicaragua.[17] Overall, Latin American economies grew only by 1.5 percent while the jobless increased from 18 to 25 million (docu-ment 5).[18]

The failures were also cultural. U.S. officials were unable to realize one of the key promises of modernization theory: the transfer of values that encouraged private investment, technocracy, and fairness in law. A 1965 USIA poll showed that 35 percent of Latin Americans rejected the notion of *any* U.S. aid, whether loans or outright grants.[19] Latin American elites resisted not the free money from Washington but the sacrifices that went along with it. Why would the 5 to 10 percent who owned 70 to 90 percent of the land give their property up just to stem the sometimes far-off chance of a Castro revolution? Most landowners resisted U.S. aid passively, refus-ing to work on legislative projects. Chilean leaders were more active: they called U.S.-like tax reform a communist tool.[20] Kennedy's rhetoric included the argument that "those who make peaceful revolution impossible will make violent revolution inevitable," but few seemed to believe that any revolution was inevitable.[21] From the Latin American end of the alliance, only $2 billion materialized.[22]

By 1963 and increasingly thereafter, Washington too proved less in-terested. Kennedy was assassinated late that year. Many in Congress saw the entire Alliance for Progress as mushy socialism. Little of the hoped-for private financing showed up. And finally, the Castro threat to the rest of the hemisphere had largely faded because of two traumatic events in Cuba: the

These before and after photos are from an Alliance for Progress project in Recife, northeast Brazil, in 1963. The first shows an area untouched by U.S. aid and the second, a finished housing project in the same village. Alliance for Progress administrators disseminated such photos to bolster their claim that the U.S. government was eager to help the poorest Latin Americans out of poverty and thus keep them away from Castro-style communism. Photo by Dave Richardson for U.S. News & World Report.

failed Bay of Pigs invasion and the dramatic Cuban Missile Crisis. In the eyes of many otherwise sympathetic Latin Americans, these two dramas made Castro seem a radical Marxist too friendly with the Soviet Union and attractive only to marginal political groups.

Playa Girón, 1961

Plans for the violent invasion of Cuba focused on a beach known to Cubans as Playa Girón and to U.S. citizens as the Bay of Pigs. In January 1960 a "Special Group" within the White House made the decision that the Castro regime should be overthrown.[23] Kennedy could have called the invasion off when he took over the following January. Had he wanted to do so, however, he would have faced a snowballing bureaucratic momentum: plans had been drawn and CIA training was underway. Some officials were skeptical (document 6), but most convinced the new occupant of the Oval Office that the exiles would take the beach easily and spark a revolt by Cubans on the island, who *must* hate Castro. If by chance the invasion failed, no one would be able to trace it back to Washington because no U.S. troops would be on the ground. CIA officials told Kennedy that the chances of success were "fair," but not that "fair" meant only one in four.[24]

Problems emerged early. Exiles trained rather openly in several locales in Central America and Florida, and tongues were wagging. When a group of exiles met a junior Foreign Service Officer at a Miami party in early 1961, they boasted, "We're going to take care of Castro just like we took care of Arbenz. It was easy then and it'll be easy now."[25] Meanwhile, the CIA did not trust the anti-Castro Cuban underground and failed to share information with it, thus minimizing the chances of the hoped-for uprising. The president also kept scaling back the size of the invasion so as to maintain "plausible deniability" and to avoid a Soviet retaliation against U.S. troops in Berlin. The navy's code for the operation suggested the growing skepticism: "Bumpy Road."[26]

Nevertheless, the assault proceeded, and it did so disastrously. On April 15, 1961, a small sortie by CIA-trained pilots taking off from Nicaragua did some damage to the Cuban air force. But more important, the sortie warned Castro that something bigger was coming and gave him time to arrest as many as a hundred thousand suspected dissidents and to move his remaining planes to safety. The next day, probably to secure support from other Cubans and especially the Soviets, Castro declared that Cuba was officially a Marxist-Leninist nation. The day after that, April 17, Castro reacted quickly to the early morning news of a force trying to take Girón. Cuban planes bombarded the Bay of Pigs Brigade, as it was called, sinking one ship and blowing up another. At that crucial moment, Kennedy refused to send in air strikes to cover the brigade. Castro himself soon showed up with 225,000 troops and militia, famously jumping off a tank in his olive-green uniform to survey his victory. It was a massive one. The revolutionaries killed about two hundred exiles and captured 1,180, whom they eventually released in exchange for medical supplies.

The failure of the Bay of Pigs invasion had far-reaching consequences. First, countless Latin Americans expressed sympathy for Cuba and anger against the United States, from radical students ready to emulate Castro to conservative statesmen shocked at the U.S. disdain for Cuba's sovereignty. Protesters gathered outside almost every U.S. embassy in Latin America. Chants of *"¡Cuba sí, Yanqui no!"* sounded everywhere. Second, heads rolled in Washington, starting with CIA director Allen Dulles's. Third, Kennedy himself suffered his first great setback as president, appearing at once a militaristic yet bumbling leader of the free world. He recovered somewhat by taking responsibility for the invasion rather than denying it.

At the same time, Kennedy approved a secret, stepped-up plan to destabilize Castro. Called Operation Mongoose, the plan enjoyed a $50 million budget and had over three hundred operatives working with two thousand agents in Cuba. Bobby Kennedy, the president's brother and attorney general, was particularly fond of Mongoose. "My idea," Bobby said, "is to stir things up on the island with espionage, sabotage, general disorder, run and operated by Cubans themselves."[27] The operatives and agents attacked sugar mills, bridges, and oil refineries, and planned eight different assassination attempts against Castro, some using U.S.-based mob figures, often without the knowledge of the State Department or the White House. Harebrained schemes ranged from placing an explosive seashell where Castro dove to dropping a depilatory in his shoes so his beard would fall out. Such plotting made one Brazilian economist and diplomat observe, "I found that Saxons are not as rational as they claim to be. In this particular instance of Cuba they were extremely emotional and quite irrational."[28]

The Missile Crisis, 1962

Most important, the Bay of Pigs convinced Cuban leaders that they would never be safe ninety miles from U.S. shores unless they had a surefire deterrent, something to scare the Yankees into not trying another invasion. In the first Kennedy trauma in Latin America, therefore, lay the roots of the second: the Cuban Missile Crisis of October 1962. The supposedly near-suicidal decision by Castro to place on his island Soviet offensive nuclear missiles that could spark World War III if discovered made more sense when one understood the conviction among Cubans that exiles and Washington were going to attack again. For the Soviets, meanwhile, the payoff lay in achieving the same threat level against the United States that the United States enjoyed against them by having missiles in Europe and Turkey. And, after all, there was nothing illegal in one nation's leader accepting another one's missiles on his soil. The missile crisis, while it could be interpreted as a story of U.S.-Cuban, U.S.-Soviet, or even Soviet-Cuban relations, had implications for the entire world as it marked the moment when the globe came closer than ever to annihilation.

For Washington and the rest of the noncommunist world, the crisis began when a U-2 spy plane flew secretly over the island on October 14, 1962, and took some unusual photos showing long tubes moved on trucks and set on large slabs of concrete. The next day CIA analysts, comparing the tubes to missiles that Soviets paraded in Red Square, identified them as medium-range ballistic missiles. This meant they could blast off Cuban soil and reach U.S. shores within minutes without a plane or submarine to carry them. And, of course, they could be armed with nuclear warheads. National Security Advisor McGeorge Bundy, thinking this was "a hell of a secret," informed the president first thing on October 16.[29]

Many details were still unknown—how many missiles there were in all, whether they were operational, how well they were defended—but the fact remained that Khrushchev had brazenly lied weeks earlier when Kennedy asked him if there were any missiles in Cuba. Historians and strategists do not agree on how much the placement of missiles in Cuba upset the nuclear balance, but they agree that it did. Before October 1962 the Soviets could have launched *some* such missiles from Europe. But now they had so many so close to the United States that they were edging toward what nuclear thinkers call a "first-strike capability." The stability of the Cold War so far relied on a grim algebra. Each country had the ability to withstand a first strike by the enemy and still launch its own counterstrike, called "second-strike capability." Now Washington perceived that it could lose that ability given the Soviet-Cuban move. At the very least, leaving Soviet offensive missiles in Cuba would deal a devastating political blow to Kennedy and the Democrats. The missiles had to go.

The U.S. response to the crisis took a few days to formulate (document 7). Virtually no one considered a purely diplomatic route. Most, especially the Pentagon brass, argued for a military strike with no warning. To consider such a sneak attack made Bobby Kennedy, who was in charge of the Executive Committee that secretly deliberated, feel pangs of guilt: "I now know how Tojo felt when he was planning Pearl Harbor."[30] Eventually, a third middling option emerged as the wisest. It called for a naval blockade of Cuba, formed by U.S. warships lining up between the ocean lanes that Soviets needed to travel to get to Cuban ports. This was the "quarantine" that President Kennedy announced on television on October 22.

The strategy was not foolproof, but it bought time—time to guess what Havana and the Kremlin were thinking; time for U.S. ambassador to the UN Adlai Stevenson to humiliate his Soviet counterpart on live television with photos of the missiles; time for the rest of the world to condemn Cuba and the Soviets for such a destabilizing move; time to attempt (too late, it turned out) back-channel diplomacy through Brazil; and time, after thirteen days at DefCon2 status—as close to World War III as it ever came—to strike a deal. The deal was this: the Soviet removal of the missiles from Cuba met with a secret U.S. promise to do the same with obsolete missiles in Turkey and a public promise not to try another Bay of Pigs.

U.S. Ambassador to the UN Adlai Stevenson (far right, behind the "United States" sign) confronts his Soviet counterpart Valerian Zorin (off-frame) with aerial photos of missile sites in Cuba in October 1962. Zorin refused to answer when Stevenson pressed him to either confirm or deny the existence of the sites. This public spectacle, much like the negotiations taking place secretly, involved U.S. and Soviet diplomats and largely left out Cubans. The crisis calmed days later when the Soviets agreed to remove the missiles, but the Cubans remained on edge, fearing a U.S. invasion. AP/WideWorld Photos.

Evidence released by Castro, the Soviets, and U.S. officials after the end of the Cold War shows that the danger of nuclear war was even greater than previously thought (documents 8 and 9). While the Joint Chiefs of Staff assumed that they could attack Cuba before the missiles were operational, Soviet participants have revealed that several of these nuclear-tipped missiles were ready to be fired in case of such an attack. Similarly, the CIA estimated they were dealing with ten thousand Soviet troops in Cuba; the actual number was forty-three thousand. Also unknown at the time in Washington was that Soviet field commanders in Cuba had the authority to fire nuclear weapons if communication with Moscow were cut off.[31] In one instance, two Soviet officers in one nuclear submarine (Washington also did not know those submarines were nuclear) agreed to launch a missile against U.S. ships that were dropping depth charges around them. It was only the veto of a third officer, a captain, that stopped them. "A guy called Vasili Arkhipov saved the world," is how a historian summed it up. In 1993, when one reporter asked Castro how close the world had come to annihilation during the crisis, he held up his thumb and forefinger, nearly touching them, and said, "This close!"[32]

Khrushchev and Cuban Insecurity

What was an end to the crisis for Washington and Moscow was the start of a generation-long insecurity for Havana. Khrushchev struck his deal with Kennedy without asking Castro. "Not only was this decision taken without *consulting* us, several steps were taken without *informing* us," Castro recalled in 1992. "The reaction of our nation was of profound indignation, not relief."[33] Moreover, Cuban leaders never believed Kennedy's pledge of no invasion, especially with the Mongoose group still running operations.[34] They felt betrayed and vulnerable, which only intensified their obsession with security. Cuba's fear partly explained why the island government sent guerrillas to Latin America and Africa throughout the 1960s and 1970s to foment revolution and thus take the U.S. focus off itself. It also explained why Cuban political freedoms became ever more stifled.

Kennedy, Johnson, and the Use of Force

A surefire way to get Washington's attention in the early 1960s was to praise Fidel Castro. Cheddi Jagan did so in August 1961 as he took over as prime minister of British Guiana, a newly independent nation in South America. Jagan had led a Mahatma Gandhi–like freedom struggle marked by dramatic hunger strikes and imprisonment. When Jagan hitched his star to Castro's, however, President Kennedy saw an opportunity to send out a message through covert operations. In early 1962 the CIA, in coordination with U.S. unions, financed demonstrations, riots, and looting that culminated in a general strike. This illegal, unacknowledged intervention brought down Jagan and ushered in a friendlier government.

The quasi-coup against Jagan might have seemed an unusual move for a U.S. president who was well liked in Latin America—even Castro praised Kennedy after he died—and who designed the Alliance for Progress. But this return to the use of force to facilitate U.S. goals in Latin America in the 1960s was a counterpart to the alliance, not a contradiction of it. Kennedy and his successor, Lyndon Johnson, repeatedly defined problems as military in nature and chose to use coercion to solve them. This proved a corrosive form of interdependence.

Policing Latin America

Kennedy and Johnson gave their approval to a host of programs that transferred the traditional "police" power of the United States to Latin Americans who pledged to resist any movement bringing about revolutionary change. The legal and diplomatic rationales for their approval were flimsy. The inter-American system forbade interference in other countries' affairs, and only outside aggression could bring about collective action from other American republics. Washington had to couch its military and police goals as "counterinsurgency," suggesting that it was helping defend Latin America against communists and, since communists *had* to be foreign, therefore against outside aggression. It was a flawed syllogism, to say the least.

By the early 1960s already more than nine thousand Latin American officers and enlisted men had trained for counterinsurgency at the School of the Americas in the Panama Canal Zone and at U.S. bases. The U.S. Army War College also now devoted one-fifth of its courses and field manuals to guerrilla warfare and counterinsurgency. Soon, the Pentagon joined the act and stationed Green Berets, also known as Special Forces, and U.S. Military Assistance Advisory Groups throughout Latin America. Transagency cooperation flourished too. In Central America, the U.S. government provided ruling oligarchies with a network of teletype machines—an early Internet of sorts—to share information on "subversives."[35] Through all these institutions, Latin Americans learned public-relations "civic action" programs such as road building, but they also studied interrogation techniques, antiguerrilla fighting, and surveillance of suspected communists.

While the training of Latin Americans for the military had a long history, new initiatives extended that training to civilians—in short, the police—thus suggesting that U.S. assistance in no way defended against attacks from abroad. In 1962 the canal zone saw the creation of the Inter-American Police Academy, which later moved to Georgetown University and changed its name to the International Police Academy.[36] In August of that same year Kennedy added a special police assistance program, the Office of Public Safety, and by 1966 38 percent of its budget boosted "internal security" in every Latin American country except Cuba. It provided the tools necessary for repression, from fire hoses to batons to wiretapping equipment.[37] As a result, in the 1960s more U.S. technicians abroad worked on police projects than in health and sanitation.[38]

Bureaucratic-Authoritarian Allies

The impact of security programs was mixed. Washington certainly saw its primary goal realized: there were no successful guerrilla revolutions after Castro's. A secondary, but important, goal was less successful. U.S. training was supposed to create professional, nonpolitical security forces. Instead it created political Frankenstein monsters, "bureaucratic-authoritarian" regimes that were not tied to a charismatic dictator but were self-perpetuating machines of repression and corruption.[39] A military that had more weapons and know-how was a military that had more political pull. From 1961 to 1966 nine Latin American countries suffered military coups and became such regimes. In 1962–63 alone representative governments fell to military coups in Argentina, Peru, Guatemala, Ecuador, Honduras, and the Dominican Republic.

Little evidence indicates that Washington produced these coups, and it strongly opposed some of them. But it did make many of them feel welcome once they were done deals. Called the "Mann Doctrine," this new willingness to place military regimes on nearly the same footing as democratic ones emerged in early 1964 out of the appointment of Thomas Mann as assistant secretary of state for inter-American affairs. The doc-

trine formulated four goals: (1) to neither encourage nor hinder social reform; (2) to protect U.S. investments; (3) to be more tolerant of military
regimes; and (4) to fight against communism in the hemisphere. As part of
this policy, the U.S. government helped organize the Central American Defense Council in 1964, uniting national armed forces into a regional military
alliance and later integrating it into the U.S. Southern Command. The Johnson
government also continued, reinitiated, or increased its support to long-time
dictators Anastazio Somoza of Nicaragua, Alfredo Stroessner of Paraguay,
and François "Papa Doc" Duvalier of Haiti.

Three crises in Latin America tested the anticommunist use of force
of the Johnson administration, showing it to be sometimes blindly reactionary and at other times sharply attuned to local conditions. The president
himself was a Texas New Dealer torn between disdain for Latinos and
other minorities and a sincere willingness to play fair and help the under-
privileged. As a young man, he had taught Mexican American schoolchil-
dren, and the paternalism of the schoolmaster seemed to linger in him. "I
know these Latin Americans," he once explained in his folksy way. "I grew
up with Mexicans. They'll come right into your yard and take it over if you
let them. And the next day they'll be right up on your porch, barefoot and
weighing one hundred and thirty pounds and they'll take that too. But if you
say to 'em right at the start, 'Hold on, just wait a minute,' they'll know they're
dealing with somebody who'll stand up. And after you can get along fine."[40]

Johnson Crisis I: Panama, 1964

Johnson applied this combination of defensiveness and understanding to
his first foreign policy crisis as president: Panama. In January 1964 Panamanians overstepped what the president considered the U.S. "porch"—the
Panama Canal Zone—and Johnson "stood up" to them. The thousands of
"Zonians" who lived in that ten-mile wide strip of land bisecting the Republic of Panama were a mixture of short-time U.S. military personnel and two
long-time populations: blacks from the English-speaking West Indies and
white U.S. civilians running the waterway since it opened in 1914. This last
group, especially, felt a strong attachment to the place. In the canal zone,
U.S. engineering, commerce, and military might radiated for all to see. The
zone was socially separate from the Republic of Panama even though parts
of it lay literally across the street. Until the 1950s Zonians enforced Jim
Crow racial segregation there. Despite the strangeness of their circumstances,
Zonians lived more or less normal, even dull, lives. They worked on the
locks of the canal and bought imported food at local military stores. Their
children went to English-speaking high schools, watched Hollywood movies, and played U.S. football. According to the Treaty of 1903 that regulated
U.S. power over the canal, the zone was to be run by the U.S. government
"as if" it were sovereign. The Zonians certainly considered themselves fully
sovereign, and they would not leave without a fight.

By 1964 several factors combined to bring that fight to the Zonians.

Panamanian nationalists had clamored for decades for greater benefits from the waterway that ran through the middle of their country. They wanted a greater annual rent, more contracts to provide services to the zone, and so on. They won some concessions in 1936 and 1955. In the late 1950s two events reinvigorated the nationalist movement: the 1956 Egyptian struggle to nationalize the Suez Canal and the Cuban Revolution. Panamanians now argued that their country was not a partner of the United States, but a colony of it. They wanted far more control over the waterway (though few wanted a complete turnover). But how to do it? More endless negotiations for minor changes? Students, professors, and other nationalists instead wanted a symbolic victory: the flying of the Panama flag in the zone. They started regularly marching into the zone to plant flags there. During one such demonstration in 1959, riots broke out when a sixteen-year-old boy wrapped his flag around a zone policeman's head and said, "It's dirty, now!"[41]

Panama City and Washington finally agreed to fly both countries' flags, but one high school principal in the town of Balboa preferred to fly no flag at all, hoping to preempt any trouble. Big mistake. When the U.S. teenagers at Balboa High School learned of the principal's decision, on January 7, 1964, they ran their makeshift Stars and Stripes up the pole in front of their school. On January 9, Panamanian students, with their own flag, marched into the zone to protest. Zone police were there to meet them, a scuffle ensued, and the Panamanian flag was torn. Within a few hours, the U.S. Army took over what had become a major riot in the roads and buildings between the Republic of Panama and the zone. In four days of confused shooting and looting, twenty-one Panamanians and four U.S. troops died. Hundreds were injured.

This incident turned out to be a perfect opportunity to try out the carrot-and-stick pragmatism of the Mann Doctrine. The Johnson administration could have appeased Panama by showering it with Alliance for Progress funds, or it could have killed more wantonly and refused to apologize or negotiate. Johnson said he was "damn tired of packing our flag and our embassy and our USIS every time somebody got a little emotional outburst. . . . They better *watch* it!"[42] But the president chose the middle route. He expressed regret for the incident and, before the year was out, promised to build a new canal and hand over the present one to the Panamanians. However, he also timed his concessions to have the ruling party re-elected and then almost doubled the size of Panama's security force. In case of another riot, local troops would do the dirty work of repression.[43]

Johnson Crisis II: Brazil, 1964

A second, more serious crisis soon followed in Brazil. There, Johnson and his staff proved more underhanded in backing a militarist regime against a perceived threat of social revolution. Brazil had long been a large, delicate piece of the puzzle of U.S.–Latin American relations. It had tremendous potential: great agricultural, mineral, and labor resources; the largest internal market in South America; and an oft-repeated faith that it was freer of racism than was the United States. During the first presidency of Getulio Vargas and his Estado Novo (1937–45), Brazil had shown impressive industrialization and wartime cooperation with the United States. But Brazil was also a counterpoint to the "Colossus of the North" and could conceivably stand up to it given Brazil's size and the distance between the two. During his second mandate especially (1951–54), Vargas pursued a nationalist foreign policy similar to Juan Perón's in Argentina.

The disappointing economy, however—including a rate of inflation between 80 and 90 percent in 1953 and 1954—lent a tragic air to Vargas's return to office. One morning in 1954 he shot himself through the heart.[44] His suicide note expressed strong anti-U.S. fatalism. "I follow the destiny that is imposed on me. After years of domination and looting by international economic and financial groups, I made myself chief of an unconquerable revolution. . . . Profits of foreign enterprises reached 500 per cent yearly. In declarations of goods that we import there existed frauds of more than $100,000,000. I saw the coffee crisis increase the value of our principal product. We attempted to defend its price and the reply was a violent pressure upon our economy to the point of being obliged to surrender. . . . I fought against the looting of Brazil."[45]

Washington did not believe it was doing any "looting" in Brazil, took exception to Vargas's rule, and grew even more opposed to two of his successors, Jânio Quadros (1960–61) and João Goulart (1961–64). U.S. observers considered these governments inefficient and feared that inflation was out of control. It did not help that Goulart backed the expropriation of a subsidiary of International Telephone and Telegraph (ITT) and announced further takeovers of refineries and underutilized lands. Washington was beginning to see in Goulart another Arbenz, or worse, another Castro. Somewhat as in Panama, Kennedy and Johnson had a carrot-and-stick policy toward Brazil. With one hand, they gave Alliance for Progress funding. With the other, the CIA funded opposition campaigns in 1962 to the tune of $5 million.[46] Johnson then increasingly withheld aid funds, in a clear message that Washington understood the addictive nature of foreign aid.

In late March 1964, recently declassified phone conversations now confirm, the U.S. embassy made contact with anti-Goulart conspirators, promised them arms and supplies if needed, and formed a naval task force that would intervene in case of civil war. "I think we ought to take every step that we can, be prepared to do everything that we need to do, just as we were in Panama," Johnson told his advisers from the White House. "I'd get right on top of it and stick my neck out a little."[47] It was an unmistakable green light for a coup. The operation's code name: "Brother Sam."

The events of March 31, 1964, were less than brotherly. A coalition of Brazilian military and civilian leaders staged a coup against Goulart, who put up little resistance—and so U.S. assistance was never needed. Wisely bowing to some constitutionality, on April 11 coup leaders had the Brazilian

Congress elect Gen. Humberto de Alencar Castelo Branco president. Back in Washington, Johnson breathed a sigh of relief. He recognized the regime twelve days later with his "warmest wishes" and showered it with $1.5 billion dollars in aid in the next four years. The regime became a model of bureaucratic authoritarianism. Generals unleashed their revenge on enemies and Castelo Branco became the first of five dictators who ruled Brazil until 1985, but Brazil also began a sustained period of growth that satisfied foreign investors.[48]

Johnson Crisis III: Dominican Republic, 1965

A third crisis, this one in the Dominican Republic, marked a qualitative jump in the use of force: the sending of U.S. troops to quell an internal revolt. Events in spring 1965 resulted from the instability following the assassination of dictator Rafael Trujillo in May 1961. Since taking power in 1930, Trujillo had been an ambivalent ally of Washington. He faithfully repressed any efforts at leftist insurgency within his own country and in much of the Caribbean. But he also strained Good Neighbor diplomacy by bribing U.S. Congress members and planting stories in the press, by attempting to blow up the president of Venezuela, and by being an all-around embarrassment with his outrageous cult of personality (he held hundreds of decorous titles and renamed the largest city and tallest mountain in the country after himself) and sadism (his secret police liked to throw dissidents in a shark tank).[49] Both Eisenhower and Kennedy thought of having the tyrant "sawed off" the U.S. tree so as to balance their efforts to eliminate Castro. Kennedy's CIA, working through the embassy, provided rifles to those who gunned down Trujillo as he was driven down a country road leading to the home of his twenty-year-old mistress.[50]

Between 1961 and 1965 Dominicans divided sharply along pro-Trujillo and anti-Trujillo lines. Among the former were the dictator's family, military leaders, large investors, and Joaquín Balaguer, who was Trujillo's prime minister and a sly politician who garnered the sympathy of the many peasants who feared revolution. Among the *anti-trujillistas* were former underground opposition leaders, exiles in New York City and Puerto Rico, and Juan Bosch, a talented writer and reformist who also had the magic touch with peasants and won the presidency but lost it to a military coup seven months later in 1963. During this period, the U.S. embassy in Santo Domingo tended to prefer "a forceful leader" in the Dominican Republic because "the people are not now politically educated to accept democracy as it exists in the United States."[51] On April 24, 1965, a civil conflict erupted, aligned behind Bosch and Balaguer and their military friends. Within days, Bosch's followers held downtown Santo Domingo while Balaguer's sympathizers surrounded the city.

The White House—and Johnson especially, as evidenced in his phone conversations—exaggerated the danger of Castro-trained and Castro-directed forces from outside the Dominican Republic. The few hundred far-left supporters later claimed that they did want to take advantage of the chaos to cause a revolution, but they also said that their prospects were dim. They had little assistance—and certainly no direction—from Havana or Moscow. Yet the White House encouraged the CIA and the embassy to provide evidence of anti-American control, no matter how flimsy (document 10). On April 28 Johnson sent hundreds of marines to protect U.S. citizens and other foreign nationals. He simultaneously considered sending thousands more troops to stop any effort at social revolution by "outside powers." On the phone, Secretary of Defense Robert McNamara explained to him:

> Well, I think you've got a pretty tough job to prove that, Mr. President. As president. The rest of us can say things like that and we don't have to prove it. But you've got a handful of people there [identified communists in Santo Domingo]. You don't know that Castro is trying to do anything. You'd have a hard time proving to any group that Castro has done more than train these people. *We've* trained a lot of people. *He's* trained a lot of people. I think this puts your own status and prestige too much on the line. . . . [The CIA has not] shown any evidence that I've seen that Castro has been directing this or has had any control over those people.[52]

Nevertheless, Johnson preferred overkill to worldly caution. Within days, over twenty thousand U.S. armed forces landed around Santo Domingo. They evacuated foreign nationals but also cordoned off the Bosch rebels in a siege of the downtown area. They also established official and back-channel diplomacy that led, in early September, to an agreement among Dominicans to create a temporary government and hold an election. In that election in 1966 voters chose the U.S.-funded Balaguer as their next president, and U.S. troops left thereafter. It was a surprisingly successful outcome for a sudden return to direct U.S. "gunboat diplomacy," a tactic not seen since the 1930s.

To many in Latin America, the Dominican episode and other uses of force laid bare the continuing power relationship in the hemisphere. There was interdependence, yes, but it was asymmetrical, or unequal. Washington, in the end, would do whatever was necessary to keep in office regimes that ensured the stability of U.S. interests.

The *Foco* Theory and Guevara's Undoing, 1967

The new military boldness of the United States may have incited some to desperate measures in order to produce blowbacks. Guerrilla warfare was such a measure. The multiplication of guerrilla groups in the early 1960s stemmed in part from the *foco* theory, formulated most clearly by French Marxist Régis Debray. The traditional, defensive vision of communism held that leftist groups needed to form a united front and work within democracies so as to eventually bring about a dictatorship of the proletariat. Not so, countered Debray. Political power was there for the taking. All it took was a small core, or "foco," of individuals determined to create an insurgency from outside the military and use the countryside to build up their forces. They would make change, not wait for it. The theory was optimistic and exhilarating.

Che Guevara became the living embodiment of the foco theory. Guevara had not only participated in a foco-like struggle with Fidel Castro but also promised that a "new man" would emerge from these victories—a humanist, nonmaterialist hero to the people. Guevara saw in the rebellion of the Viet Cong in Southeast Asia a model, and he called for the worldwide disruption of U.S. strategies through "one, two, many Vietnams" in Latin America and elsewhere.

Guevara's fervor was also his demise. In 1965 he left Cuba for what he felt was his real mission in life. He wrote to Castro, "I carry to new battlefronts the faith that you taught me, the revolutionary spirit of my people, the feeling of fulfilling the most sacred of duties: to fight against imperialism wherever it may be."[53] Guevara traveled throughout Latin America and Africa, joining and inspiring guerrillas, but rarely seeing them succeed. Eventually he joined a ragtag outfit in the mountains of Bolivia. In October 1967 Bolivian authorities, helped by CIA agent Eddie González, captured and shot many of the hungry, tired guerrillas, including Guevara. To prove his death to those who might want to believe that he survived, the authorities circulated a grim photo of his corpse. A week later Castro called Guevara's death "a fierce blow, a very hard one."[54]

The harshness of the blow was partly a realization that few Latin Americans were willing to follow Guevara into near-suicidal violence. Compared to the tens of thousands whom U.S. officers trained in counterinsurgency, only a few thousand ever took Cuban or other guerrilla training. Guerrillas needed a weak state to attack, and the U.S. use of force had made bureaucratic-authoritarian states stronger than ever.[55]

Migrants and Militants

In the late 1960s Latin Americans increasingly turned to less violent solutions as blowbacks against the perceived U.S. control over destinies that were not getting any richer or more secure. Whether they voted with their feet and migrated north, or whether they voted for leaders who promised to separate their economies from Wall Street's so as to modernize them, ordinary Latin Americans increasingly played a part in inter-American affairs.

Immigration Reform, 1965

In 1965 the United States suddenly seemed to open its doors to greater immigration from the region. President Johnson stood at the base of the Statue of Liberty, the traditional greeter of immigrants to the East Coast, and announced amendments to the Immigration and Nationality Act. The amendments eliminated the quota system in place since the 1920s, which had discriminated against immigrants from Asia and Eastern Europe. Many have suggested that Latin American immigrants benefited from this new system, but the record is mixed. The Western Hemisphere was exempt from quotas *before* 1965. Back then, hemispheric migrants came in either legally through labor arrangements such as the Bracero Program (1942–64) or illegally by simply crossing over from Mexico. In the early 1960s immigration from Mexico and farther south was about equal parts legal and illegal. The 1965 law placed limits on visas granted to Latin Americans for the first time. The impact was to convert many legal immigrants who were unable to obtain new visas into illegal, or—here was born a new word— "undocumented" immigrants.

The post-1965 side-by-side existence of "legals" and "illegals" brought about a greater politicization of Latinos, that is, Latin Americans now living in the United States. Much of that politicization followed the African American model. Before World War II, like blacks, Latinos had organized into mutual aid societies. After the war the American GI Forum and the League of United Latin American Citizens increasingly defended Latinos who were kept from the ballot box by requirements similar to those forced upon African Americans. In the mid-1960s, César Chávez, a self-taught union organizer whose family had been farming in the United States since the 1880s, spearheaded the integrationist model through labor organization. His group, the United Farm Workers, helped win major concessions for those who toiled long hours in the grape fields of California.

Mexican migrant worker Clemente Mendoza is being fumigated at an immigration processing center in El Centro, Mexico, 1958. Mendoza was headed for California to harvest carrots. Under the Bracero Program (1942–64) a half million workers like him were taken each year by bus or train to the border, where they underwent medical exams, questioning, fumigation, and inoculation. At the U.S. farm camps, they worked for 80 cents an hour. Photo by Earl Thiesen for Cowles Communications.

Chicano Pride and Protest

Also like African Americans in the late 1960s, cultural pride boomed among Latinos and with it came calls for separation from the "Anglo" mainstream. Many used the term for poor Mexican Americans, *chicanos*, and conflated it with *la Raza* ("the race" or "the people"), meaning that all Latin Americans derived their uniqueness from the blending of linguistic and ethic heritages. They also claimed ownership of a land that once belonged to their ancestors and now encompassed much of the U.S. South and West. In 1971–72 La Raza militants handed out a manifesto that announced

> We the people of the Southwest hereby declare ourselves a nation, and as a nation that has been the subject of a profit-making invasion. We are a nation with a land that has been temporarily occupied. And we are a nation with the ability to survive. We are a nation with great natural culturability. We are a nation, we who come from different ways, combining ourselves in one nation.[56]

One of the more militant La Raza groups, the Brown Berets, emulated an African American group, the Black Panthers. They sought empowerment through separation, not integration, had a ten-point program for attaining it, and adopted the symbols and solutions of militarism. The somewhat more moderate Young Lords, formed in 1969, produced many of the future activists of the 1970s.

Throughout Latin America in the late 1960s, blowbacks did not end, but they fractured, like the antiwar and civil-rights struggles in the United States. When Mexican students erupted in a general revolt against authority in 1968, for instance, it seemed that they were undergoing the same tumult that was rocking much of the world at the time. But it also appeared to many in Washington that Latin Americans chose to vent their anger on U.S. symbols. From 1968 to 1979 the CIA counted 455 attacks against U.S. targets in Latin America. Four of every ten anti-U.S. assaults around the world were in the region.[57] These attacks included bombings of U.S. embassies and USIS centers, sabotages of U.S. corporations such as Goodyear, Chrysler, and Pepsi-Cola, and kidnappings of U.S. ambassadors—including Burke Elbrick, whose ordeal was captured in the 1997 Brazilian film *Four Days in September.*

The United States offered no overall response. Policymakers were distracted by the growing commitment in Vietnam and the protest against it, running out of patience with radicalism in general, and wary of formulating another massive commitment such as a new Good Neighbor Policy or an Alliance for Progress. Washington dealt with problems on a case-by-case basis while suspecting all progressive change as radicalism.

Military Militancy: Peru, 1968

In Peru, the actions of a new military government discredited Washington's views on such regimes' inherent stability. Rather than loosening land ownership and tax laws for investors, it nationalized the International Petroleum

Company, a subsidiary of Standard Oil of New Jersey. Immediately, the embassy mentioned the Hickenlooper Amendment of 1963, which called for the termination of U.S. economic aid to any country that failed to compensate appropriately when expropriating. But Peru in 1968 was not Guatemala in 1954. It was bigger, farther away, and not likely to follow the Castro path. The expropriation in this case was a reasonable nationalistic move to increase control over the economy. The Department of State opposed sanctions against Peru, and President Richard Nixon agreed. Further, polls showed that U.S. investors thought enforcing the Hickenlooper Amendment in Peru could backfire. Instead, investors wanted a more open environment, e.g., closer cooperation with local governments, firmer rules of the game, shared management between U.S. and Peruvian citizens, and investment insurance.[58] Taking the middle road, Nixon delayed aid until Peru convinced the United States to invest further, and both reached a settlement in 1974.

The Consensus at Viña, 1969

At the end of the tumultuous 1960s, the foreign ministers of Latin America met without their U.S. counterparts to review recent U.S.–Latin American affairs. On June 11, 1969, they presented to Nixon their conclusions, called the "Consensus of Viña del Mar" after the posh Chilean resort town where they stayed. Weeks before the moon landing set off a celebration of U.S. technological savvy, the consensus dolefully reported on Latin America's underdevelopment. Since World War II, it said, programs such as the Alliance for Progress had not responded to Latin American desires, which were, in the end, to have the United States practice what it preached. While the United States promised free trade, it imposed tariffs that made it impossible for poor countries to crack its markets. While it provided economic aid, it forced recipients to buy U.S. goods with the money.

∎ ∎ ∎

What Latin Americans at Viña and elsewhere prioritized was not an obsessive fight with communism. Polls consistently showed that few were afraid of Castro-like takeovers and that fewer still would accept one, a point they had made repeatedly with blowbacks against U.S. power during the previous decade. Washington's response to the blowbacks, however, had been mostly to prevent them through increased repression and the preemption of attempts, like Castro's in Cuba, to uproot U.S. power from Latin America. The 1970s would offer another opportunity for readjusting the path of integration of the hemisphere. Latin Americans, after all, had rarely said that they opposed interdependence. But they wanted it achieved fairly, openly, and while keeping in mind each nation's cultural distinctiveness and path toward development. While more U.S. political leaders grew attentive to such requests, many others felt more secure in allowing the development of "dirty wars" against Latin American opposition groups.

CHAPTER 3

DIRTY WARS

Industrialization, Human Rights, and the Violence
of Poverty, 1970–80

FIRST PUBLISHED IN SPANISH IN 1976, the Argentine Manuel Puig's novel *The Kiss of the Spider Woman* introduced a subtle new interweaving in U.S.–Latin American affairs. Its story revolves around two prisoners sharing a Buenos Aires cell during Argentina's repressive "Dirty War." One of these is Valentín, an atheist Marxist jailed for organizing workers and a man who rejects sensual pleasures as bourgeois indulgences. His cell mate, Molina, is an unabashedly gay man who could not care less about politics. Throughout the book, Molina entertains Valentín by making up elaborate romantic stories of femmes fatales, evil Nazis, and a mysterious panther woman. *Kiss of the Spider Woman* reached large audiences both in Latin America and the United States, first as a novel, then as a play and as a movie. But what did it have to do with U.S.–Latin American relations? Very little explicitly; the United States was rarely mentioned in Molina's stories. However, the liberated gay man's eventual seduction of the—up to then—heterosexual Valentín suggested a new kind of liberation for Latin Americans: not an external liberation from Yankee imperialism, but an internal liberation from a culture of repression against "deviants" from rigid social orders. In *this* liberation, Puig seemed influenced by a more open U.S. society. Molina's visions were embellishments on Hollywood film noir. In contrast to Latin America's socially realist novels of the 1940s and 1950s, which pitted virtuous peasants against evil U.S. plantation owners, *Kiss* brought psychological depth and mature social themes to Latin American literature. It also heralded both more *and* less dependence on the United States.

As subtle as *Kiss of the Spider Woman*, 1970–80 is often perceived as a less dramatic decade in U.S.–Latin American relations, mostly because it lacked a military confrontation with the United States like the Bay of Pigs in 1961 or the Contra War of the 1980s. But below the surface, major changes were brewing. The decade saw another cycle in the growing interdepen-

dence—and not necessarily the pacification—of U.S.–Latin American relations. It introduced an increased push for economic integration, this time
through greater globalization of capital, which led to a growing gap between
the few rich and the many poor. Many of these poor identified the United
States as lying at the root of their misery and organized to reduce or eliminate the North's presence from Latin America. The U.S. response to this
new round of upheavals was also cyclical. Washington optimistically backed
integration, then reacted to misery and protest with a rare show of concern
for human rights, but then took a sharp turn away from encouraging
antidictatorial struggles and toward defining them as regional battles in a
worldwide communist assault.

Dependency Versus Diffusion, Round Two

Debates over economic models continued to divide Latin American and
U.S. citizens in the 1970s and 1980s just as they continued to define political
allegiances. But the world economy itself had changed, and each side in the
debate between dependency and diffusion that began in the 1950s now had
sharper tools with which to carve out its arguments.

State Control Over Economic Growth and Integration

The dependencistas held sway over most Latin American intellectuals and
public-university students and over similar U.S. groups. In the 1970s Marxist sociology and economics, often explained in hackneyed language about
the inevitabilities of capital's expansion abroad and the proletariat–business
owner struggle, pervaded university curricula in Latin America. These views
were often based on observations that were a century old and far removed
from the economies of Latin America. More up-to-date, and more likely to
get Washington's attention, were the many intellectual and political leaders
who observed that significant state control was still necessary even if free
markets and globalization had their benefits. These "neo-Marxist" nationalists largely rejected the vision of a Moscow-supported revolution, partly
because they witnessed its failure to bring good sugar harvests to Cuba.

What the neo-Marxists *did* observe was that economic growth was
revving up. Latin America's real GDP rose on average by 4.1 percent per
year in the 1970s, more than any other developing region and more than in
the Alliance-for-Progress days of the 1960s. This increase was partly due to
shifts in the basic structures of Latin American economies: away from
agricultural products, such as sugar and corn, and cheap consumer goods,
such as textiles and shoes, and toward big-ticket items such as steel, machinery, automobiles, and electrical products. Some countries, especially Brazil,
Argentina, Mexico, and Uruguay, underwent major industrial overhauls. And
Mexico, Venezuela, and Ecuador all benefited from the dramatic rise in the
price of oil on world markets. Oil profits enhanced desires for self-empow-
erment and dreams of massive social programs. Economic change brought
social change: more women in the workforce, more doctors per person,

more hospital beds, and more access to potable water and sewage disposal. Life expectancy, education, and literacy all rose. Much of this indeed seemed like a victory for modernization theory. Yet all these improvements were achieved while Latin American governments spent on their economies more than twice what Washington did—the sort of industrial subsidy that dependency theorists had championed.[1] Who would want smaller government in this situation?

The U.S. near-monopoly over foreign capital and trade was also no longer so monopolistic. From the early 1960s to the late 1970s, the proportion of Latin America's exports that was shipped to the United States decreased from 37.2 percent to 35 percent while its share of imports from the United States diminished from 41.8 to 32.9 percent.[2] Who filled the gap? Europe, as always, but Japan, Canada, and the Soviet bloc were also "in on the action."

In addition, Latin Americans increasingly traded with each other. The 1960s saw several common-market schemes hatched, some with limited achievements, but all with a shared sense of self-sufficiency achieved through a lowering of trade tariffs and barriers. Among these were the Latin American Free Trade Association (founded in 1960); the Central American Common Market (1961); the Caribbean Free Trade Community (1967; later the Caribbean Community and Common Market); the East Caribbean Common Market (1968); the Andean Group (1969); and the Latin American Economic System (1975).

The "Chicago Boys" and Free Trade Zones

Meanwhile, in the United States and among many U.S.-educated Latin American elites, an opposite consensus grew around the idea that state control had to be kept to a minimum, that eliminating nationalizations was not enough, that the door to the hemisphere's resources must be fully open to any foreign investor. One group of about one hundred University of Chicago–trained economists, mostly returning to Chile to work in government, led this charge for "neoclassical" economics. They were known as the "Chicago Boys." Their beliefs were not only economic: they also argued that the free market was the best guarantee of *political* freedoms, including democracy. State control, they said, only brought about a monster bureaucracy and lazy public servants, both of which corrupted politics. They championed strict spending so as to curb inflation and bring Latin American currencies more in sync with world markets.

The mindset shared by the "Chicago Boys" allowed the expansion of export processing zones (EPZs), commonly referred to as *zonas francas,* which proliferated after the late 1960s. EPZs were industrial parks, usually found near ports, where mammoth modern factories employed thousands of workers in a variety of manufacturing—some of it was light, such as t-shirts and underwear, while some was hi-tech, for instance, the assembly of computers. These factories paid no taxes on what they imported or exported, or on profits, so they would not raise revenue for the host governments directly. This did not bother the diffusionists, who believed government was the problem. Besides, the government would get something from the EPZs because they would provide jobs to those living in shantytowns. Employed citizens would pay income and perhaps property taxes, would consume more, and would not be leeches on government services. Practically since their creation, EPZs elicited mixed feelings. While employees often appreciated the steady jobs and wages, they and outside observers complained that "sweatshop" owners denied the right to unionize and that managers abused the mostly female workers physically, mentally, and sexually.

Border Towns

Industrialization most dramatically transformed the Mexican border towns, the front lines of globalization. In the early twentieth century locals mostly raised cattle or worked on farms along the two-thousand-mile U.S. border. But *maquiladoras*, or assembly plants, almost all owned by U.S. investors, sprang up along the border as trade barriers became looser and looser. The mid-1960s Border Industrialization Plan (BIP) hammered out between the United States and Mexico sped up this process. From 1966 to 1988 maquiladoras mushroomed from 57 to 1,481, while the jobs they provided went from about 4,000 to nearly 400,000.[3] The BIP encouraged U.S. factory owners to create "twin plants" along the border to reduce immigration but ended up moving the factories themselves. In one year alone General Motors opened twelve new maquiladoras in Mexico while closing eleven factories in the United States. In the process, it fired twenty-nine thousand workers.[4]

The result was chaos along the border. From 1940 to 1970 employment in towns such as Tijuana, Mexicali, Nogales, Ciudad Juárez, Nuevo Laredo, and Matamoros grew tenfold while employment in Mexico as a whole only doubled.[5] Mexicans living and working along the border had increasingly indirect relationships with those who signed their paychecks. Few, if any, were unionized. Culturally, denizens of border towns became what anthropologists called "deterritorialized." They lived in a place where few laws seemed to apply, where drugs flowed northward to U.S. consumers and U.S. youths flowed southward for a night of tequila shots. Whatever culture there was seemed neither American nor Mexican, neither Spanish- nor English-speaking, neither Protestant nor Catholic. It was purely money-driven.

Perhaps most seriously, the environmental and health devastations were dramatic. The Rio Grande became an open sewer in parts. More children living there had cancer or were born deformed because of the uncontrolled release of toxic chemicals. Rates of liver cancer and hepatitis rose for border-town residents. And accident rates at factories grew to among the highest in the world.[6] To be sure, life was better in some ways—there were more schools, more doctors, and more cars—but were they worth it?

This 1976 poster contained a wealth of information on its back, both to help migrants integrate better into Arizona life and to help Arizonans better understand the migrant experience. It emphasized that "Arizona has always had migrant workers" and listed books on immigration, services offered, and agencies that could help migrants. Such programs were the long-term result of decades of Latino self-help and activism. Designed by William Jeffrey Harttner. Reprinted with permission of the Tucson-Pima Public Library, Tucson, Arizona, 2005.

In unity there is strength
La union hace la fuerza

MEXICAN MIGRANT LABOR IN ARIZONA

Fears of Cultural Hegemony

Latin Americans increasingly feared the effects of U.S.-led globalization not only on their pocketbooks but also on their minds. By the 1970s Western intellectuals were exploring the many ways that global media, operating through publishing, radio, and the new Latin American medium of television, quickly changed local cultural values. The fear of globalization was largely generational. Older Latin Americans reared on pious Catholic values and strict gender roles found it dreadful that their sons and daughters grew obsessed with their physical appearances, associated happiness with consumer goods, and challenged the "proper place" of women in society. Some called this process "cultural imperialism," others called it "hegemony." Both terms implied, at the very least, a system of informal social control that required some participation on the part of those controlled: shopping for Levi's jeans, dancing to rock 'n' roll, sitting in front of the TV set.

In 1972 two Latin American scholars successfully made the link between abstract theories and popular culture in a short book titled *How to Read Donald Duck*. This odd study of el Pato Donald was a hit despite its hard-to-read jargon. It reproduced several pages of Disney comic books, hugely popular among Latin American children, and analyzed them creatively. It argued that the supposedly innocent characters of Donald Duck cartoons subtly taught children that the highest civilization was that which celebrated greed (the thirst for hidden treasures), disdained "natives" (the ignorant tribes who stood in Donald's path to riches), and denied any responsibility for the future (through the absence of a parental link between Donald and his nephews). Critics of this study pointed to its many shortcomings: that the argument against Donald was stretched too thin and that, in any case, the comic books were sold also in industrialized countries and so were not meant to "brainwash" Latin Americans. Regardless, the authors struck a chord with many Latin Americans, and their concerns would only multiply in the coming years as more and more Latin Americans moved into towns and cities wired with electricity. There, they consumed ever-greater amounts of U.S. film, music, and, by the early 1980s, the swirling cultural chaos of cable television.

Nixon, Kissinger, and the Chilean Coup

"You come here speaking of Latin America, but this is not important. Nothing important can come from the South. . . . The axis of history starts in Moscow, goes to Bonn, crosses over to Washington, and then goes to Tokyo. What happens in the South is of no importance." So spoke National Security Adviser Henry Kissinger to Chilean Foreign Minister Gabriel Valdés during a White House meeting in June 1969. Valdés, insulted, answered that Kissinger knew nothing about South America. "No, and I don't care," Kissinger replied.[7] Kissinger's dismissal of the Chilean lacked tact, but it honestly expressed one influential approach to U.S.–Latin American affairs during the presidency of Richard Nixon: Realpolitik.

Kissinger, a Jewish German immigrant who had been a star academic at Harvard University, spent a career honing the concept of a "realist" foreign policy and adapting it to the Cold War. This Realpolitik held that events in small, powerless countries such as Chile were only important if they affected, by some "linkage" with larger countries, the centers of power of the world. Morality did not enter the equation. So if a dictator in Latin America, say, unleashed brutal ethnic violence that killed millions of his own people, it was a horrible tragedy but not "realistic" for the United States to respond. However, if the violence set off a mass migration that closed down major transportation routes and weakened U.S. commerce vis-à-vis the Soviets, then the massacre took on "geopolitical" importance. As long as Chileans ran a stable society, therefore, Kissinger paid them no mind. Kissinger and Nixon also agreed that the most effective U.S. tool for ensuring stability was the Latin American military. As Nixon said to aides in 1970, "I will never agree with the policy of downgrading the military in Latin America. They are power centers subject to our influence. The others [the intellectuals] are not subject to our influence" (document 11).[8]

The Rockefeller Report

Nixon's Latin American policy—and, by inference, his Chilean policy—was also embodied in another, more ambivalent analysis. In 1969 the president tapped Nelson Rockefeller, who had years of experience in Latin America, to investigate conditions there and make recommendations for future U.S. policy. Traveling to the region four times with a slew of experts, the former New York governor touched down in twenty countries and interviewed over three thousand public and private leaders. Rockefeller's trips were not uneventful. While they were not a repeat of the Nixon riots of 1958,

Rockefeller and his entourage did encounter several hostile demonstrations. Peru, Chile, and Venezuela refused to host the delegation, and a student died during an anti-U.S. riot in Honduras.

The Rockefeller Report on the Americas that resulted represented a well-intentioned reading of Latin American politics that could easily be distorted by Realpolitik. Moved by the expressions of anti-U.S. sentiment during the trip, Rockefeller counseled against a "paternalistic attitude" when dealing with Latin Americans.[9] While this was a nod to cultural sensitivities, President Eisenhower's brother Milton and Nixon himself had both said about the same a decade earlier (see chapter 1). One of the few changes brought about by the report and welcomed by Latin Americans was Nixon's announcement that U.S. economic aid to Latin America would no longer have to be used to buy U.S. goods. Overall, in the economic field, Nixon ran with the theories of the "Chicago Boys." For instance, he created the Overseas Private Investment Corporation to encourage the use of private rather than government money to develop poor nations (document 12).

Most ominously for Chile, Rockefeller welcomed "a new type of military man" in Latin America, who was "becoming a major force for constructive social change" and "prepared to adapt his authoritarian tradition to the goals of social and economic progress." Again, while these observations may have been accurate, they reiterated Thomas Mann's conclusions from several years earlier (see chapter 2). Rockefeller called for lifting the cap off military aid to help these supposedly new and enlightened military leaders. Perhaps the report's most surprising recommendation was to leave Latin America alone. Whereas previous surveys reported that Washington could spark the right kind of "revolution," Rockefeller largely counseled the status quo. "We know that we, in the United States, cannot determine the internal political structure of any other nation, except by example."[10] A speech delivered by Nixon in October 1969 used a "Kissingerian" lesson from the report: "We must deal realistically with governments in the inter-American system as they are."[11]

Allende's Election: Chile, 1970

As *it* was, however, the new Chilean government would not do. In 1970 Chilean voters had embarked on radical social and political experiment by electing a Marxist, Salvador Allende, to the presidency. Through the 1960s Allende and his socialist allies had consistently run for office and lost. At that time, power belonged to those who collaborated with Washington, especially when Alliance for Progress funds flowed freely, but efforts by U.S. aid administrators to control how Chile spent the funds led to disillusion. In 1967 President Eduardo Frei even penned a famous article arguing that the Alliance for Progress had "lost its way."[12] Workers in Chilean copper mines especially were angry at U.S. capital. When U.S. investors took over but remained far away, they said, local managers pretended to no longer have the authority to negotiate with their workers. In 1970 the traditional center-right coalition was divided over these and other failures, and Allende won a plurality of the votes—36 percent—with his proposal to nationalize the copper industry. The Chilean Congress, while divided, insisted on following constitutional protocol and confirmed Allende as president.[13]

No to the Chilean Way

The Nixon White House saw great danger in the socialist victory. One young NSC staffer recalls that his superiors were "wringing their hands" over Chile, "almost as if they [the Chileans] were an errant child."[14] Kissinger saw in Allende a man with "linkages" to geopolitics. Allende was dangerous because, like Fidel Castro a decade earlier, he offered a workable alternative to U.S.-led free market globalization. Worse, Allende had been freely elected. He showed a *democratic* path to socialism—*la via chilena*, the "Chilean Way." "I don't think anybody very fully grasped that Henry saw Allende as being far more serious a threat than Castro," recalled a Kissinger aide. "If Latin America ever became unraveled, it would never happen with Castro. Allende was a living example of democratic social reform in Latin America."[15] Two days after the Chilean's inauguration, Kissinger cabled, "What happens over next 6–10 months will have ramifications far beyond U.S.-Ch[ilean] relations." It "will have effect on what happens in rest of Latin America and developing world; our future position in hemisphere; on larger world picture . . . even effect [*sic*] our own conception of what our role in the world is."[16] He could not allow such chaos: "We set the limits of diversity," he apparently told his staff.[17]

FUBELT and Economic Warfare

On September 15, 1970, while Allende was still president-elect, Nixon ordered the CIA to begin covert operations against him. CIA director Richard Helms scribbled down notes after a meeting with the President:

> 1 in 10 chance perhaps, but save Chile!
> worth spending
> not concerned risks involved
> no involvement of embassy
> $10,000,000 available, more if necessary
> . . . make the economy scream[18]

The next day Helms interpreted this to mean that "the President asked the Agency to prevent Allende from coming to power or to unseat him." This was the essence of project FUBELT. Nixon repeated his desire to see Allende unseated to several others. When meeting with the U.S. ambassador to Chile, for instance, he struck his fist against his open palm and swore against "that son of a bitch Allende. We're going to smash him."[19] Some considered a military coup. But a coup was not a sure means of overthrow, and talk of coups against elected heads of state made some uncomfortable.

Kissinger's top aide in Latin America told him that "what we propose is patently a violation of our own principles and policy tenets. . . . Is Allende a mortal threat to the U.S.? It is hard to argue this."[20]

Nevertheless, the White House, the CIA, and private U.S. corporations attempted to keep Allende from taking office. This cooperation lent credibility to dependency theorists, who argued that self-interested corporations exerted an unusual and secretive influence on U.S. foreign policy. For instance, when Allende's future lay in the hands of the Chilean Congress in late 1970, ITT offered $1 million in support of FUBELT. And in the twenty-four hours before Nixon gave that famous order to "make the economy scream," two key meetings took place. Nixon talked with Donald Kendall, the U.S. head of Pepsi-Cola and a major campaign contributor, and Kissinger had breakfast with Agustín Edwards, a Chilean media magnate. Both Kendall and Edwards pressed for U.S. intervention against Allende.[21]

This intervention came mostly through CIA support for the removal of Gen. René Schneider, the Chilean army commander in chief who controlled the confirmation of Allende. The agency also provided plotters with submachine guns, gas grenades, and masks, and encouraged kidnapping Schneider as a prelude to a coup.[22] The would-be kidnappers tried twice and twice failed. On October 22, 1970, essentially the same Chilean military men kidnapped and gravely wounded Schneider.[23] The attempt on the general's life backfired when horrified Chilean legislators elected Allende to the presidency two days later. Schneider died the day after that. Some concluded that U.S. intervention had failed; others, that it had not been resolute enough. For the moment, Allende was safe.

Once Allende took office in late 1970, he embarked upon la via chilena. To U.S. observers, Allende's nationalization of U.S. copper companies Anaconda and Kennecott was his government's most dangerous maneuver. The Chilean government promised to compensate these capitalists, after it subtracted from their total compensation the "excess profits" they had earned since 1955. According to Allende's math, profits exceeded the value of the companies. In September 1971 the Chilean president presented Kennecott not only with an order to evacuate Chile but with a *bill* of $310 million; he presented Anaconda with one of $78 million.[24]

Allende also fueled the State Department's anger with his socialist diplomacy. He was friendly to communist countries such as North Vietnam and North Korea, reopened diplomatic relations with Cuba against the wishes of the OAS, and erected a statue of Che Guevara. Lest he be accused of likening himself to Castro, however, he promised to maintain good relations with the United States and to harbor no Soviet bases.

This mattered little. Nixon's response "on the economic side" was to give Allende "cold turkey."[25] From 1970 to 1973 the CIA spent $8 million to fund opponents of Allende's Popular Unity coalition, to pay for radio stations and newspapers, and possibly to conduct break-ins.[26] Out in the open, meanwhile, Nixon nixed new Export-Import Bank guarantees to Chile, stopped all new aid programs except for food, delayed existing programs, and pressured foreign investors to pull out of Chile.

Allende called the measures "the invisible blockade."[27] To make things worse, Allende's own policies battered the Chilean economy. He tried to control the prices of farming goods, a move that helped double food imports, fired up inflation, and caused a sharp drop in foreign exchange. Supported by CIA funds, a major strike uniting truckers, merchants, and professionals drew great sympathy and increased middle-class discontent among a population that, after all, had given Allende barely one-third of its votes in 1970.

In March 1973, in mid-term elections, Allende's coalition won 43 percent—still not a majority, but better than 1970 and enough to go on ruling. This continued democratic push for socialism might have convinced Washington to reignite the idea of a coup. Washington had never stopped funding the military, and the "40 committee"—the White House group in charge of covert actions—now gave $1 million to opposition groups.[28] This was not a direct order to overthrow Allende, nor did the U.S. government help plan the coup. But the acts of pressuring Allende on one hand and letting conspiracies unfold on the other were a clear go-ahead to coup plotters. Several groups activated plans, and they reported their moves faithfully to the CIA and the Department of Defense. The most important of these had as its leader Gen. Augusto Pinochet.[29]

The Coup

On September 11, 1973, Pinochet and the Chilean military rolled their tanks into major Chilean cities. In Santiago, they bombed government buildings, including the presidential palace, inside of which Allende apparently committed suicide. Pinochet, who fancied himself as a Rockefeller-defined enlightened military man rather than a dictator, nevertheless sent out an edict the next day saying that anyone with a "belligerent attitude" would be "executed on the spot."[30] Back in Washington, Kissinger publicly claimed to be "neutral," but privately he pledged to "cooperate with the military junta and to assist in any appropriate way."[31] Assist he did: Nixon immediately recognized the Pinochet government, and less than one month after the coup, the president promised the dictator a loan for the purchase of U.S. wheat. The money was eight times more than all the commodity credit ever given Allende.[32]

The long-term impact was tremendous. For Chileans, the most serious effect was on human rights. Pinochet murdered more than thirty-one hundred people, and another eleven hundred were never heard from again. Thousands more suffered torture or jail. Fear and repression stifled all democratic opposition for the next seventeen years.

The Church Committee, 1975

As for U.S. policymakers, many suffered moral qualms over the support of dictatorship in Chile. In 1975 a Senate committee headed by Frank Church

(D-Idaho) ordered a massive investigation into this and other episodes. The Chilean coup had kick-started a debate about U.S. involvement in human-rights abuses, and one of the Church Committee's reports was titled *Covert Action in Chile, 1963–1973*. The committee also uncovered a string of, as another report title described them, *Alleged Assassination Plots Involving Foreign Leaders* in which the United States had played a role. Among these were Operation Mongoose schemes against Fidel Castro and help for the assassins of Rafael Trujillo in the Dominican Republic. The Church Committee blamed most of the covert U.S. involvement in Chile and the assassination attempts on the CIA, which it called a "rogue elephant rampaging out of control."

Despite all the revelations—and the Bill Clinton administration's release of twenty-four thousand new documents—controversies remained decades later. Secretary of State Colin Powell in April 2003 said of the Allende overthrow, "It is not a part of American history that we're proud of." Immediately, Kissinger, still active in international affairs, responded angrily, and William Rogers, secretary of state during the 1973 action, called the accusation of U.S. participation in the coup a "canard." In 2004, when a reviewer at the periodical *Foreign Affairs* failed to condemn a book faulting the United States in the Allende overthrow, Rogers and Kissinger strong-armed his resignation.[33]

The Human Rights Approach

Many factors moved Jimmy Carter to place a premium on human rights protection when he assumed the presidency in January 1977. First, Nixon's political practices had been rotten in general, as the Watergate investigation had revealed. Watergate, disillusionment with the war in Vietnam, and the Church Committee's findings led to a number of actions aimed at limiting the power of the Oval Office. Second, many U.S. allies, especially those in Latin America, were of a brutal nature. "Bureaucratic-authoritarian" regimes, not surprisingly, were more authoritarian than bureaucratic. They offered few services and little administrative efficiency to the people, but they certainly curtailed many freedoms and repressed criticism of the government. These regimes had often obtained green lights for repression from Nixon and Kissinger, who sympathized with calls for help in the Latin American "war on terrorism" long before September 11, 2001.[34] Finally, Carter, a born-again evangelical from Georgia, had long expressed sympathy for the victims of poverty and violence both at home and abroad. This was his chance to do something.

So for reasons of domestic politics, foreign affairs, and personal conviction, Carter said in his inaugural address, "our commitment to human rights must be absolute." Once in office, he intoned, "Human rights is the soul of our foreign policy." He created the office of assistant secretary of state for human rights and named a veteran of the U.S. civil rights movement, Patricia Derian, to head it.[35]

Respect for human rights did not mean the end of U.S. intervention. Instead, it meant intervention that was more respectful of democratic regimes, that might even make democracy a condition of U.S. friendliness. In this sense, it further acknowledged U.S.–Latin American interdependence. Senator Tom Harkin (D-Iowa), a supporter of Carter, perhaps expressed it best: "We are going to influence Latin America. We will influence every country there. The question is how. Are we going to keep supporting these dictators down there who violate human rights with some sense of security? Or will we forcefully, once and for all, say 'No, we won't put up with it'?"[36] To demonstrate his seriousness, Carter reduced aid to Bolivia, Chile, Haiti, and others because of human rights violations. He also relaxed relations with Cuba, setting up limited diplomatic relations within the Swiss Embassy through a U.S. "Interest Section," which still existed in 2005 (document 13).

Human Rights Test I: Argentina

The biggest test of the human rights approach, however, was the Dirty War. A military junta took over Argentina in 1976 and, for the next six years, unleashed a repression on its opponents rarely seen in Latin American history. Particularly in the first three years, armed gangs clearly identified with the junta roamed the cities and countryside and "disappeared" dissidents. "To disappear" was a new verb, meaning to kidnap without leaving a trace. This emotionally scarring experience left anxious mothers, wives, and children wondering if a loved one was alive or dead. Some relatives of the *desaparecidos* organized a group called the "Mothers of the Plaza de Mayo" after the site in Buenos Aires where they held vigils during the Dirty War. The Mothers enjoyed resonance through international organizations such as Amnesty International, which, founded in 1961, lobbied for the release of political prisoners. Together, these activists inside and outside Argentina pressured Washington and other world leaders to do something about the estimated 8,960 dead and desaparecidos of the Dirty War, some of whom had been thrown into the ocean from airplanes while still alive.[37]

The Argentine regime's inhumanity tested the U.S. human rights approach because, unlike with Chile, Washington had not directly aided the regime and so felt no collective remorse. Nor did a Realpolitik approach suggest action since the Dirty War did not threaten global U.S. interests. Carter could have ignored the junta in Argentina and not suffered any political setback. In other words, Carter's decision to move against Argentina was close to a purely moral decision, true to his Christian conscience. In February 1977 Secretary of State Cyrus Vance cut foreign aid to Argentina by more than half, and in July Congress cut off the rest. The administration also blocked loans to Buenos Aires through the Inter-American Association Bank and restricted Export-Import credits. Washington criticized the Argentines in public and in private. As a result, Argentina gave promises of fair elections and released some political prisoners.[38] Overall, however, the human rights approach did not stop the abuses or bring about the end of the regime.

Human Rights Test II: The Panama Canal Treaties

In Panama, the problem was not that human rights were being endangered directly, but it did involve the same proclaimed U.S. commitment to morality. In this case, Carter struck a moral tone with his successful support for agreements to hand over the Panama Canal to the Republic of Panama.

After the riots of 1964 (see chapter 2), Panamanian nationalists such as military man Omar Torrijos cleverly framed their demand for total control of the waterway in anticolonial terms. It helped that the Zonians increasingly looked like relics of old-time imperialism. After a failed effort in 1967, Panamanians reached an agreement on principles with Kissinger in 1974, which suggested that the then–secretary of state understood that visible U.S. control of a small country hurt its support for the war in Vietnam. U.S. negotiators were also willing to give away the canal because it was much less useful militarily and commercially in the 1970s than it had been in previous decades. Militarily, the United States had fleets in both the Atlantic and the Pacific, and nuclear strategy was less reliant on the urgent movement of battleships from one ocean to the other. Commercially, "supertanker" ships had outgrown the locks. Plans to enlarge the canal—namely, by nuclear explosions—had proven too expensive, dangerous, and environmentally ruinous.

The logic—Realpolitik, symbolic, or otherwise—seemed flawless. In August 1977 U.S. and Panamanian negotiators announced two treaty proposals. The first provided Panamanians with increased revenues from the canal and the training to eventually run it. It also set up joint U.S.-Panamanian authority until December 31, 1999, after which Panamanians would have complete control. The second treaty defined U.S. rights to defend the canal after that date. National Security Advisor Zbigniew Brzezinski called the proposed treaties "the ideal fusion of morality and politics" for Carter. "He was doing something good for peace, responding to the passionate desires of a small nation, and yet helping the long-range U.S. national interest."[39]

For many others, however, neither the morality nor the politics were self-evident. First, Panamanian voters had to approve the treaties, and these voters worried about a U.S. amendment that allowed Washington to use force to keep the canal open after 1999. Only after Torrijos reluctantly agreed to keep this amendment out of Panamanian voters' hands did the treaties pass in Panama. Second, U.S. public opinion was divided. Although a wide array of U.S. conservatives, including Kissinger, the Catholic Church, the Pentagon, and even tough-guy actor John Wayne supported the treaties, Republican presidential candidate Ronald Reagan headed a group of ultraconservatives—as many as one hundred thousand—who fiercely opposed them. The John Birch Society, the Conservative Caucus, and the American Legion criticized the human rights approach for lacking patriotism and strength. The proposed treaties risked making the United States "number two" in the world, Reagan said. In this debate, Reagan brazenly ignored the facts, claiming, for instance, that the canal zone was sovereign U.S. territory.

"We bought it, we paid for it, it's ours, and we're going to keep it!" Audiences cheered.[40] "We stole it fair and square," added Senator S. I. Hayakawa (R-California), somewhat more candidly.[41]

All that mattered constitutionally in the United States, however, was the Senate, which had to ratify the treaties. Their passage became the single-most time-consuming effort in the first two years of Carter's mandate. The president spent hours and political capital promising senators with payoffs unrelated to the topic of the treaty—a process known as pork-barrel politics. If they did not comply, Carter might threaten to not support their agendas—"arm-twisting," also common in Washington. In March and April 1978 the Senate finally passed both treaties separately, each with a sixty-eight to thirty-two vote—a shift of two votes would have meant defeat. Carter eked out a victory at great cost.

Human Rights Test III: Central America

Meanwhile, in the tiny countries of Central America, a far more serious struggle percolated slowly to the top of the U.S. foreign policy agenda. Poverty and the violence it engendered had deep roots and far-reaching branches. In Central America, as far back as the 1950s, two of modernization theory's target sectors were taking off: capital-intensive industrialization and export-oriented crops, including coffee, bananas, coca, and sugar. So far, so good. But cotton and cattle, especially, required large farms and so created a landless class by eating up smaller farms. As a result, countless persons became agricultural wage laborers, poor workers in cities, or homeless or jobless drifters.

By the early 1970s Central Americans were helpless before world markets. The prices of the raw materials they produced declined while those of the finished products they bought rose. Barriers to foreign investment eased with each passing year but legal obstacles to emigration remained. And the oil shocks of the 1970s, which occurred when oil-producing countries in the Middle East protested U.S. policies there by cutting back production, hit Central Americans especially hard because they were importers of petroleum.[42] As a result, Central American economic growth slowed from 2.2 percent per capita in 1970–74 to 0.4 percent per capita in 1975–79.[43]

It would have been one thing if all Central Americans had suffered together, but a yawning chasm between the many poor and the few rich who now owned these monster farms and factories worsened the social crisis. In Guatemala, the crisis was particularly cultural and racial, as most of the poor were indigenous groups who spoke little Spanish and had been banished to isolated mountain villages by the concentration of land.

Liberation Theology

Poverty fed a rising movement uniting middle-class reformers and the poor. Its motivation was to put an end to military dictatorships in Central America.

What distinguished this from previous antidictatorial movements was its religious flavor, which gave it the name Liberation Theology. Liberation Theology was founded on the Vatican's encyclicals and Council II of the early 1960s and could be interpreted as a purely intellectual movement. But it also had a political message. Defying the traditional Catholic habit of accepting suffering as spiritually cleansing, liberation theologians suggested that the poor could free themselves from suffering through raising consciousness and organizing. They preached that Jesus Christ was a social reformer, a revolutionary leader of men and women in struggle. Clearly, the liberation theologians had been listening to dependency theorists. They blamed poverty and the violence that emerged from it not on providence but on changeable economic "structures" (document 14).

In 1968 the Latin American bishops met in Medellín, Colombia, where they defined this "institutionalized violence" and endorsed the organization of the poor at the local level. Ecclesiastical Base Communities (CEB), already forming across Central America, multiplied. A CEB sympathizer in El Salvador, Maryknoll Sister Ita Ford, said that "the Christian base communities are the greatest threat to military dictatorship throughout Latin America." She was tragically correct. A short while later, a death squad raped and killed her and three other churchwomen.[44]

In Sister Ford's El Salvador and in Nicaragua, Washington became deeply involved. While crises also raged in Guatemala and Honduras, they did not destabilize those countries' central governments as much and so did not arouse as much concern along the Potomac.

Nicaragua, the Sandinistas, and Carter's Responses

In Nicaragua, the seeds of discontent were sown as deeply as anywhere—in 1977 a third of farmers owned only 1.7 percent of the land and sixty thousand were completely landless.[45] But perhaps the largest contributing factor to the political crisis was Anastasio Somoza Debayle. The second son of the dictator who had taken power shortly after the departure of the marines in the 1930s (see the introduction), Somoza owned so much farmland in Nicaragua that his property came to be called Latin America's "biggest private ranch."[46]

After an earthquake hit in the early morning hours of December 23, 1972, Somoza moved to enrich himself, his family, and his supporters even more. The massive shock killed ten thousand, injured twenty thousand more, and left another three hundred thousand homeless. It destroyed 589 blocks and damaged 80 percent of Managua's buildings—including the U.S. embassy, which collapsed. The Nixon government provided Somoza with $32 million in emergency aid, but the Nicaraguan treasury listed the aid as only $16 million. With the money he had not stolen, the dictator proceeded to rebuild the capital—on land he owned and by awarding contracts to companies he owned. For their part, the troops of Somoza's National Guard, or police force, spent the days after the disaster looting, and when the relief supplies arrived, they *sold* them to the needy.[47] This made Nicaraguans angry. Unions stepped up work stoppages and strikes. Students rallied. Peasants, with the help of the clergy, organized into CEBs and labor unions. Even capitalists expressed outrage at this open corruption. This was society-wide discontent, but when faced with the guns and tanks of the National Guard, it stopped short of an open confrontation.

It took the Sandinista Front for National Liberation (FSLN) to bring down Somoza. In 1959–62 the FSLN was only one among twenty or so new groups in Nicaragua inspired by Fidel Castro's barbudos (see chapter 2). In the mid-1970s an internal debate within the FSLN ended with the triumph of the *terceristas*, who, following the foco theory, advocated violent actions by small groups to set off broader changes. In December 1974 and again in August 1977, the FSLN boldly staged dramatic hostage takings, first at a Christmas party in honor of the U.S. ambassador (who had already left) and then of the National Palace. In both instances, the Sandinistas got away, winning also the release from prison of *compañeros* and large cash ransoms.[48] The second hostage taking even saw Managua residents cheering the departing Sandinistas as they boarded planes to Cuba. By this time, Somoza had already launched a three-year war in the countryside, which eventually moved to the cities.

In January 1978 opposition newspaper editor Pedro Joaquín Chamorro was assassinated. Immediately, an important section of moderate and middle-class supporters of Somoza abandoned the dictator. The FSLN, newly divided by Somoza's attacks but feeling that Somoza was also weakened, regrouped and launched its final offensive in May 1979. In mid-July Somoza and his mistress fled the country, and the FSLN marched into Managua triumphantly. Somoza eventually landed in Paraguay, where the Sandinistas later fired a rocket into his Mercedes and killed him.

In late 1979 Nicaragua finally enjoyed freedom from right-wing repression—but not from poverty or war. During the insurrection, as many as forty thousand lives had been lost and forty thousand children had been orphaned. These numbers proportionately dwarfed the U.S. Civil War. Economically, Nicaragua's growth in 1975–79 was actually negative 6.8 percent; in 1979 alone it was negative 24 percent. The treasury had a debt of $1.5 billion, and Somoza's escaping with $100 million had not helped.[49]

The Sandinista rebellion showed the human rights approach's limited ability to influence events in a polarized Central American society. Throughout the late 1970s Carter's advisers looked in vain for Nicaraguans who would walk down the middle of the political road, somewhere between the radicalism of Sandinista leader Daniel Ortega and the ruthlessness of Somoza. Ambassador Lawrence Pezzulo counseled against any moves to weaken the Sandinistas: "We should stay out of the 'foreign devil' role, which they'd just love to put us in." For Brzezinski, a believer in power and linkages, Nicaragua tested U.S. resolve "in our own backyard." "We have to demonstrate," he said, "that we are still the decisive force in determining political outcomes in Central America and that we will not permit others to intervene."[50] The "others" he referred to were the Soviets and Cubans; Ortega had friendly relations with both, and after his triumph, he took $100 million in aid from Moscow (document 15).[51]

Even before the Sandinista revolution, Carter was vacillating between shoring up Somoza and encouraging his opponents. He listened to those, like Representative Edward Koch (D-New York) and Senator Ted Kennedy (D-Massachusetts), who counseled using Nicaragua as a testing ground for punishing dictators. But when Somoza refused to let the OAS supervise elections in Nicaragua, Carter terminated military aid, withdrew embassy officials, and cut economic assistance to the dictatorship. When Somoza eased repression in late 1977, Carter rewarded him with $2.5 million in arms while continuing to hold back economic aid.[52]

After the Sandinista takeover, Carter vacillated even more. In mid-1979 he sent the insurrectionists $20 million, and he requested an extra $75 million for them in the fall.[53] But to the Sandinistas, this was too little, too late; the aid did not address the deeper causes of poverty. The Nicaraguans were not following in Cuba's shoes, however. Although they nationalized Somoza's properties and the banks, they welcomed U.S. investors, retained private farms (which were the most productive farms in the 1980s), and kept their foreign policy relatively separate from that of the Soviets and Cubans (as Castro himself advised them to do).

Their foreign policy also included funneling arms to a similar insurrection in neighboring El Salvador. Up to now, the Sandinistas' offenses had been limited to advocating a different *internal* path to development, but Carter interpreted sending arms across borders to El Salvador as aggression against another American republic. As a result, the president funded the anti-Sandinista press, clergy, unions, and parties, and he interdicted arms transfers to El Salvador.

El Salvador and the Death Squads

In El Salvador, the country densest in population in Central America, the economic and political crises of the 1970s were similar to, and perhaps worse than, those in Nicaragua. As in Nicaragua, part of the reason for the trouble was the misapplication of the Alliance for Progress from the Kennedy era. Under the alliance, El Salvador received more funding than any other Central American country. Hundreds of industries popped up, and the country reached the extraordinary growth rate of 12 percent in 1964–65.[54]

Then things went awry. Oligarchs passed the reform laws called for by the alliance but put few of them into effect. Alliance funds went into the industries of these lawmakers, and they used the profits to buy up still more land. Growth was real, but it benefited only a small group of leaders. The best lands, therefore, ended up in the hands of owners who grew beef and cotton. This forced out subsistence tenants, squatters, and smallholders. As a consequence, landless peasants grew from 12 percent of the population in

1961 to 41 percent in 1971.[55] El Salvador had an even greater concentration of land than did Nicaragua, except that it belonged not mostly to one family but to several, known collectively as the "Fourteen Families." By the late 1970s these families, in reality a few thousand people who made up about 10 percent of the population, owned all the banks, most of the factories, and almost 80 percent of the farms.[56]

Repression grew apace. Violent deaths per year doubled between 1965–66 and 1977–78. In El Salvador especially right-wing paramilitary groups, or "death squads," were omnipresent agents of repression. Death squads operated outside the formal government but with its tacit approval. Since the 1960s one of the scariest of these groups bore the acronym ORDEN ("order") and commissioned peasants to inform on who the "communists" in their communities were. The unlucky fingered ones were then executed or disappeared.

When the gap between rich and poor in El Salvador grew too wide and wages fell, the inevitable happened: unions, student groups, CEBs, and peasant leagues sprang up. In the 1970s, cooperatives more than doubled. Most important, from 1970 to 1979, five guerrilla groups arrived on the scene, most combining labor, peasant, student, and guerrilla organizations. Then, the Sandinistas' success next door set off a crisis as they funneled resources to the Salvadoran revolutionaries. A few months after the triumph in Managua, on October 15, 1979, a coup within the Salvadoran military promised the end of repression and a moderate civil-military power-sharing coalition. But in January 1980 an extreme conservative countercoup broke this coalition. A greater wave of attacks, which included kidnappings and executions by death squads, followed.

Murder in 1980

The year 1980 was the darkest in a dark era in El Salvador. First, *massive* murder left its mark. Violent deaths that year were up eightfold from the previous, averaging a thousand a month, and most of them were political killings done by the government or death squads. Second, 1980 was a year of *dramatic* killings. On March 24, 1980, while Archbishop Oscar Romero gave mass, a sniper gunned him down. His crime: speaking out against the violence that tore apart his country. At his funeral—the largest gathering in Salvadoran history—the army fired on fleeing, panicked mourners, killing some thirty and wounding hundreds.[57] Handouts from paramilitary groups that year read, "Be a patriot! Kill a priest!" On December 2 of that year Ita Ford and the other churchwomen were savagely murdered. Events in El Salvador were more of a massacre than a civil war.

The year 1980 ended ominously for El Salvador as Ronald Reagan won the U.S. presidential election in November. Salvadoran society split even more widely. On the right of the political spectrum, oligarchs rejoiced in Reagan's triumph with lavish parties, during which they shot off guns and firecrackers and mariachis and marimbas blared joyful music. On the left, sixteen Salvadoran groups, including guerrillas, Christians, communists, and social democrats who feared that Reagan would side with the most extreme military officers, fused into the Farabundo Martí National Liberation Front (FMLN), a close cousin to Nicaragua's FSLN not only in name (in the 1920s Salvadoran Agustín Farabundo Martí had fought alongside Nicaraguan Augusto Sandino, the namesake of the Sandinistas) but also in tactics and financing.

The two groups' ideologies were also similarly anti–United States. Just as the FSLN's anthem called the United States the "enemy of humanity," the FMLN chanted "Down with the Yanqui invader." One twenty-three-year-old Salvadoran guerrilla named Marcos explained his compañeros' politico-religious vision. "The Bible says man should love his fellow man. We are putting that lesson into practice as Marxists-Leninists. . . . We are going to create a new society, a clean society full of love, whatever it costs."[58]

A final similarity between El Salvador and Nicaragua was the confused, desperate inability of the human rights approach to achieve U.S. aims. Carter played his usual carrot-and-stick game with military juntas. In 1977, for instance, Gen. Carlos Humberto Romero (no relation to Oscar) seized power in fraudulent elections. In reaction, Carter blocked an Inter-American Development Bank loan and maintained an embargo of weapons sales to El Salvador. In late 1979 Carter again took away aid but then restored it when the new junta accepted within its government some Christian Democrats, who were civilians and relatively friendly to Washington. The killings of religious figures, especially Westerners, tended to arouse the indignation of the U.S. president and most foreign observers. After the murders of the churchwomen, Carter again suspended military aid.

In early 1981, however, from his perch as a lame-duck president in the White House, Carter watched helplessly as events spiraled out of his control in El Salvador and the FMLN launched its offensive against the right-wing regime. Carter then made a fateful decision. Using special presidential funds that allowed him to circumvent Congress, the White House approved $25 million in military aid to the Salvadoran government. One month later it gave an additional $19.5 million and almost doubled the number of U.S. military advisors sent to train the Salvadoran army to expand the civil war.[59] Unlike in the 1960s, however, the military increase did not come with the pretense of social reform. Carter witnessed the end of a cycle in the 1970s. The decade had begun with the promise of industrialization and reached a peak of optimism with the White House adoption of a human rights approach. Yet those raised expectations met with the reality of continuing inequality and repressive regimes and the plain bad luck of a tanking world economy.

The dirty wars of the 1970s, therefore, were not limited to Argentina. Events in Chile, Nicaragua, and El Salvador were just as malicious, and perhaps dirtier because the U.S. government could have done more there to prevent their brutality. In 1981 one Argentine editor, who in 1979 had been released from prison by his country's military regime, felt that the short attention span of U.S. citizens had helped sink Carter's human rights approach. "America gets impatient with human rights, restless. You don't see the accomplishment," he reflected. "No, if you want to change a government you have to send in the Marines. What a human rights policy does is save lives. And Jimmy Carter's policy did. How many? I don't know. Two thousand? Is that enough?"[60] Enough or not, it no longer mattered. Ronald Reagan's presidency would take Central America, and much of the rest of Latin America, in a sharply different direction.

CHAPTER 4

WRECKAGES

Proxy Wars, Debt, and Defiant Strongmen,
1981–90

O N DECEMBER 1, 1982, President Ronald Reagan was on a tour of Latin America. At one of his stops, he toasted his hosts during a state dinner. The former actor, a flawless performer when given a proper script, made a gracious and elegant beginning. Then he raised his glass to "the people of Bolivia." Trouble was, he was in Brasília, Brazil. President João Figueiredo was terribly embarrassed. Reagan was too and tried to correct himself by saying, "That's where I'm going next." But this was also incorrect. He was going to Colombia. The White House attempted to change the official public transcript to have Reagan toasting "the people of Bogotá," but the damage was done and the compounded mistakes made news throughout the continent. And Reagan was not done. Heading home on Air Force One, he told reporters he had "learned a lot" in Latin America. "And you'd be surprised, yes, because, you know, they're all individual countries."[1]

Students of U.S.–Latin American relations should remember Reagan's gaffes because fudging the difference between Bolivia and Brazil—a difference equal to that between England and the United States—revealed the president's larger inability to see that Latin America was far more complex than the black-and-white Cold War battleground he imagined. Because of Reagan's misconceptions, the 1980s became one of the most tragically destructive decades, and certainly the most destructive since 1945, in the history of U.S.–Latin American relations. Far more than had the Carter administration, the Reagan administration intensified military struggle in the smallest, weakest Latin American countries thanks to fears of an ideological world struggle that did not correspond to events on the ground. By the end of the 1980s, the results were a series of wreckages—a catastrophic loss of life, the devastation of Latin American markets and natural environments, and a complete disillusion among the Latin American left with the possibility of humanistic reform.

Ronald Reagan's Wars

If the Vietnam War has come to be known as "Lyndon Johnson's War," then the events in Central America in the 1980s should be as tightly connected to Ronald Reagan. These were society-wide orgies of violence in which leftist revolutionaries enjoyed wide popularity with the masses while a minority of oligarchs, military commanders, and middle-class supporters held up their end of the struggle only by being proxies, or stand-ins, of the U.S. president. Through it all, Reagan, perhaps more than any other person in Washington, was single-minded in his financing and training of counter-revolutionaries and in his hope of eradicating communism from the Western Hemisphere, consequences be damned.

Three Questions

But why war, why Central America, and why proxy wars? War was necessary, the Reagan Republicans insisted, because the ongoing civil conflicts threatened U.S. national security. A secret April 1982 NSC paper explained the perceived threat. "Strategically," the United States must prevent "the proliferation of Cuba-modeled states which would provide platforms for subversion, compromise vital sea lanes and pose a direct military threat at or near our borders. This would undercut us globally and create economic dislocation and a resultant influx to the U.S. of illegal immigrants."[2]

The Reagan administration therefore abandoned diplomatic solutions such as support for human rights, economic pressure, and negotiation. The Republican platform of 1980 judged that Carter's "undifferentiated charges of human rights violations" had caused a "precipitous decline" in U.S.–Latin American relations.[3]

The Reagan administration defined the problems of Central America as military ones, and so moved the resolution of those problems largely out of the hands of the State Department and into those of the Defense Department. Even within State, the "hawks" quickly overpowered the "doves." Secretary of State Alexander Haig was of the first flock, consistently arguing for war over diplomacy. Speaking about Cuba—the still-defiant communist island—he once pleaded with Reagan, "You give me the word and I'll turn that fucking island into a parking lot."[4] Reagan gave no such word, but he did give taxpayer dollars. While between 1950 and 1979 U.S. military spending on Latin America averaged $7.5 million yearly, it increased to $8.8 million in 1980 (under Carter), $44.8 million the following year (Carter and Reagan), and $109.1 million in 1982.[5]

Why Central America? Haig's response again was blunt: "Mr. President, this is one you can win."[6] Central America could be won because it was small and because it was close. The subtext—the war the United States *couldn't* win—was Vietnam. The humiliating retreat from Southeast Asia back in 1975 still weighed like an albatross around Washington's collective neck. There, U.S. policymakers had made two mistakes: overestimating their chances and buying wholeheartedly into the domino-effect theory. According to this theory, one country's fall to communism would prompt neighboring countries to succumb to communist revolutions one after the other, like toppling dominoes. In 1981 what registered more was not the desire to learn from the mistakes of Vietnam but to try again somewhere else. Reagan himself argued that a symbolic line in the sand must be drawn in Central America, and he warned of falling dominoes if that line were crossed. In one speech, the president placed El Salvador "on the front lines of the battle that is really aimed at the very heart of the Western Hemisphere, and eventually at us."[7] Jeane Kirkpatrick, the U.S. ambassador to the UN, announced the new status of the region in early 1981: "Central America is the most important place in the world for the United States today" (document 16).[8]

Vietnam also answered the third question: Why a proxy war? After the deaths of over fifty thousand U.S. citizens in Southeast Asia had put an end to several political careers, the "Vietnam syndrome" gripped Washington and stopped politicians from sending troops abroad to fight communism for fear of the political costs. Central America, therefore, could also be won because it could be paid for by U.S. taxpayers but fought by local mercenaries.

The Santa Fe Report, 1980

In January 1981 Reagan walked into the Oval Office with his crusading spirit stoked by a just-published document that outlined future policy in Latin America to the U.S. public, press, and Congress. *A New Inter-American Policy for the Eighties* was the brainchild of the so-called Santa Fe Commission, a group of five conservative men who soon moved into jobs at the State Department and the NSC.[9]

In the economic sphere, the *Policy* recommended an expected—and, in Latin America, often welcomed—increase of U.S. investment in neoclassical entrepreneurship in Central America and the Caribbean, a region known for the first time as the Caribbean Basin. The overall role of the basin in the U.S.-led free-market global economy, according to the *Policy,* was to exploit its comparative advantage in "extractive" industries such as petroleum and in industrial and nuclear energies. In the sphere of agriculture, the basin was to pursue cash crops destined for the U.S. market, such as sugar. The U.S. Agency for International Development was also to help small cooperatives and "communal-tribal enterprises" rather than government-funded programs. Similarly, the AFL-CIO would encourage labor organization free from the taint of communism. The Santa Fe commissioners, in short, reaffirmed their belief in diffusionist modernization—the transfer of technology and values that promoted free markets, free investment, and free labor.

But the most striking passages of the Santa Fe report concerned security. Using alarmist language, the Santa Fe commissioners warned that "survival demands a new U.S. foreign policy." The report did not provide evidence of an imminent outside attack on Central America, not even from Cuba. Instead, it clearly stated that the threat was internal, from leftist insurgencies. Nevertheless, it called on Washington to "reaffirm the core principle of the Monroe Doctrine: namely, no hostile foreign power will be allowed bases or military and political allies in the region." This meant that a completely internal insurrection was somehow "foreign" if it gave the appearance of being a sympathizer of Moscow. The correct response, therefore, was to drop the pie-in-the-sky human rights policy of Jimmy Carter (document 17).

Diffusion did *not* apply, the men of Santa Fe noted, to political freedom. "The United States must reject the mistaken assumption that one can easily locate and impose U.S. style democratic alternatives to authoritarian governments and the equally pervasive belief that change *per se* in such situations is inevitable, desirable, and in the American interest." "Human rights," they declared, "is a culturally and politically relative concept [that] must be abandoned and replaced by a non-interventionist policy of political ethical realism."[10]

Renewed Support for Military Regimes

What the Santa Fe report meant by "non-interventionist," of course, was intervention. It supported the active backing of dictators and other military regimes. Guatemalans have alleged, for instance, that during the 1980 campaign, Reagan emissaries came to their country and told leaders not to negotiate with the Carter government because they would have a freer hand once Reagan was in power. Reagan personally spent part of the 1980 campaign with Guatemalan Gen. Luis Mans, whose death squads in the 1980s swept through and annihilated, according to one doctor, at least 662 Mayan villages. When Reagan reached the White House, he gave his full support to Gen. Efraín Ríos Montt (1982–83), whose military unleashed fierce violence against dissidents and indigenous Guatemalans.[11] In 1999, after a truth commission report found that the Guatemalan government and its allies were responsible for nine out of every ten of these deaths, President Bill Clinton visited Central America and publicly apologized for past U.S. support (document 18).

Increased repression also came from the U.S. Army School of the Americas. In 1983 it moved out of the Panama Canal Zone (in accordance with the Panama Canal treaty) and reopened at Fort Benning, Georgia, yet its mission remained unchanged, "providing military education and training to military personnel of Central and South American countries and Caribbean countries."[12] Reflecting Reagan's new geopolitics, however, Central Americans were now the majority of the school's attendees; the Salvadoran class alone grew from fourteen thousand to fifty-five thousand.[13] By 1983 Salvadorans were almost as numerous as all other students combined.[14] Training included seven manuals that the army published for the first time in 1982 and distributed throughout the 1980s. Declassified in 1996, these manuals chillingly taught students the best techniques for "executing guerrillas, blackmail, false imprisonment, physical abuse, using truth serum to obtain information, and paying bounties for enemy dead."[15] Roberto

D'Aubuisson, a man widely believed to be responsible for death squads in El Salvador, was a graduate.[16]

The Grenada Invasion, 1983

While much of the anticommunist, prodictatorial training and funding was messy and expensive, the Reagan administration got the most "bang for its buck" in Grenada. In March 1979, on this tiny island of one hundred thousand inhabitants north of Trinidad, a leftist insurgency similar to Nicaragua's FSLN, called the New Jewel Movement, overthrew strongman Eric Gairy. Once rid of this strange leader who believed in his own divinity and in imminent contact between humans and extraterrestrials, New Jewel Prime Minister Maurice Bishop established ties with Cuba and the Soviet Union and in 1982 declared his island a socialist republic. Understandably, the Reagan government kept a close watch on the island, looking for any sign of a Soviet takeover—or, as critics said, any excuse for invasion.

It eventually came down to the meaning of an airport. In March 1983 Reagan was shown photos of a landing strip whose construction was multinational—financed by Venezuelans and Europeans and undertaken by the British (the island was a British colony until 1974) and a Cuban work brigade. The Grenadians said the strip was built to boost tourism. The U.S. president countered that it was meant to land Soviet or Cuban planes, perhaps even missiles. He called Grenada "a Soviet-Cuban colony being readied as a major military bastion to export terror and undermine democracy."[17]

In October 1983 Grenada surged further to the left when Bernard Coard, a self-described Marxist and the deputy prime minister, overthrew the popular Bishop and killed him. Soon after, on October 23, a bomb ripped through marine barracks in Beirut, Lebanon, killing 241 U.S. troops. Reagan, shattered, now worried about U.S. citizens being taken hostage in Grenada. He signed the order to invade. On October 25 Operation Urgent Fury landed nineteen hundred U.S. marines on the island, supposedly to protect a group of U.S. medical students there. Thousands more landed in the next six days, fighting Grenadians and Cubans alike. They won, of course, leaving 24 Cubans dead and 59 wounded and 45 Grenadians dead and 337 wounded. Eighteen U.S. troops died and 116 were wounded. The U.S. government now had a new ally open for business. It had also shown to Central American leftists such as the Sandinistas that it had no compunction against landing troops in a tiny country with no proven extrahemispheric threat. And it had done all this relatively cheaply: $75.5 million for the invasion and $110 million in aid to the new government over the next five years.

While critics accused Reagan of using Grenada to look tough on terrorism in the wake of the Beirut bombing, U.S. citizens celebrated the invasion as a much-needed show of strength. In 1986, for instance, the film *Heartbreak Ridge* used the Grenada invasion as a backdrop to its climactic battle scene. Its main character, a marine gunnery sergeant and veteran of the Korean War played by Clint Eastwood, is close to retirement but, as his final tour of duty, has to whip into shape lazy recruits who have never known war. He himself is eager for a last war to prove his worth, and he gets one in Grenada. The film in no way tries to portray the motivations of Grenadians or Cubans, who only serve as props for an entirely U.S.-centric drama. If, as film historians have shown, 1985's *Rambo: First Blood Part II* had Sylvester Stallone refighting the Vietnam War and winning, Eastwood's character served a similar patriotic purpose in flexing U.S. muscles in a symbolic struggle against the Soviet bloc in the Western Hemisphere.

War in El Salvador

But it was across the water from Grenada, in El Salvador and Nicaragua, that Reagan most disregarded the nature of conflicts on the ground. Although the two wars overlapped in time, El Salvador's emerged earlier as the crisis of the day for Washington. Reagan's election had set off a final offensive by the leftist FMLN, and a panicked Carter had circumvented Congress and funded the counterinsurgency through discretionary funds (see chapter 3). Throughout the 1980s Reagan's advisers increased funding to the successive military regimes in El Salvador. In 1981 alone Reagan doubled economic aid, to $126.5 million. Military aid grew eightfold that same year, to $40 million. By 1984 military aid alone to El Salvador was $196.6 million.[18] The tiny nation was now the third best-funded U.S. ally in the world, behind Israel and Egypt. Each Salvadoran received on average one dollar per day in U.S. aid.[19]

The Reagan White House met revolution not with development or even caution but with paranoia and might. To counter accusations of disregarding poverty, the right-wing Salvadoran governments drafted plans for agrarian reform but then implemented them only halfheartedly. Secretary Haig framed El Salvador within the Cold War ideas of containment and domino theory, saying he wanted to "draw the line" there. In 1984 Reagan explained why on television: "What we see in El Salvador is an attempt to destabilize the entire region and eventually move chaos and anarchy toward the American border."[20]

Reagan may have stopped one kind of instability—the FMLN never won on the battlefield—but he intensified another—the massive movement of Salvadoran refugees northward. Between 1980 and 1982 the number of Salvadorans in the United States skyrocketed from ninety-four thousand to perhaps half a million.[21] In 1981 forty-six of every one thousand Salvadorans left the country, eleven times more than six years earlier. (War also displaced another half-million Salvadorans inside their country.) Ironically, Reagan had argued for the Central American wars to *avoid* a "tidal wave" of "feetpeople" soon "swarming into our country."[22] By the mid-1990s, after hostilities ended, one million or so Salvadorans lived in the United States.

Salvadorans in the United States often improved their lives by migrating, but they remained poor and steeped in a different kind of violence. Salvadoran youths in Los Angeles, for example, often joined gangs such as the Mara Salvatrucha 13. In 2005 *Newsweek* called MS-13, as it was known, "the most dangerous gang in America."[23] Members of this and other gangs who were caught and deported by the U.S. government re-created their criminal behavior in El Salvador. By the twenty-first century Salvadoran gang members had grown to be tens of thousands strong, and they re-emerged in U.S. cities such as Washington, D.C. (in 2000 the U.S. capital had 11,741 Salvadorans, far more than any other Central American group, and 25 MS-13 gangs).[24] The film *El Norte* (1985) partially told this story of migration through its two central characters, Guatemalan siblings whose parents die in the U.S.-supported conflict and who suffer the indignities that come with migrant status both in Mexico and in the United States. In a way that Reagan did not expect, therefore, chaos and violence indeed moved toward the American border, then inside it.

Chaos and violence reigned inside El Salvador also. But it was doubly important for the White House to ignore repression by the Salvadoran government because Congress—which, constitutionally, controls the budget and the authority to go to war—required the White House to show that foreign aid did not support violations of human rights in order to pass a yearly "certification."

El Mozote, 1981

The massacre at El Mozote revealed the fraud behind congressional certification. In late 1981 the people of El Mozote found themselves in an area considered to be a free-fire zone by the Atlacatl Battalion, a unit trained by U.S. Special Forces and armed with the latest U.S.-made M-16s, M-60 machine guns, 90-millimeter recoilless rifles, and 60- and 80-millimeter mortars. In December the batallion showed up in El Mozote, looking for sympathizers of the FMLN. Rufina Amaya Márquez, who hid from the men with guns and miraculously survived, recalled the day in these words:

> They said we were collaborators. They were angry. They kept asking us where our pistols were, where the men had hidden our guns, and when we kept saying, again and again, that we didn't have any, they'd push at us with the bayonets. Then they'd say, "Shut up, old woman, what are you crying about." They said they'd kill us if we didn't tell them.

The soldiers went from house to house, killing everyone, men and women, infants, and elders. One investigative reporter said it "may well have been the largest massacre in modern Latin American history." A man in a village nearby later recalled that "the soldiers would pass by, coming from there, and they'd talk about it. You know, they were talking and joking, saying how much they liked the twelve-year-olds. . . . We could hear the women being raped on the hills."

The operation, like the My Lai massacre during the Vietnam War, was not an isolated case of soldiers run amok. It was, rather, a particularly brutal instance of widespread violence, ordered from above and actively ignored by Washington. One of the Atlacatl soldiers was overheard saying to another, "We have to finish everyone, you know that. That's the colonel's order. This is an *operativa de tierra arrasada* here [a scorched-earth operation] and we have to kill the kids as well, or we'll get it ourselves."[25]

Church leaders alerted the U.S. embassy, which supposedly investigated. Six weeks after the killings, the *Washington Post* and the *New York Times* both reported the massacre on their front pages, thus putting pressure on the White House and Congress to release the findings. The internal embassy cable following the *Post* and *Times* articles did not deny the massacre but neither did it confirm it. In other words, the United States would do nothing. Elliott Abrams, the assistant secretary of state for human rights and humanitarian affairs, explained why the pressure eventually eased. "Congress didn't cut off aid, because it didn't want to risk being blamed, if the guerrillas won as a result, for 'losing' El Salvador." And so Reagan got his much-needed certification renewed.

The results of the first full investigation of the massacre were not published until November 1991, almost ten years later. The report included the names of 794 dead. El Salvador's own truth commission found that at least 500 died in El Mozote and nearby villages. Still, the fighting continued.

The Contras in Nicaragua

It was one thing to protect an allied government against an insurgency but quite another to fuel an insurgency against a sovereign government. In Nicaragua, Reagan did just that, and for that reason, his actions there demanded a wholly different level of secrecy and moral and legal rationalization.

Reagan's first major legally ambiguous move in Nicaragua was his approval of National Security Decision Directive 17 (NSDD 17), which increased aid to $19 million for five hundred anti-Sandinista guerrillas originally funded by Carter, in November 1981.[26] These guerrillas came to be infamous as the *contras* (short for *contrarevolucionarios,* or counterrevolutionaries) and were trained by Argentine officers in Honduran bases. Their stated role was legal: to interdict the transfer of weapons between the FSLN in Nicaragua and the FMLN in El Salvador.

In 1982, however, the Argentines dropped out of the effort because the White House supported Great Britain against Argentina in the Falklands War. The CIA took over training the contras, increased their ranks to twelve thousand and their funding to $150 million by 1984, and expanded operations to engage Sandinista soldiers and attack schools and hospitals inside Nicaraguan territory.[27] Reagan characterized the contras as "freedom fighters" and "the moral equivalent of the founding fathers." Congressman Tom Harkin (D-Iowa) disagreed. He thought them "vicious cutthroat murderers . . . remnants of the evil, murderous National Guard."[28]

U.S. Involvement Deepens

Eventually, the U.S. government participated more directly in this "low-intensity warfare." CIA-backed planes bombed airports in Managua, and the CIA and Special Forces also launched nineteen attacks, mostly against oil storage facilities, to choke the energy flow to the Sandinistas. The NSC and the State Department contributed propaganda to the CIA's efforts. The Office of Public Diplomacy, as one NSC staffer explained, gave itself the job of "gluing black hats on the Sandinistas and white hats" on the contras. Public Diplomacy did the expected—publishing pamphlets and briefing books—but also engaged in more unorthodox activities, such as pressuring journalists and editors, secretly funding private pro-contra ads, and accusing the Sandinistas of anti-Semitism. It also booked over fifteen hundred speaking engagements, placed publications in sixteen hundred libraries, and sent anti-FSLN and anti-FMLN materials to hundreds of editorial writers and religious organizations.[29] The Pentagon, for its part, conducted large-scale military exercises in the Caribbean to intimidate the Sandinistas.

Most serious, in late 1983 and early 1984 operatives trained by the CIA dropped mines in three of Nicaragua's harbors, without telling Congress, damaging a British ship and a Soviet tanker in the process. Given the brazenness of these assaults, the secret CIA role could not stay hidden for long. When accusations of this illegal mining surfaced in March 1984, the contras claimed, "We are responsible for placing the mines, not the United States." Secretary of Defense Caspar Weinberger also swore that "the United States is not mining the harbors of Nicaragua." Both were lying—CIA operatives had done these things, and Reagan had ordered them done in late 1983.[30] The CIA later revealed that it had taken over the fight against the Sandinistas in November 1983 because it had concluded that the contras were too incompetent and corrupt to win their own war. To note one instance, Congress's General Accounting Office reported in 1986 that more than half of $12 million handed to the contras ended up in their leaders' bank accounts in Miami.[31]

The secret mining was a breach of international law and of the U.S. Constitution, not to mention acts of war in the absence of any declaration by Congress. So, the International Court of Justice found the United States guilty of "unlawful use of force." But only Congress could truly limit the White House's authority, and it moved to do so. In 1983 Representative Edward Boland (D-Massachusetts), chair of House Intelligence Committee, shepherded the first Boland Amendment onto an appropriations bill. The amendment prohibited the CIA and the Defense Department from providing the contras with any aid other than that aimed at restricting the smuggling of arms into the country. In 1984, in the face of continued lies and illegalities from the White House and Pentagon, another amendment, Boland II, broadened the restrictions. It cut off funding to support, "directly or indirectly, military or paramilitary operations in Nicaragua by any nation, group, organization, movement, or individual."[32] This amendment was supposed to end all shipments of lethal weapons to the contras. One of its side effects, however, was to encourage the contras to found a crack cocaine distribution network to fund their movement and fill their pockets.

Despite clear directives from Congress to stop the war in Central America, Reagan and the Pentagon would not give up. Early on, the president cut Nicaragua's sugar quota by 90 percent, and he consistently played up the Sandinistas' weaknesses, such as their shoddy treatment of the Miskito Indian minority on the Caribbean coast and the trip that Sandinista leader Daniel Ortega unwisely took to the Soviet Union. In 1984, in the face of Boland I and II and to win reelection, the White House publicly accepted the ban on aid to the contras and downplayed the issue during the campaign. All the while, however, it secretly circumvented Congress and continued to fund the contras—a choice that blew up into the Iran-contra scandal (described below). After Reagan handily won reelection in November 1984, he imposed a full economic embargo on Nicaragua and persuaded Congress to vote for military aid for the first time (all military aid up to that point had been from the White House or the CIA).

The Contadora and Esquipulas Peace Plans

Intent on keeping the war alive, Reagan killed the peace. Luckily for him, as long as Haig was secretary of state, peace could not even be discussed. For instance, when Thomas Enders, assistant secretary of state for Latin American affairs and a "dove" in the Reagan administration, approached the topic of peace in secret talks with Spain's foreign minister, he was fired. In January 1983 a new effort emerged—called the Contadora peace plan—that was completely autonomous from the White House. Contadora is an island off the coast of Panama where, in January 1983 Panama, along with Mexico, Venezuela, and Colombia, hammered out a twenty-one-point peace agreement between the five Central American states. Surprising everyone in Washington, the Nicaraguans agreed to it in principle.

At this point, the State Department had a new secretary, George Shultz, who was more moderate than Haig. Shultz might have been inclined to support Contadora, but the NSC, CIA, and Pentagon were not. Reagan sank it. He demanded that all Soviets and Cubans leave Nicaragua and that the Sandinistas reduce their army drastically. He offered nothing in return. Ortega and the Sandinistas of course refused. When they did, Reagan convinced most opposition groups not to participate in the 1985 Nicaraguan election, which then appeared as a sham contest that the Sandinistas won easily.

In 1984 a background paper frankly admitted, "We have effectively blocked Contadora group efforts." A few weeks later the NSC summed up its strategy: "Continue active negotiations but agree to no treaty, and agree to work out some way to support the contras either directly or indirectly. Withhold true objectives from staffs."[33] In 1986 the Department of Defense argued that if Contadora had passed, the Nicaraguans would have violated it and the United States would have found itself forced to invade.

The *New York Times* exposed this twisted thinking, worthy of George Orwell's *1984,* with the headline, "Pentagon Predicts Big War if Latins Sign Peace Accord."[34]

In the late 1980s the "Latins" tried peace again, this time with more success. Nicaragua's neighbors were clearly tired of the chaos in Central America. "We had to choose between rationality and madness," said the leader of the new plan, Costa Rican president Oscar Arias Sánchez. The Arias plan, also called the Esquipulas plan, was similar to Contadora, asking for cease-fires, negotiations, and elections. The Reagan administration again tried to strangle the peace, this time by wringing the neck of its main broker. The White House slashed economic assistance to Costa Rica and failed to support the restructuring of its debt. In addition, a shady Republican-party affiliate called the Republican Institute for International Affairs funneled $433,000 of quasi-public money to Arias's political opponents.[35] Resisting such pressure, the five Central American nations signed the Esquipulas plan in August 1987, and Arias earned the Nobel Peace Prize.

Deepening Ambivalence in Latin America

Ronald Reagan's wars aroused the indignation of much of Latin America. Mexican writer Carlos Fuentes, like countless others, was saddened by the spectacle of destruction that seemed to serve only symbolic politics. He called the United States the "Land of Jekyll and Hyde," "a democracy inside but an empire outside; Dr. Jekyll at home, Mr. Hyde in Latin America." Embracing ambivalence, he pledged:

> We will continue to praise the democratic achievements and the cultural values of the society of the United States. But we will continue to oppose its arrogant and violent policies in Latin America. We will do so painfully, because we love so many things in the United States. We will not confuse the United States and the Soviet Union, or indeed accept their moral equivalence. The problem is far more tragic: the Russians act as an empire inside and outside. They are perfectly coherent. The United States, by acting like the Russians in its sphere of influence, becomes profoundly incoherent and hypocritical.[36]

Reagan's wars also angered U.S. citizens. The public's anger explained why the president downplayed Central America before the election of 1984 and then turned up the volume after his victory. One poll, from April 1983, revealed that fewer than one in three respondents supported "involvement in El Salvador." By the mid-1980s more than sixty thousand U.S. citizens pledged civil disobedience if the United States invaded Nicaragua. At the height of the war, the White House's Nicaraguan policy never received more than 35 percent support in polls.[37] These numbers did not necessarily reflect high-minded opposition to intervention. Most respondents seemed to think that the vague threat of Soviet influence was not worth risking U.S.

lives in Central America. One pollster reported "a strong aversion to the region that goes from misinformation to racism."[38]

New Activist Networks

Thousands of U.S. citizens actively participated in efforts to end U.S. involvement, mostly through nongovernmental organizations (NGOs). In 1982 Human Rights Watch was founded in New York; the same year the Inter-American Dialogue was born in Washington, D.C. Other groups who fought the Reagan wars from outside the government included the Sanctuary Movement, Witness for Peace, the Committee in Solidarity with the People of El Salvador, Amnesty International, Americas Watch, and the North American Congress on Latin America (NACLA). The Catholic Church also became involved, moved by the example of Liberation Theology in Central America. Its members wrote letters, made speeches, and marched in massive demonstrations.

For perhaps the first time in modern U.S.–Latin American affairs, these private citizens created a network of activists pursuing peace in Central America. They uncovered abuses that otherwise might have remained hidden. In its 1985 report, for instance, Americas Watch catalogued the human rights abuses in Central America, concluding that "the Reagan administration had done harm by its public praise for governments that systematically abuse human rights . . . by its public embrace of those responsible for gross abuses . . . by attempting to discredit victims of human rights abuses and those who report on abuses . . . in attempting to shift the blame for human rights abuses . . . by systematically disregarding U.S. law and international law on human rights."[39]

Other nongovernmental protests included the production of feature films that denounced the anticommunist paranoia in Washington, the continuing obsession with "winning" Vietnam in Latin America, and the targeting of peasants, priests, activists, and press in Central America. Among these films were *Under Fire* (1983), *Salvador* (1986), *Walker* (1987), and the little-known *Sandino* (1990).

NGOs and U.S. public opinion arguably had an impact on the passage of the Boland amendments in the U.S. Congress and on otherwise keeping an eye on Reagan. They certainly irritated the executive branch, which lashed back. The administration's methods included secret wiretapping, photographing participants at peace marches, and illegally breaking into offices and searching files. From 1981 to 1988, the FBI investigated more than thirteen thousand people and eleven thousand organizations active in Central American affairs.[40] Reagan also called on the Internal Revenue Service to harass NACLA and other organizations. In 1988, when several abuses by the FBI surfaced, Director William Sessions apologized, but the punishment he meted out was limited: a two-week suspension of three employees.

Peace at Last, 1990–1992

Reagan long wanted the Sandinistas in Nicaragua to, as he put it, "say uncle."[41]

They never did. But in 1990 they did the next best thing—they collapsed from exhaustion. For a decade after coming to power in 1979—and this, after a years-long civil war—they had never ceased being under attack. Defense swallowed up 4 out of every 10 dollars of the budget, inflation ran at 14,000 percent in 1988, and of Nicaragua's state farms, only 4 out of 102 were profitable.[42] The Sandinistas had nevertheless remained remarkably popular with Nicaraguans despite the autocratic, male-chauvinist tendencies of some of their leaders. Poor Nicaraguans had recognized the Sandinistas' efforts to improve healthcare, spread literacy to the countryside, promote culture, and never again allow the return of a dictatorship like the one they had defeated.

In 1990 the Sandinistas gambled on that popularity and subjected themselves to another election. This time, however, everyone participated. President George H. W. Bush backed the National Opposition Union, led by Violeta Barrios de Chamorro, with millions from the U.S. Congress's National Endowment for Democracy. He also pressured Soviet leader Mikhail Gorbachev to suspend aid to the Sandinistas that now reached almost $800 million annually. On November 25, 1990, voters gave the presidency to the smiling Violeta, clad in white—the color of peace, which they no longer associated with the red-and-black Sandinistas.[43]

War weariness also set in on El Salvador. There, too, the U.S. government benefited from a liberal pacification. In 1989 right-wing candidate Alfredo Cristiani won the presidency. Soon after, death squads murdered six Jesuit priests at the Central American University. Reactions to this crime revealed that both sides were growing tired of the violence. After all, seventy-five thousand Salvadorans had died (as had twelve U.S. citizens) with no battlefield victory anywhere in sight. Moreover, the devastation to the environment had been almost total: 94 percent of the original forests, 80 percent of natural vegetation, and 77 percent of arable soil were gone. Financially, the war's cost had reached $6 billion.

It ended on New Year's Eve 1991, a few minutes before the clock struck midnight, when guerrillas and the government reached an agreement to lay down arms and curb abuses. Bush, unlike Reagan, supported this negotiation. On January 16, 1992, Cristiani and the FMLN met in Mexico City's Chapultepec Palace, site of the 1945 conference, and formally put an end to twelve years of war. One thousand UN peacekeepers moved in to oversee the peace.[44]

Crimes and Misdemeanors: The Iran-contra Scandal

The White House's determination to continue funding the contras after Boland II specifically prohibited that funding led to a secret operation. When it erupted into public consciousness in 1986, what came to be called the Iran-contra scandal revealed one of the greatest abuses of power committed in the history of U.S. foreign relations. Not only did officials inside the White House operate a war directly against the orders of Congress, but many of them—including President Reagan—repeatedly lied to Congress and to the U.S. public about the operation.

North and the Enterprise

The operation was originally called "The Enterprise" and was largely run by U.S. Marine Col. Oliver North, who worked for the NSC. The NSC, founded in 1947, was an office separate from other executive departments and was intended only to advise the president on, not to make, foreign policy. By the 1980s, however, the NSC had appropriated much of the foreign-policy making initiative not only from Congress, but also from the State Department and even the Pentagon.

North was the perfect tool for chipping away at the Constitution by inflating the NSC's power. Unusually ambitious, he was a patriotic anticommunist but also a man ready to fib for his nation. "Ollie North. God, the man could speak a blue haze of bullshit," recalled a CIA specialist on Latin America. "And at times, I was convinced he was mad." Under oath, North lied that he had been a Special Forces company commander in Vietnam. He also lied that he accompanied Secretary Haig on shuttle diplomacy during the Falklands War. He even falsely bragged about how he met with Reagan in the Oval Office and in his living quarters, sometimes praying with the president. The truth was that he never spent any time alone with Reagan. A former aide to UN Ambassador Jeane Kirkpatrick said about North, "I've concluded that not only is he a liar, but he's delusional, power-hungry, and a danger to the president and the country."[45]

In mid-1985 North began to pull in private contributions from several noncongressional sources to continue funding the contras. Private and government funds came from Costa Rica, El Salvador, Guatemala, Honduras, Israel, Panama, Saudi Arabia, and Taiwan. The Saudi government gave $32 million, and the Sultan of Brunei, $10 million. In the United States, former crooner Pat Boone and beer magnate Joseph Coors also contributed. These donors' motivations ranged from gaining favor with Reagan to helping achieve stability on their borders with Nicaragua to hoping sincerely for the failure of communism in the hemisphere.

In an initially separate operation, North and associates also overcharged Islamic fundamentalists in Iran about $30 million for about $12 million worth of antitank missiles and weapons parts. In return, the Iranians helped free hostages held in Lebanon. This endeavor was a potential scandal in itself, since it placed missiles in the hands of supporters of terrorism and millions in the pockets of arms dealers.[46]

The Diversion of Funds

The contra and Iran operations became "Iran-contra" in 1986, when North hit upon the idea of linking the two operations. The NSC would use "residuals," or profits, from these Iran sales to fund the contras. In ten months

$3.8 million went to the Central American war. Little of that went to the contra soldiers on the ground, however, since their leaders stole 37 percent of North's funds through currency conversion.

Effective or not, U.S. actions were illegal, unconstitutional, and against established policy in at least four respects: First, flying planes full of weapons down to Central America directly defied Boland II. Second, selling weapons to Iran ran against the U.S. policy, as Reagan stated it, "that America will never make concessions to terrorists," especially those who held U.S. hostages. Third, helping Iran fight Iraq contradicted the official U.S. support of Saddam Hussein, who was no friend of the United States but a convenient ally against the Iranians, with whom the United States had had no official relations since 1979. And fourth, diverting funds from Iran to Nicaragua demanded a level of secrecy and underhandedness that shocked most, even in Washington. With the president praising the contras as patriotic heroes, however, North could easily justify his actions morally if not legally. "I don't think it was wrong," he later said. "I think it was a neat idea."[47]

The edifice of lies and illegalities came crashing down with the plane of Eugene Hasenfus. In October 1986 Hasenfus, a cargo handler, was working on a plane full of arms destined for the contras when the Sandinistas shot it down and captured him alive. Luckily for Hasenfus, he was wearing a parachute, despite the Enterprise's policy of not providing them (perhaps to reduce the likelihood of crash survivors revealing secrets). On October 9 he told a news conference what he had already told his captives. Claiming that "this is not my war," he described how CIA agents in El Salvador had supervised his flight.

At this point, the CIA could have dismissed Hasenfus as a liar unconnected to the White House, but the Sandinistas had also found a card in a wallet of one of the dead crew members linking the flight to the then-obscure Oliver North.[48] Upon hearing the news, CIA director William Casey, a mastermind of the operation from the beginning who died from a brain tumor soon after the allegations came out, had North immediately begin to shred documents. Secretary Shultz and Elliott Abrams both denied White House involvement. When a House committee asked Abrams about any link between Hasenfus and the U.S. government, he lied, "Absolutely not." Because of the evidence, however, Attorney General Edwin Meese publicly began an investigation.[49]

The investigation might have uncovered only the illegal contra funding if not for the work of a small Lebanese magazine, *Al Shiraa,* which, one month after the Hasenfus crash, uncovered the Iran link in a Swiss bank account. On November 13 Reagan appeared on television to say he had sold arms to Iran, but he continued to deny that he had traded them for hostages. Meese's investigation soon uncovered a key North memo that revealed the diversion. "Oh, shit," said Meese, when he learned of the memo. He then informed the president, who, by all accounts, seemed genuinely shocked.[50]

Eugene Hasenfus, an air cargo handler for the Enterprise, was shot down and captured by Sandinista soldiers in 1986. The Enterprise was a White House operation to continue funding the anti-Sandinista contras in Nicaragua against explicit orders from Congress not to do so. Hasenfus's confession set off the investigation that became the Iran-contra affair. Wreckage from the plane is on the right. AP/WideWorld Photos.

The Investigation and Hearings

In the months and years that followed, what rivaled the Watergate scandal of the Nixon era in the seriousness of its crimes became, symbolically and often literally, more like a series of misdemeanors that saved the Reagan administration from historical ignominy. Democrats in the 1980s were kind to the Reagan administration despite the seriousness of the allegations. They did hold hearings in summer 1987, but they let them become media circuses in which the personality of North—testifying in a military uniform, boldly taking responsibility for the Enterprise—became almost as central as the findings of criminality. Perhaps half the country considered North a Boy Scout figure who bent the Constitution only for the worthwhile purposes of freeing U.S. hostages and fighting communism (neither goal was clearly attained: a few U.S. hostages were freed but others were kidnapped, and not one Nicaraguan village was won by the contras). While North testified, the camera angled upward so as to make him appear more heroic (the angle was lowered for other witnesses). North's lawyers stacked up thousands of telegrams of support around him so as to impress upon the members of Congress the political implications of asking tough questions. One pop music group wrote a song titled, "Go, Ollie, Go," set to the tune of Chuck Berry's "Go, Johnny, Go."

Throughout the proceedings, witnesses dodged questions, refused to answer on the grounds that they might incriminate themselves, or claimed not to remember recent events. National Security Advisor John Poindexter, a man with a photographic memory, said "I don't recall" or "I don't remember" over 180 times.[51] Many seemed to be protecting the president by claiming that he had not been involved in any way, and Reagan himself could rely on his famous amnesia (which might have been the onset of Alzheimer's disease) to exculpate himself. Few in the Democratic Party or in the office of independent counsel Lawrence Walsh called for the president's resignation or even for a motion of censure from Congress. Reagan's attitude toward North was enigmatic. Hours after he permitted North to be threatened with criminal charges, he called him to thank him for his work. "You are an American hero," said the president.[52]

One Democratic senator, Patrick Moynihan of New York, looked back with grief on the whole episode. "In the history of the American Republic, I do not believe there has ever been so massive a hemorrhaging of trust and integrity. The very processes of American Government were put in harm's way by a conspiracy of faithless or witless men: sometimes both."[53]

The Whitewash

The investigations led to a happy ending for the Republicans. To be sure, fourteen officials were indicted and eleven of those convicted—the highest being Secretary of Defense Weinberger. Their crimes ranged from perjury to conspiracy, tax evasion, mail fraud, theft, destroying documents, and withholding information from Congress or otherwise obstructing its work. Poindexter and North resigned. But most plea bargained for light sentences (Abrams and others), got their convictions overturned on technicalities (Poindexter and North), or were pardoned by President George H. W. Bush (Weinberger) (document 19).

When Bush's son took office in 2001, the Republicans welcomed a trio of Iran-contra characters back into the fold. Abrams was put in charge of human rights in the Middle East, and Otto Reich, who as head of the Office of Public Diplomacy had concealed much of the diversion of funds from the Congress, became assistant secretary of state for Western Hemispheric affairs at the State Department. Former U.S. ambassador to Honduras John Negroponte enjoyed the most spectacular ascent. He first became U.S. representative to the UN, then ambassador to Iraq, and finally was appointed the first director of national intelligence.

Not so highly placed as these three, John Poindexter also returned to government in 2001 and raised another controversy when he headed a program called "Total Information Awareness," which purported to keep track of all U.S. citizens through their credit card purchases and other schemes. Oliver North, finally, made a living as a conservative talk radio host and a commentator for the Fox News network.

Debts Rise, Tyrants Fall

Reagan's wars were crude efforts at taking control of the region militarily, but in two other ways, Latin America was changing largely beyond U.S. control. Many of its economies were collapsing under crushing debt burdens, and some of its tyrannical regimes were ending under pressure from rising democratic movements. While the U.S. government was not directly responsible for many of these sweeping structural and political changes, it did try to respond so as to integrate Latin America into a new hemispheric community of free-market democracies that would stand as a model of U.S.-led globalization.

Economic Collapse

After uplifting economic prospects in the 1970s, Latin American economies crumbled in the 1980s. From 1982 to 1989 the average Latin American's real income fell by one-tenth, and GDP growth was actually negative in 1981, 1982, 1983, 1988, and 1989. Latin America was doing not only badly but comparatively worse than other regions of the world. In the 1980s, for instance, while its exports increased by half, Latin America's share of world commerce fell from 6 to 3.5 percent. By 1990 the region had 45 to 50 million new poor people. "Translated into human terms," wrote one leading scholar, "the statistics on Latin America's plight mean hunger, infant death, boat people and feet people, stunted education, epidemics, street crime and delinquency, and mounting unrest."[54] The 1980s in Latin America came to be known as the "lost decade."

The culprit commonly blamed was not necessarily dependency but skyrocketing debt levels. From a manageable $30 billion in 1970, the region's debt rose to $220 billion in 1980, $378 billion in 1985, and $448 billion by 1990. At mid-decade Latin America's external debt was equal to that of the rest of the so-called developing world.[55]

Three factors, primarily, caused the debt. First, war, affecting mostly the nations of Central America, forced them to borrow in order to import arms, food, and consumer goods. Second, the price of petroleum rose from $10 a barrel in the early 1970s to more than $40 a barrel in 1981. As in the United States, rising costs for imported oil rippled through the economy through pricier energy for almost every industry and household.

The third cause of massive debt was borrowing in the 1970s at low but variable interest rates. When bills came due in the early 1980s, the financial markets happened to be operating at much higher interest rates—they rose 8 percent in just three years—which made repayment excruciating. In response, governments borrowed more. In five years the debt increase due solely to rising rates amounted to as much as $50 billion.[56] This third contributor can partly be attributed to U.S. policies because the U.S. Federal Reserve responded to global inflation with a "tight money" policy, which meant rising interest rates. And, policies aside, 38 percent of these loans were owed to U.S. banks.[57] In short, Latin American governments had gambled on the world markets and lost. The result was a transition from U.S. dependence to global dependence.

The Mexican Bailout, 1982

They say that tragedy brings neighbors closer together. In 1982 this was certainly the case as Mexico's currency collapsed and the U.S. government moved in with a "bailout." Mexico was one among many countries that had taken out massive high-interest loans with international bankers. The country could do so while it did well in oil, selling ever increasing amounts at rising prices. In 1980 and 1981, however, dependence struck back. Overproduction of oil flattened sales. Investors sensed that Mexico was too dependent on petroleum and pulled out. In reaction, in 1982 the government of José López Portillo announced the nationalization of banks to stop the outflow of investment, devalued the peso by 100 percent, and informed Washington that it could no longer service its debt of $83 billion.

The Reagan administration at first did little. Then it realized that several U.S. banks might collapse if Mexicans stopped paying their loans. All involved were seeing firsthand one of the effects of globalization and interdependence—the U.S. need for Latin American financial stability, even in poor nations. It turned out that Wall Street, too, was dependent. The Federal Reserve, along with the International Monetary Fund, moved into action. They arranged a restructuring of Mexico's debt, a process typically involving smaller payments at lower interest rates for a longer time. The U.S. government also bought $1 billion of Mexico's oil in advance and promised another billion for farm goods. The price to Mexico for the bankers' generosity? Selling oil and natural gas at favorable prices, and keeping out of the Central American wars.

Unwelcome Strongman I: Duvalier

Another development that grew subtly in the 1970s and 1980s was the declining legitimacy of dictators. Even in the poorest Latin American nations, it now seemed, there existed substantial merchant and middle classes who found their desires for capitalist profit and democratic freedoms stifled by old-style autocrats. Those leaders who went too far in repressing their people sensed that their days were numbered. Between 1978 and 1990 fifteen Latin American countries got rid of dictators and began to elect their leaders. As of 2005 no civilian constitutional president elected in free and fair elections had been overthrown by armed forces, with one exception.

This exception was Haiti, where Jean-Bertrand Aristide was overthrown in 1991 and again in 2004. Aristide's overthrows were rooted in the 1980s. Even before the 1980s, graft and violence marked the regimes of Haitian dictators Jean-Claude "Baby Doc" Duvalier (1971–86) and his father (1957–71). Poverty was both cause and consequence of these regimes. In the mid-1960s Haitians ranked the absolute lowest in almost all measures of social well-being in the Americas, including GDP per capita, literacy, doctors, hospital beds, newspapers, radio, televisions, expenditures on education, and rates of unionization and urbanization.[58] Meanwhile, the Duvaliers remained staunch Cold War allies of Washington, benefiting from economic aid and in return voting with the United States at the OAS.

By the mid-1980s the prevailing concern in the White House toward Haiti seemed to be stemming the flow of boat people to the shores of Florida and other states. In 1981 the Reagan administration and Baby Doc established a compact under which the Coast Guard could intercept Haitians on rafts and boats and send them back to Haiti if they did not satisfy Coast Guard officials in on-board hearings. These hearings turned out to be largely for show. Over ten years U.S. immigration intercepted 22,716 such Haitians and admitted only 28.

In 1986 a strong student and middle-class movement ousted Duvalier. Military regimes ruled Haiti for the next four years. In 1990 Jean-Bertrand Aristide, a modest parish priest influenced by Liberation Theology, won 67 percent of the votes for president in a field of thirteen candidates, without the support (but also without the opposition) of Washington. Representing Haiti's poor, Aristide rooted out some corruption and repression, disbanded the army, and allowed free speech. Many foresaw in the Duvalier-Aristide transition the flowering of democracy in the poorest nation in the hemisphere.

Unwelcome Strongman II: Noriega

Across the Caribbean in Panama, another dictator left power much less quietly. Manuel Noriega had presided over one of the most unequal societies in Latin America since the mysterious death of Omar Torrijos in a plane crash in 1981. During Torrijos's reign, Noriega headed the brutal military intelligence service, a position he used to torture prisoners personally. In 1983 he took control of the national guard and renamed it the Panamanian Defense Forces (PDF). From then on Noriega could dictate his will to civilian leaders.

What mattered more in the end was the Panamanian strongman's shifting relationship to the U.S. government. Noriega had enriched himself through friendships with the CIA and Vice President George H. W. Bush, to whom he was an informant in the struggle against drug trafficking. Having been cut off from the CIA payroll under Carter, Noriega was reinstated under Reagan—at a salary of $200,000 per year.[59]

For Washington, however, Noriega soon proved unreliable. He was an opportunistic man, if nothing else, helping whatever side in a conflict would enrich and empower him. Both Oliver North and Fidel Castro were his partners. In Central America, while he helped train the contras, he also bought arms from Cuba and sold them back to Salvadoran guerrillas. And in the "drug war," he not only informed the CIA but represented Colombia's Medellín drug cartel and laundered its money in his banks. By 1989 the State Department assessed that he was worth $300 million.[60]

When Congress reopened the money spigot to the contras in 1986, Noriega was suddenly not so essential but more of a nuisance. In 1988 a Miami grand jury indicted him on drug charges. Meanwhile, he refused to sanction elections in his own country. When protests erupted, the now out-of-control dictator sent gangs of youths called "Dignity Battalions" ("dingbats" is what U.S. personnel in Panama called them) to beat opponents in broad daylight in front of rolling television cameras. Not satisfied, Noriega banged a machete against a podium and dared the U.S. government to take him down.[61] In May 1988 Reagan accepted the challenge. He declared that the U.S. goal in Panama "must be the removal of Noriega from power."[62]

By 1989, no longer needing Noriega as an informant, embarrassed by his erratic public behavior, and perhaps feeling he would reveal some nasty secrets, now-President Bush ordered the dictator captured and brought stateside to stand trial on those 1988 drug charges. To capture the strongman, Bush took the dramatic step of invading Panama in the early morning hours of December 20, 1989, with twenty-four thousand U.S. troops. The "Christmas invasion" targeted PDF headquarters and blocked off all escape routes from Panama City. Noriega was caught unawares in the middle of a drunken, drug-addled fiesta. He took refuge in the Vatican embassy. U.S. troops installed massive speakers outside Noriega's hideout and played ear-splitting rock music to wear down his resistance. Within a few days the Panamanian surrendered, but not before U.S. troops burned down the nearby poor neighborhood of El Chorrillo, in the process killing perhaps as many as three thousand Panamanians.[63] As president, Bush had now destroyed the monster he had helped create while he was the director of central intelligence in the 1970s. As for Noriega, he was tried in a U.S. court and sentenced. In 2005 he was still a U.S. prisoner somewhere near Miami.

Was this the revival of gunboat diplomacy, as critics said? It certainly seemed a lot like the 1983 Grenada invasion: a small nation falling prey to U.S. unilateral aggression. The OAS condemned the action 20 to 1, as did the UN, 75 to 20. Polls showed, however, that Panamanians approved the invasion at least 3 to 1. They were especially grateful for the restoration of a democratic process after Noriega's departure. Significant corruption continued, but the system brought to power rule-through-election through the 1990s. In late 1999 the Panama Canal changed hands as planned for in the treaties of the 1970s (see chapter 3).[64]

Around 1990 one door closed and another opened. The wars in Central America were the last gasp of the Cold War in Latin America. Washington relaxed its proxy war in light of the failure to produce military victory, the heavy political price at home, and especially the collapse of the Berlin Wall in November 1989, which pulled the rug out from under the ideological legs of the Reagan crusade. The Panamanian and the Haitian episodes can therefore be seen as early post–Cold War events. In both, the U.S. government was concerned not with the ideological alignments of leaders but with the rising transnational problems of the Western Hemisphere: in Haiti, migration, and in Panama, drug trafficking. Also because the Cold War was winding down, Washington was willing to experiment with "irresponsible" democracies that might bring about political and economic uncertainty. The new president, George H. W. Bush, argued that the crumbling of the Soviet bloc meant a new life for democracy and the free market. "Out of these troubled times," he said, "a new world order can emerge: a new era—freer from the threat of terror, stronger in the pursuit of justice, and more secure in the quest for peace. An era in which the nations of the world, East and West, North and South, can live in harmony."[65] This was not altruism but a sharpening of self-interest: U.S. officials coalesced around the idea that free markets could only truly flourish where political freedoms and optimism for the future existed. An irony of this shift was that U.S. citizens largely lost interest in Latin America. A 1990 poll revealed that only 2 percent of U.S. respondents expressed genuine concern for the problems of the region.[66] From 1985 to 1996 U.S. aid to Central America fell from $1.2 billion to $167 million; military aid wound up being virtually nil.[67] U.S. aid to Latin America as a whole dropped from over a third of overall U.S. foreign aid in 1990 to less than a tenth in 1995.[68]

CHAPTER 5

TRANSNATIONALISMS

Neoliberalism, Drugs, and Latina *America,*

1991–2005

IN 2000 ECUADOR MADE A REMARKABLE MOVE. It adopted the U.S. dollar, replacing the *sucre* as its official currency. The following year, El Salvador and Guatemala followed Ecuador's lead. Up to then "dollarization" had existed only in tiny Panama, whose economy had always depended heavily on the United States. Ecuador's reason for dollarization was not dependence, but its belief that converting to a trusted global currency would even out Ecuador's finances and trade. The switch brought some benefits: Ecuador's prices stabilized and economic growth increased. But problems also arose almost immediately. Counterfeiters circulated good fakes, and cashiers in Ecuador had no training or technology to tell the difference. To make matters worse, one in eight Ecuadoreans was illiterate and relied on the different colors of the *sucre* to help tell denominations apart; the always-green Yankee dollar was confusing. Drug traffickers, in contrast, loved the dollar because it made savings more valuable and shipments easier to move. A final casualty of dollarization was its main champion, President Jamil Mahuad. Following his announcement in January 2000, indigenous groups supported by military officers led protests that forced the president out of office (his vice president took over and stuck with Mahuad's plan).

Ecuador's dance with the dollar suggested that the sharp black-and-white simplicities of the Cold War gave way to blurrier, grayer complexities from 1991 to 2005. When the Soviet Union imploded in 1991, transnationalism—the state of existing *across* several nations rather than within one single nation—emerged from below the surface to reveal itself as the main dynamic in U.S.–Latin American relations. The Cold War had been "hiding" many integrative trends of the post–World War II era. No single transnational issue took the place of the East-West conflict, however.

In fact, U.S.–Latin American relations in the 1990s and 2000s were defined by the absence of defining issues—no dominating concern around which to plan economic growth or pitch political battles. Instead, new ideas and new energies flowed pell-mell in almost every aspect of human endeavor. Even the *channels* of U.S.–Latin American relations diversified. No longer were they overwhelmingly government-to-government. No matter the issue—trade, the environment, drugs, immigration, popular culture— several governments were generally involved at the same time. Moreover, nonstate actors such as migrants, indigenous groups, unions, NGOs, and corporations featured more prominently in the transnational era. By 2005 many of those long kept out of political power were back with a vengeance. They demanded—and often caused—the overthrow of traditional leaders and of the U.S. ties that defined them.

Economic Transnationalism: From Washington Consensus to Cancún Dissension

When the cloud of the Cold War dissipated, along with it disappeared both the utopian appeal of communism as a worker's paradise and the suspicion of the free market as a ruse of imperialists. Instead, a new orthodoxy swept through Latin America: the so-called Washington consensus, a "neoliberal" embrace of the free market. Yet others soon came to believe that unregulated free trade led to greater inequality and devastated the environment. Parallel to the growth of neoliberalism, therefore, grassroots organizations and populist leaders formed alliances to derail what they saw as U.S.-dominated economic interdependence.

Washington's New Prescriptions

Coined in 1990,[1] the term "Washington consensus" aimed to turn back the clock on many of the policies that Latin American governments, influenced by dependency theory, had pursued since 1945 (see chapter 1). The consensus's three core prescriptions for what ailed Latin America were (1) to allow supply and demand to set prices and wages, (2) to sell off state-owned enterprises and use the money to pay off the crushing debt, and (3) to concentrate on exports rather than substitute imports. This was not a return to modernization theory from the 1950s, which assumed that nations would all industrialize one day. Rather, it looked like a return to original eighteenth-century "liberal" political economy, in which each nation struggled to find its own "comparative advantage" in the global economy largely free from government interference save for basic social welfare and central banks. Whatever the remedy, there was certainly widespread agreement behind the idea that economic globalization was the primary issue in post–Cold War U.S.–Latin American relations.

Not only did the goals of integration change, but so did its mechanisms. Within the U.S. government alone, the handling of policy expanded from traditional bodies such as the Department of State, the CIA, and the Pentagon, to a larger group of bureaucracies that dealt with issues beyond national security. These included the Treasury Department, the Office of the Special Trade Representative, the Export-Import Bank, the Drug Enforcement Administration (DEA), the Environmental Protection Agency (EPA), the Immigration and Naturalization Service (INS), the Coast Guard, and after the terrorist attacks of September 11, 2001, the Department of Homeland Security.

U.S. corporations and investors especially wanted to create an aura of consensus because Latin America remained an important trading partner. To be sure, the share of Latin American exports that went to the United States had fallen—from almost half after World War II to a third in 1990—yet the United States maintained its place as the largest trading partner for every single country in the hemisphere and Latin America remained a greater buyer of U.S. exports than Japan or Germany.[2]

The consensus seemed to work at first. In the late 1980s and early 1990s sell-offs by states were quick and massive. Argentina unloaded fifty-one firms for $18 billion in three years while Mexico auctioned off more than one thousand of them for $12 billion. New cash from the sales filled state coffers and helped pay off debts. Tariffs also nose-dived. Costa Rica's average tax on imports went from 92 to 16 percent; Brazil's, from 80 to 21 percent; and Colombia's, from 83 to 7 percent. Finally, U.S. exports to Latin America in 1990 grew 50 percent faster than those to any other region. The impact on inflation was immediate, as it receded from an average of 450 percent per year to around 10 percent. From 1990 to 1995 economic growth grew at a yearly average of 4 percent.[3]

Latin Americans seemed to be finding their comparative advantages. In the circum-Caribbean, for example, those advantages were tourism and cheap labor for manufacturing. In 1992 export-processing zones in Mexico, the Caribbean, and Central America numbered more than two hundred. Their three thousand plants employed 735,000 workers and produced $14 billion in exports to the United States every year.[4] In Mexico, the border shared with the United States saw the further expansion of maquiladoras. By 1999 1.3 million Mexicans and others worked in 4,420 plants. General Motors had become the largest private employer in Mexico, with over fifty thousand workers.[5] "The so-called lost decade in Latin America is a fading memory," announced President Bill Clinton in December 1994 as the recovery became apparent. "These reforms are working wonders. These are remarkable, hopeful times."[6]

NAFTA

The U.S. government was especially excited about its own brainchild for speeding up economic transnationalism: the North American Free Trade Agreement (NAFTA) between the United States, Mexico, and Canada. When the three nations agreed to NAFTA in 1992, reforms had already lowered tariffs between the United States and Mexico from 24 to 11 percent, making Mexico the third-largest U.S. trading partner. And in the late 1980s the

United States had signed its largest partner, Canada, onto a trade agreement. Major export-import and financial firms then doled out large contributions to U.S. members of Congress so that they would bring Mexico into the fold of NAFTA. The pact was unveiled in the middle of a U.S. presidential election in August 1992, and Democratic presidential challenger Clinton seemed to compete with the incumbent, George H. W. Bush, to see who would most enthusiastically back NAFTA. By the eve of its implementation, Mexican tariffs had dropped to 5 percent and U.S. tariffs to about twice that figure (document 20).[7]

NAFTA created a trading bloc second only in size to the European Union, with 370 million producers and consumers and a GDP of over $6 trillion. After its implementation in 1994, NAFTA boosted investment, competition, and productivity. Workers in export-oriented industries enjoyed the greatest wage increases in their economies. Mexico's exports nearly doubled those of the rest of Latin America put together, to the point where, in 1998, Mexico became the United States's second-largest trading partner and was on its way to bumping Canada from the top spot.[8]

The consensus over free trade even spurred Latin American economies to integrate *without* the United States. In 1991 Brazil, Argentina, Uruguay, and Paraguay created the Common Market for the South (MERCOSUR), which made 90 percent of trade duty free starting in 1995. In the three years after that, intra-MERCOSUR trade quintupled. Others organized too. The Andean Community united Bolivia, Peru, Ecuador, Colombia, and Venezuela. The Central American Common Market revived free trade between Costa Rica, Nicaragua, Honduras, El Salvador, and Guatemala. And the Caribbean Common Market (CARICOM) lowered barriers between the countries of the English-speaking Caribbean and the United States.

The Zapatista Revolt and Other Responses to NAFTA

But was there truly a "consensus"? The very day that NAFTA went into effect, January 1, 1994, a shout of protest arose from a poor, rural region of Mexico. Three thousand indigenous members of the Zapatista Army for National Liberation (EZLN) launched a revolt and quickly took over seven towns in their state of Chiapas.

The Zapatistas shrewdly combined opposition to NAFTA with age-old grievances. In the name of all indigenous peoples, they foresaw NAFTA threatening land ownership, democracy, and basic services. They feared that maize and beans, for instance, would lose government subsidies, and that those who produced them would lose their livelihood. They warned that the IMF and World Bank would force Mexico to cut social services. In larger sense, the Zapatistas saw NAFTA as the latest salvo in a five-hundred-year-old conquest of the original inhabitants of the Americas by European colonists.

Yet they did not argue for a return to the past. Their support came partly from friends in the United States and elsewhere in Latin America, many of them known only through the Internet. They also emphasized their own lack of hierarchy and ideological doctrine. One of their spokespersons, the mysterious and charismatic Subcommandante Marcos, explained the democratic structure of the EZLN:

> You can't put so much emphasis on the old, traditional vertical guerrilla discipline—the you're-with-us-or-you're-dead school of thought. You can't raise the step so high that nobody can climb it; you have to make room for all the people to participate to the best of their abilities, and so you are always in the process of looking for what unites people, and not what separates—what adds, and not what subtracts.[9]

Marcos himself kept his identity secret behind a ski mask meant to signify how the organization's leaders were less important that its members. (He was later revealed to be a former university professor.)

The Zapatista war cry, "the Indians are no longer afraid!" rang true with the convictions of other indigenous peoples in the Americas, especially Mayan activist Rigoberta Menchú, who won the Nobel Peace Prize in 1992 (document 21). The Zapatistas survived violent attacks from paramilitary groups and eventually gained significant property and community rights in Chiapas but did little damage to NAFTA. The Clinton administration supported the Mexican government's efforts to assuage some of the Zapatistas' social demands while containing them militarily.

Outside the Zapatista struggle, the case against NAFTA slowly garnered evidence and arguments. The voices that made Congress members most hesitant to back NAFTA were those of U.S. labor organizations and of two-time presidential contender Ross Perot. Both had warned against a loss of U.S. jobs to cheap-labor Mexico. And, a decade after NAFTA, most computations indeed found a net reduction in the number of jobs in Canada and the United States somewhere in the hundreds of thousands. Even in Mexico, the agricultural sector lost 1.4 million jobs, intensifying an already-existing trend. In all three countries, the rich got richer and life for the poor got more expensive. The middle class was being squeezed and the "working poor"—those who worked full-time but could not make ends meet—became a standard socioeconomic category. In 2001 the AFL-CIO declared that NAFTA "utterly failed to deliver the promised benefits to ordinary citizens in any of the three North American countries."[10]

NGOs concerned with poverty and human rights also argued that NAFTA worsened inequalities between Mexico and the United States. Already in the early 1990s the United States and Mexico were the most unequal economies of any two countries sharing a border. Many NAFTA cheerleaders had left unmentioned that Mexico provided only $200 billion of the $6 trillion in common GDP. NAFTA might have widened the gulf. From 1981 to 2001 the proportion of Mexicans living in poverty climbed from one-half to three quarters.[11] Rural poverty was even worse: it increased from 79 percent to 82 percent.[12] Cheap maquiladora labor—one of the few advantages Mexico had at the outset—seemed also to be limited. Border-area employment peaked in 2001, then declined because of a U.S. recession, high peso values, and competition from Chinese laborers.[13]

And because the U.S. government—contradicting all free trade principles—continued to prop up U.S. farmers with subsidies, it was able to undersell Mexican corn. As a result, small corn farmers in Mexico, many of them indigenous peoples, found themselves buying from the United States a crop that had assured Aztec, Mayan, and Mexican survival for five thousand years. This would have been called "unthinkable" except that it was exactly what the Zapatistas had warned against.

On the ground, other changes brought predictions to life. One working-class Mexican woman called Doña Josefina observed that, since NAFTA, many small artisans in her community had disappeared: the curtain makers, the carpenters who made the furniture, the boys and girls from the umbrella factory. "If you go shopping," she observed, "everything is from another country, radios, grills, dishes, pots, batteries, games, like that. If you go to the supermarket there's also a lot of meat from the United States." Her neighbor, Jorge, agreed. "The small industries used to have more chance of offering work here in Mexico, but now they have to compete with transnational companies. Games, a lot of other things they used to make here. But no longer. Why? Because they shut [the plants] down. Now the big North American chains, like Home Mart and I don't know what can offer everything less expensively."[14]

Perhaps NAFTA's greatest defect was the unwillingness of its corporate sponsors to allow workers the same right to ignore borders as investors now enjoyed. NAFTA destroyed jobs that were unionized and created ones that were not. Mexico's president, Vicente Fox, recognized that NAFTA was "an instrument . . . too limited for the kind of neighbor relations we can build. . . . Here a worker earns five dollars a day; there, he earns sixty."[15] When, in late 2003, U.S. Trade Representative Robert Zoellick announced a Central American Free Trade Agreement (CAFTA) lowering tariffs between Central America and the United States, AFL-CIO president John Sweeney looked back on a decade of NAFTA results and predicted that its little cousin CAFTA would be "yet another job-destroying free trade agreement that will undermine workers' rights here and around the world."[16] The five Central American countries and the Dominican Republic signed CAFTA in May 2004, and in summer 2005 the U.S. Senate ratified it.

The Environment and Inter-American Diplomacy

During the NAFTA negotiations, the environment was an important side debate, which produced a supplementary agreement in August 1993. Reached after consultation with NGOs and approved by the EPA, the side agreement made NAFTA the "greenest-ever" trade pact—on paper. The agreement promised to "promote sustainable development" and to "strengthen the development and enforcement of environmental laws and regulations." This meant not only protecting the environment but also cleaning it up. Under the agreement, organisms would disseminate information, enforce the rules, and settle disputes. Furthermore, another side agreement specifically addressed the U.S.-Mexico border, laying out a three-year program to help, for example, purify water and treat sewers.

Here again, NAFTA failed to deliver. The environmental agreements tied down the EPA in red tape. Funding from NAFTA for the environment in Mexico remained low, at roughly $3 million per year—a fraction of the $36 *billion* yearly price tag in environmental damage. And Mexico's own investment in the agreements actually decreased 45 percent after 1994 while pollution from its manufacturing nearly doubled. Worst of all, under the agreements, any corporation could sue any of the three governments that tried to diminish its profits with environmental protection. One California firm, for instance, received a $17 million judgment in its favor against the government of Mexico, which had denied it the ability to treat hazardous waste in a sensitive location.[17] One study group in 2000 found that NAFTA did not worsen the environment and that it was better to have NAFTA than no agreement at all, but also that its minimal results were disappointing.[18]

Outside of NAFTA, Latin America and the rest of the world began to grasp the seriousness of pollution. In the 1980s an area of Amazonian rain forest the size of Connecticut disappeared each year, thus reducing Earth's ability to recycle carbon dioxide. Scientists warned that half the ozone layer over the Antarctic had disappeared because of this added pollution, and this locked in greenhouse gases such as chlorofluorocarbons. These environmental crises were leading Earth to the most potentially disastrous event in human history: global warming.

In response, at the 1992 Earth Summit in Rio de Janeiro, Brazil, the largest international conference ever, the governments of the world adopted an environmental agreement called Agenda 21. It was a comprehensive but flawed plan that demanded far too much consensus. President George H. W. Bush showed up in Rio, but when he spoke, he criticized one of the summit's achievements, the Biodiversity Treaty, meant to protect endangered species. To Bush, the treaty failed to protect intellectual property, a theoretically worthwhile cause but one that tended to protect corporations rather than the environment. Bush also thought that the treaty reduced carbon dioxide too much, cost too much, and gave too much control to developing countries. He refused to sign it.

Despite failures, NAFTA and Rio set precedents. First, environmental issues became legitimate matters for heads of state to discuss at summits. Second, all future trade pacts might be expected to include protections for the environment. When the Democrats returned to the White House, Clinton signed the Biodiversity Treaty, but the Senate, lobbied by food and drug corporations, never ratified it.

Crisis and Poverty Again

By the late 1990s Latin America's newly recovering economy was sliding back into turmoil. A financial meltdown that hit Asia in 1997 and Russia a year later crept over to Latin America in 1999. The regional GDP per capita fell from 3.5 percent in 1997 to –1.2 percent in 1999.[19] In January of that year Brazil let its currency fluctuate and it collapsed by 36 percent. As world prices for many Latin American goods fell sharply—oil by 30 percent, coffee by 43 percent—the proportion of poor people in Latin America and the Caribbean grew from 40 percent of the population in 1990 to nearly 50 percent in 2000.[20] Inequality grew apace. By 2003 the top tenth of income earners made 40 percent of the income while the bottom 30 percent made 8 percent. Latin America was now, perhaps more than ever, the most unequal region in the world.[21]

Interdependence grew so quickly that Washington, Wall Street, and their friends at the IMF became Latin America's saviors and whipping boys all at once. The savior role emerged when the Mexican peso suddenly collapsed just nine days after Clinton's optimistic words about "remarkable, hopeful times" in December 1994. The White House first thought to "let the market sort it out" but then accepted Mexico's recovery plan. Recalling the U.S. bailout of Mexico in 1982 (see chapter 4), another followed in January 1995. The cost of this bailout had gone up to $53 billion for the United States and included a strict economic program for Mexico that stabilized the peso but caused a 7 percent drop in GDP in 1995.

The whipping boy label also stuck to the United States when many Argentines blamed it either for causing the meltdown of their economy in 2002 or, alternatively, for abandoning Argentina. In the eyes of one family about to be evicted in 2003 the U.S.-dominated IMF could "go to hell" and take with it the policy of "structural adjustment," which they blamed for the crisis. Other Argentines admitted that their own politicians and bankers had laid the groundwork for collapse by locking in the peso's conversion rate with the dollar at one to one since 1991. This had distorted the true value of the peso and pushed foreign debt to half of the GDP.

Launching the FTAA

As soon as NAFTA was off and running, U.S. diplomats moved to expand the agreement to include more Latin American countries under the Free Trade Area of the Americas (FTAA). This effort promised to balloon NAFTA to 655 million people and a GDP of $9 trillion. In December 1994 in Miami, Clinton convened the Summit of the Americas, the first meeting of all Latin American heads of state in a quarter century (thirty-four showed up; Fidel Castro of Cuba was not invited). There Clinton concluded an agreement to form the FTAA by 2005.

By its target year of 2005 the FTAA had not materialized. Critics pounced on the proposal for the control it would give corporations over the economic decisions of ordinary people and even governments. The FTAA, more than NAFTA, aimed to let capital run amuck. Under it, free traders would define "investments" as anything that could be given a monetary value, such as national forests, oil reserves, hospitals, even water. They could sue national governments for placing not just direct but also indirect limits on the exploitation of those "investments." This might, for example, remove protections on toxic chemicals or consumer warnings on dangerous products because those might *in theory* reduce profits. A first setback came when Clinton could not secure fast-track authority for the president—that is, the right to submit trade agreements to Congress for a straight yes or no vote without amendments—which would have eased the inclusion of more countries into the FTAA.

When George W. Bush campaigned for the presidency in 2000, however, the FTAA seemed to speed up. "Our future cannot be separated from the future of Latin America," he said, and enthusiastically endorsed the FTAA.[22] And at the third Summit of the Americas in Quebec City in April 2001, now-President Bush reinvigorated the FTAA by proposing to sign bilateral agreements instead of an everyone-or-no-one gamble. He notably criticized Clinton for having "dropped the ball" on the FTAA but did not mention that a Republican-controlled Congress had thwarted Clinton's fast track. In 2001 and 2002 a Bush-friendly Congress granted the president fast-track authority.

Opposition From "Below"

Against such bold advances, grassroots organizations mobilized. In 1999–2000, on a small but effective scale, Bolivians in Cochabamba forced the retreat of the international water conglomerate Bechtel when it announced rate increases. Small groups also coalesced and protested several summits and conferences, and most prominent among these were the protests against the World Trade Organization (WTO) in Seattle in 1999 and against the FTAA in Quebec City in 2001 and Mar del Plata, Argentina, in 2005. When Bush visited Latin America, especially, major protests tended to break out. Most embarrassingly, anti-U.S. groups booed him in Santiago, Chile, in November 2004, and the Chilean government canceled a dinner planned for hundreds of dignitaries when the U.S. Secret Service insisted on having guests pass through metal detectors.

Grassroots activists articulated perhaps their clearest alternatives to capital-led globalization when over twenty thousand of them gathered for the first World Social Forum (WSF) in Porto Alegre, Brazil, in January 2001. The WSF's motto, "Another World Is Possible," helped shape a broad agenda of "one no and many yeses."[23] In tents, classrooms, and stadiums, participants said "no" to the growing power of international financial institutions—also called IFIs, or "iffies." At the first meeting, French farmer José Bové, who earned a fanbase fighting McDonald's restaurants back home, occupied a farm near the conference where the U.S. biotech company Monsanto, a leader in genetically-modified crops, was allegedly experimenting with what critics called "Frankenfood." The "many yeses" of the WSF, meanwhile, ranged from building peace to canceling debts, fighting AIDS, and working for the equality of women. The only rule of the WSF was that political parties could not be planned there. The forum was, as the name implied, a "space" in which activists could compare notes and strategies. Scheduled to overlap with the World Economic Forum of wealthy nations held in the isolated Swiss Alps, the WSF was a smash. Its attendance doubled yearly. By 2005 over 155,000 participants attended more than twenty-five hundred events. To mark its global presence, in 2004 it moved temporarily to Mumbai, India, and in 2006 it was scheduled to meet in several venues around the world.

Protests against U.S. economic prescriptions for Latin America also sprang from governments, when several populist leaders rose to the highest office of their country with the overwhelming support of the poor but not necessarily the wealthy or the middle class. To be sure, Hugo Chávez in Venezuela (first elected in 1998), Ricardo Lagos in Chile (2000), Luiz Inácio "Lula" da Silva in Brazil (2002), Lucio Gutiérrez in Ecuador (2002), Néstor Kirchner in Argentina (2003), and Tabaré Vasquez in Uruguay (2004) ran widely different regimes. At one extreme was the virulent anti-U.S. and authoritarian Chávez; at the other was the market-friendly, moderate Lagos. What united them most was that, to some degree, they redirected their nations away from U.S.- and IMF-led globalization. In early 2005, too, when the OAS had to elect its new leader, Latin American diplomats defeated two pro-U.S. candidates from El Salvador and Mexico and instead elected Chile's socialist Interior Minister José Miguel Insulza.

Some of these men had distinctly modest backgrounds. Lula of Brazil, for instance, had once been a shoe-shine boy and was a metalworker at the age of fourteen. He won office with the support of two grassroots movements, the *sem terra* (the landless) and the *sem teto* (the roofless, or homeless). These movements often represented or championed ethnic social groups such as indigenous peoples or Afro-Latin Americans.

Populist groups, long out of power, would at times use violence if necessary to unseat traditional elites from power. They were also not averse to identifying those elites as puppets of Washington. In 2003, for instance, protests by Aymara Indians in the highlands of Bolivia led to riots that caused seventy deaths and President Gonzalo Sánchez de Losada's flight to Miami. The exiled president, nicknamed *El gringo* for his accented Spanish, was hated for his plan to export the country's natural gas to California while the Aymaras, living thirteen thousand feet above sea level, continued to live without heat. One Bolivian described the "gas revolt" as part of a "mountain chain of indigenous uprisings in reaction to U.S. neoliberalism in Latin America, the most radical thing that has appeared in thirty years." An indigenous leader, known as the "condor," suggested a more unforgiving, race-based vision. "Whites are here as renters on our land, and we need to put a giant fence around them, a reservation, a safe place for white people to be."

He felt himself at war "against gringo neoliberalism and racism, and [wanted] to change our government to an Indian one."[24] In June 2005 Indian protests brought down another president in Bolivia: Carlos Mesa.

The hemisphere's political economy thus threatened to turn against the United States. During his 2002 campaign Lula warned that the FTAA would lead to the "annexation" of Brazil by the northern nation. "Brazil ha[s] not only the right, but the obligation to define a project that will be favorable to all countries, principally the poor countries," he later added.[25] Most dramatically, in 2003 Brazil led in derailing a meeting of the WTO in Cancún, Mexico. Also that year, a meeting of foreign ministers in Miami broke up early over the rejection of the FTAA. The Bush administration got the message and intensified its turn toward what some called an "FTAA lite" through bilateral agreements (document 22).

In January 2004, when the OAS met at the Summit of the Americas in Monterrey, Mexico, Lula again led in rejecting the FTAA and expanding MERCOSUR (Venezuela joined in July of that year). The Brazilians also began courting powerful nonhemispheric powers such as China and India. And local resistance continued. In July 2004 farmers in Panama blocked several intersections of the Pan-American Highway to protest the negotiation of a free-trade agreement between Panama and the United States that they said would devastate the agricultural sector. By 2005, when the FTAA came up to its target date set a decade earlier, Latin America no longer looked to Washington for modernization under schemes such as the Alliance for Progress. Instead, it created its own transnational networks inside and outside of the hemisphere.

The Chávez Challenge in Venezuela

Of all Latin American leaders, Hugo Chávez most worried the Bush administration. At the beginning of the twenty-first century, Venezuela stood alongside Mexico, Brazil, and Colombia as one of the most important countries of Latin America for the United States. One word justified Venezuela's inclusion: oil. The country held the largest petroleum reserves outside the Middle East, a fact that emboldened Chávez. To make things worse for Washington, Chávez was popular with Venezuelans. He was elected twice to the presidency, survived a coup in April 2002, and saw his rule confirmed 59 percent to 41 percent in a referendum in 2004. During this time, he pumped about $100 million of oil revenues into programs for the poor, earning their undying gratitude. Yet Washington saw in him an unstable, undemocratic leader with an unreliable hand on the oil spigot. Chávez purged the state oil company and repeatedly threatened to turn off oil exports to the United States. He also took over government branches when they disagreed with him, endangered the independence of the media and the judiciary, befriended Fidel Castro of Cuba, and criticized U.S. wars in Afghanistan and Iraq.

Tensions rose to a fever pitch when U.S. diplomats failed to condemn the botched attempt to overthrow Chávez in 2002 and even contacted plotters while the Venezuelan president temporarily sat in a prison cell. Venezuelans publicly suspected foul play from Washington, especially after they discovered in late 2004 that the CIA had failed to warn Chávez of coup rumors. Chávez also railed against alleged U.S. efforts to influence the referendum of August 2004. Convinced that Bush was "financing this mad opposition [in Venezuela]," he claimed to be confused. "I thought since Bush came from an oil family, and given his political trajectory, that we would understand each other. I can't believe that a government is willing to put at risk its supply of oil."[26] Washington started looking for connections between Chávez and drug-fueled guerrillas or even Middle Eastern terrorists.

After the terrorist attacks of September 11, 2001, Bush policy increasingly conflated economic fears, like the drying up of oil, with security fears, like the spread of terrorism. In Latin America, this dynamic was eerily familiar. The reforms of Guatemala's Jacobo Arbenz in 1954 had similarly conflated Washington's fear of agrarian reform with its fear of communism (see chapter 1). The memory of Arbenz's overthrow by the CIA caused some to suspect that security and economic fears would reinforce each other once again. At the WSF in 2003 Chávez showed up and warned, "If we don't put an end to neoliberalism, neoliberalism will put an end to us."[27] He may have been right. In August 2005 evangelist Pat Robertson called for Chávez's assassination on his television program. The Venezuelan government angrily protested Robertson's "terrorist" statements, and the White House limited its intervention to calling the preacher's comments "inappropriate."

Military Transnationalism: From Haiti's Boat People to Colombia's Drug Lords

In the 1990s many Latin Americans began to view U.S. military influence in their countries as an unwelcome relic. On the tiny island of Vieques, Puerto Rico, militarism was not an abstract concept but a concrete experience. Since the 1940s the U.S. Navy had occupied two-thirds of the small island, built a base, and used it to conduct war games. For decades many Puerto Ricans accepted the navy as a bulwark against communism and a provider of jobs. But in 1999 that changed when an errant bomb accidentally killed a civilian guard during one of these games.

The incident set off some of the most serious civil disobedience against U.S. power in Puerto Rican history. Sit-ins, marches, and candlelight vigils in and around Camp García attracted U.S. critics, including the Reverend Al Sharpton and Robert F. Kennedy Jr. They joined Puerto Ricans in protesting the environmental and physical dangers of military exercises on such a small island (but their evidence was inconclusive). In July 2001 a nonbinding referendum showed that two-thirds of Vieques residents wanted the navy out. Cheers in town squares greeted news of the symbolic vote.

"Let the Navy pack their bags and go right now. If they let me on the base, I'll even help them pack," joked one local woman. In May 2003 she finally got her wish. The U.S. Navy left for good.[28]

Bush, September 11, and Militarism

The rest of Latin America would not be rid of U.S. militarism so easily. In fact, militarism made a comeback in the early 2000s. "Should I become the president, I will look south not as an afterthought, but as a fundamental commitment."[29] Bush's pledge during the 2000 campaign was half right. He made a commitment but he made it very much as an afterthought of the post–September 11 "war on terror."

In Latin America, the 2001 terrorist attacks were not so much a transforming moment as an intensifying one. As expressed in Bush's 2002 National Security Strategy, one new global reality was the overwhelming military power of the United States, a power that convinced many—especially the Pentagon and the vice president, Richard Cheney—that military solutions could be quicker and more effective than the usual diplomatic means. Washington could use force—or allies who used force—not only against international terrorists but against drug traffickers and even opposition groups. In this view, even the violence arising from poverty and the rejection of neoliberalism might be best answered with unilateral military solutions. Thus, while the disappearance of the Cold War threat might have reduced the U.S. military presence, the early 2000s saw military transnationalism become common in U.S.–Latin American relations. Here again the lifting of the Cold War veil revealed the true nature of post-1945 integration. In military matters, the U.S. arming of autocrats and police forces had long ceased to be about extrahemispheric threats. They served mainly against domestic challenges to neoliberals in power. It was in Colombia that militarism made its clearest comeback.

Drugs and Inter-American Security

In the 1990s the movements of drugs across borders became the main issue in military transnationalism in the region. As the decade advanced, marijuana, cocaine, and other substances seemed to pass through every Latin American country on their way to the lucrative markets of the United States and Europe. Drug trafficking affected entire societies, from the campesinos who grew the coca leaves and cannabis plants on poverty-stricken hills to the financiers who laundered the profits in glass-enclosed skyscrapers.

In this respect, the School of the Americas again held a mirror up to U.S.–Latin American relations. In the 1990s no longer were Central Americans the favorites at Fort Benning. Three quarters of the students were now Mexicans, Colombians, Peruvians, and Bolivians. What did their countries all have in common? Drugs.[30] Drugs even plagued Haiti. Anti-drug hearings led by Senator John Kerry (D-Massachusetts) in 1993, for instance, showed that Colombians supported the military there in exchange for the right to land their planes in Haiti.

Colombia and the War on Drugs

It was no accident that Haiti's patrons in the drug trade were from Colombia. The Andean nation had grown into the world's premier producer and exporter of cocaine and was now the main target of U.S. efforts at remilitarizing Latin American policy.

To be sure, anti-drug efforts existed before the 1990s. President Richard Nixon coined the term "war on drugs" to describe his domestic efforts. And at least since the 1960s the U.S. government had attempted to reduce shipments crossing the Mexican border; the DEA was created in 1973 largely for that reason. In 1986 the United States began "certifying" Latin American countries for their anti-drug efforts. Governments that did not pass certification faced sanctions ranging from aid reduction to the blockage of international loans. Mexico condemned the certification practice and remained an important gateway for drug shipments to the United States. In 1984 Mexico alone accounted for 36 percent of the heroin, 30 percent of the cocaine, and 9 percent of the marijuana consumed in the United States. U.S. drug consumers spent more than $50 billion on their habits.[31]

In the 1990s Colombia ignominiously dethroned Mexico as the main source of drugs (or, more accurately, Colombia produced the drugs while Mexico moved them). The most important factor in Colombia's rise was U.S. demand. In the 1980s addiction to Colombia's product of choice—cocaine—skyrocketed in the United States, especially with the appearance of "crack" cocaine. Crack was a purer, more addictive, and more dangerous use of coca leaves that spread like wildfire because it was cheaper than powder cocaine and was smoked rather than snorted. By about 2000 Colombia alone produced 80 percent of the cocaine consumed in the United States and Europe and most of the heroin consumed on the East Coast.[32] With armies of gun-toting shippers and pen-wielding lawyers on their flanks, drug cartels in Colombia easily bested any government effort to reduce their profits. In show of that power, in 1985 the Medellín cartel offered to pay off Colombia's national debt, estimated at $11 to $14 billion. Bogotá refused.[33]

Traditionally, drugs might have kept only the DEA and the State Department busy. But what elevated drugs to a prime concern for the Department of Defense and the White House in the 1990s was that drug traffickers formed alliances with guerrillas, paramilitaries, and allegedly, governments. On the left, the eighteen-thousand-strong Armed Forces of the Colombian Revolution (FARC), self-described as Marxists, and other groups came to control an area of Colombia the size of Switzerland. On the right, groups such as the United Self-Defense of Colombia (AUC) claimed to fight the FARC in defense of the Colombian government and were often rumored to be commanded by the army itself.

Though both sides claimed to be idealists, in practice they both lived off protecting coca growers, or *cocaleros*. One Colombian guerrilla explained the racket: "We don't look after coca fields, we don't grow coca, and we don't transport it. But we do charge taxes, as we do on everything else." Those "taxes"—voluntary or not—netted the FARC and similar groups between $200 and $600 million per year, about half of the FARC's revenue (but nothing compared to the $200 million a *week* one Mexican drug dealer made).[34]

The other half of FARC's revenue came from the kidnap-and-ransom business. In 1994 Colombia alone accounted for four thousand abductions, and a decade later, three of every four kidnappings in the world took place in Latin America.[35] Since the kidnapping business tended to focus on foreigners, such as U.S. tourists and employees of oil companies, it helped suck into the drug vortex not only the State Department but also nonstate actors such as human rights groups and corporations.

Drugs were a problem ripe for the type of military solution that the U.S. government preferred because men with guns protected drug dealers and so other men with guns could perceive victories through violence. Not surprisingly, it was the Reagan administration and Congress that first defined the drug problem in military terms and argued that the U.S. military be used in interdiction and eradication while fighting the Central American wars. In 1986 Reagan's National Security Directive No. 221 stated for the first time that drug production and trafficking threatened U.S. security. The document also set a precedent in blaming Latin Americans as suppliers, rather than U.S. citizens as consumers, for the drug-trafficking problem. Enforcement then moved its focus from the border with Mexico to the fields of Colombia. The "war on drugs" expanded in 1989 under George H. W. Bush's five-year, $2.2 billion plan, meant once again to stop cocaine "at its source."

In 1994 Clinton softened the rhetoric about a "war" on drugs but nevertheless framed his response as a "Security Strategy for the Americas." One U.S. defense attaché summed up the now-standard military transnationalism of drugs by saying, "We are now faced with a world that is somewhat gray and blurred, in which fear of communists has been replaced by fear of international terrorism, drug corruption, organized crime, contraband arms trafficking, and even industrial espionage."[36] In 1996, in an indication of how rotten U.S. partners had become, Colombia's president Ernesto Samper was "decertified" because the Clinton administration believed Samper had taken money from the Cali cartel during his 1994 campaign. But decertification was not attaining its goals. It did not reduce drug production, nor did it improve democracy in Colombia. The government and rebels again and again failed to sue for peace.

In such a failed political context, militarization slid down a slippery slope as the line between anti-drug and antiguerrilla aid blurred. Already in 1998, hundreds of U.S. Special Forces trainers operated in over fifteen countries, and almost two hundred military operations were now aimed at destroying cocaine and heroin laboratories rather than guerrilla camps.[37]

Frustrated by Bogotá's inability to deal with the FARC or restrain the AUC, the U.S. Congress in 2000 approved Plan Colombia, a $1.3 billion aid package primarily focused on military aid.

"All Fight, No Talk"

The events of September 11, 2001, sealed the relationship between anti-drug and military operations. The pervasive fear of "terrorists" came to resemble the Cold War fear of "communists" and policy toward the Andes was now almost exclusively focused on security. In early 2002 the White House persuaded Congress to allow Plan Colombia to apply to counterinsurgency, not just anti-drug, operations. The U.S. military was now fighting in an internal Colombian war. Meanwhile, Colombia's new president, Álvaro Uribe, a hard-liner whose father was killed by rebels and who himself survived four assassination attempts, transformed the government's policy from "all talk, no fight" to "all fight, no talk." By 2004 U.S. aid reached $3.3 billion. Because of Colombia, the U.S. military found itself training nearly twenty-three thousand Latin Americans, and in the 2005 U.S. budget, military aid almost equaled economic aid to the region.[38]

Despite all the new resources, results were mixed. In early 2005 the Office of National Drug Control Policy reported that, despite massive spraying of coca fields, the area of coca cultivation remained "statistically unchanged." Humble cocaleros either replanted after the spraying was over or cut new fields out of precious rain forests, or else cultivation sprang up in neighbor countries.[39] Furthermore, transportation that was halted in Mexico got diverted to almost every other country in the circum-Caribbean, resulting in a steady supply of cocaine and heroin and even drops in the price of both drugs.[40]

Yet militarization continued, prompting revolts against U.S. policy. Peasants began to protest eradication because it robbed them of their livelihood without offering alternatives. U.S. policymakers, in response, classified protesters within the catch-all category of "narco-terrorists." There seemed to be no middle ground in this struggle. Commenting on indigenous cocalero revolts in Bolivia, the head of the U.S. Southern Command warned that "if radicals continue to hijack the indigenous movement, we could find ourselves faced with a narco-state that supports the uncontrolled cultivation of coca."[41] Indigenous leaders such as Evo Morales of Bolivia responded that "coca is not a drug within the Aymara and Quechua [indigenous] cultures" and argued for continued cultivation.[42] The end to the drug war, it seemed, would come only when users stopped using.

Aristide Out, In, and Out Again

U.S. actions in Haiti were far less unilateral than in Colombia. In the end, however, the preferred solution was to use the military repeatedly to force political change. Haiti emerged on the U.S. security radar screen because of its boat people, who were desperate to escape what indicators in 1990 still showed was the worst society in the hemisphere. The nation of seven million souls had about one thousand doctors, two-thirds illiteracy, massive soil erosion and deforestation, a life expectancy of fifty-six years, malnutrition in seven of every ten children, and an average yearly income per person of $370.[43] Jean-Bertrand Aristide, the first democratically elected president in Haiti's more than two centuries of independence, presented himself as a voice for the masses and allowed democracy to thrive, but a military coup in 1991 forced him into exile (document 23).

Bill Clinton worried about his Haitian dilemma. On one hand, NGOs, such as TransAfrica, and African American members of Congress lobbied hard to change the prevailing U.S. policy whereby the Coast Guard stopped Haitians on the water and sent them back, and Clinton eventually loosened those rules for Haitian political refugees. On the other hand, Clinton knew that the swing state of Florida would surely swing away from any president who allowed poor, desperate Haitians to wash up on its shores. Potential refugees numbered three hundred thousand.[44] As long as political instability in Haiti continued, this dilemma sharpened.

From 1991 to 1994 the UN and the United States tried nonmilitary approaches, primarily economic sanctions, to restore democracy in Haiti. When these failed to move the Haitian government, now headed by strongman Raoul Cédras, the military option resurfaced. In October 1993, for both political and humanitarian reasons, U.S. and Canadian peacekeepers sailed to Port-au-Prince to enforce a UN-supported settlement between Aristide and the military. However, when, as they approached the harbor, they spotted a band of hostile Haitians waiting on the docks with machetes, they turned their ship around. Clinton clearly did not wish "another Somalia"—a phrase that referred to the recent murders of U.S. peacekeepers by Somalian warlords on global television (the racial aspects of these reverse lynchings also did not escape attention). But the humiliation of U.S. soldiers retreating because of a few thugs stung no less.

Clinton welcomed a July 1994 UN Security Council vote supporting a forcible intervention to restore Aristide. When Cédras expelled the UN's human rights observers shortly after the vote, Secretary of State Madeleine Albright warned him, "You can depart voluntarily and soon, or you can depart involuntarily and soon." Clinton was blunter still: "Leave now, or we will force you from power."[45] A last-ditch diplomatic effort followed, headed by former President Jimmy Carter and Chairman of the Joint Chiefs of Staff Colin Powell. Carter and Powell were unable to get Cédras to commit, but the Haitian strongman broke down when the news that U.S. planes were headed his way reached him. Soon, fifteen thousand troops met little resistance and restored Aristide.

"We're still gonna have a shitload of people in boats wanting to go to America," predicted one U.S. peacekeeper after landing in Haiti.[46] The presence of U.S., Canadian, and other peacekeepers over the following decade did little either to stem the tide of refugees or to promote honest government in Haiti. Aristide returned to power, but he increasingly adopted the sordid habits of Haitian politics, which included allying with paramilitary gangs and cheating at the ballot box. After accusations of fraud in 2000, a far less friendly Republican administration in Washington reduced U.S. funding to Haiti by more than half. The Republican Party, operating through the International Republican Institute (IRI), also funded Aristide's opponents to the tune of $1.2 million.

In January 2004 these IRI-supported groups, now organized as the Democratic Convergence, took advantage of a violent uprising in Haiti's provinces to call for the departure of the discredited Aristide. As the rebels closed in on Port-au-Prince, Aristide warned of a "coup d'état in motion." Powell, now secretary of state, claimed there was "no enthusiasm" in Washington for military action either to protect or depose Aristide. Secretary of Defense Donald Rumsfeld similarly maintained that the "threshold" for U.S. military action had not been crossed.

On February 24 the opposition rejected a power-sharing agreement and Aristide spoke the magic words: "The wave of violence sweeping through here is going to provoke the flight of many Haitians."[47] Aristide was desperate now to have international forces protect his government from advancing thugs. And Haitians were, as he said, spilling out into the sea and also across the border into the Dominican Republic. In all likelihood, the flood of boat people was the "threshold" of which Rumsfeld spoke because within days of Aristide's comment, President Bush hinted at U.S. intervention.

Congressman Mark Foley (R-Florida) specified what the United States would present as Aristide's options: "He's either going out in a Learjet or he's going out in a body bag."[48] Still, the Pentagon insisted it only considered a "political" solution.[49] However, the very next day, February 28, 2004, a Coast Guard vessel carrying two thousand U.S. troops showed up in Haiti. In the early morning hours of February 29, U.S. officials knocked on Aristide's door with an ultimatum to either suffer the fate presented to him by the opposition or go into exile under U.S. protection—immediately, on a plane. Aristide signed a declaration choosing the latter—"I agree to go with the hope that there will be life and not death," it read—though he claimed shortly after that he was "kidnapped" by U.S. forces.[50] Powell shot back, "He was not kidnapped. We did not force him onto the airplane. He went onto the airplane willingly. And that's the truth."[51] U.S. officials, to their credit, refused to let thuggish rebels take over after Aristide's ouster and ushered in a civilian interim government, and U.S. troops soon operated under a UN stabilization force. Fifteen years after Aristide's rise to power in 1990, Haiti's now eight-million-strong population still hoped for a stable government amid continuing polarization. But despair grew as hurricanes easily flooded helpless villages, and Haiti suffered the highest rates of HIV and AIDS outside of sub-Saharan Africa.[52]

Democratization and U.S.-Mexican Relations

Increased attention to security in Colombia, Haiti, and elsewhere left the

U.S. government paying little mind to the unprecedented democratization taking place in Latin America. Several markers were set in 2000 alone. That year, Guatemala's President Alfonso Portillo began a reconciliation process to heal the wounds of the country's thirty-six-year civil war. In the Dominican Republic, clean elections eroded the power of traditional strongman Joaquín Balaguer. And in Peru, Alberto Fujimori stepped down from his near-dictatorial position.

Perhaps most important for the United States, 2000 was also the year Mexico's Vicente Fox and the National Action Party handed the Institutional Revolutionary Party its first presidential defeat in seventy years. Fox was the most gringo-friendly Mexican leader in decades. The grandson of a U.S. immigrant of Irish descent, he was tall, fair-skinned, divorced, personally honest, and savvy with the media.

Relations between Fox and Bush began well. Bush visited Fox during Bush's 2000 campaign and, with his characteristic grammar, called the U.S.-Mexico relationship "of the most importance."[53] Both men dressed in cowboy boots and hats (a sign of their shared Southwestern heritage), and Bush flattered his Mexican counterpart with his first foreign visit as U.S. president. During that visit at Fox's ranch in February 2001, the U.S. and Mexican presidents defined an agenda promising an integral approach to trade, drug enforcement, and border security. For Mexican immigrants, specifically, Bush foresaw letting in more Mexicans as temporary workers and speeding up the transition to citizenship.

September 11, 2001, changed that plan too. The attacks refocused attention on the U.S.-Mexico border as a potential site of terrorist infiltration, and Bush set aside all efforts at immigration reform. Mexico's foreign minister, Jorge Castañeda, a former leftist who had recently become optimistic about interdependence and joined Fox's conservative government, grew disenchanted again and resigned. He reflected on Bush's turnaround: "The United States has replaced its previous, more visionary approach to relations in the Western Hemisphere with a total focus on security matters. This disengagement is dangerous because it undermines the progress made in recent years on economic reform and democratization."[54] Only in 2005 did the tide promise to change back. The U.S. president resumed discussion of border issues after winning reelection in late 2004. And in mid-2005 Senators John McCain (R-Arizona) and Ted Kennedy (D-Massachusetts) introduced legislation, supported by both immigrant rights advocates and business leaders, that proposed amnesty for illegal immigrants.

The Bush focus on security had a final cost—a loss of Latin American support for the 2003 invasion of Iraq and for the counterinsurgency that followed. During the run-up to the invasion, Mexico and Chile, both members of the UN Security Council at the time, refused to vote in favor of the U.S.-led invasion. When Iraqi dictator Saddam Hussein was toppled anyway and an uprising followed, all the Latin American governments that had sent troops in support—Honduras, Nicaragua, and the Dominican

Republic—pulled out. Latin Americans as a whole were highly critical of U.S. policy in the so-called war on terror. In late 2004 one poll indicated that, while 75 percent were concerned about terrorist attacks, only 15 percent agreed with U.S. actions in Iraq.[55]

Cultural Transnationalism: Who's Afraid of a Latina America?

Perhaps the most widespread and fertile ground for U.S.–Latin American connections was in the daily lives of ordinary people and the meanings they attached to those lives. By the start of the twenty-first century, migration to the United States had had major sociocultural impacts. First, more than other U.S. immigrant populations, Latinos kept strong ties to their homelands—the very stuff of transnationalism. Second, the now-critical mass of Latin Americans changed the face of the United States as a whole. Latino immigrants faced a tension between their two cultures. On one hand, they wanted to protect and celebrate their cultural distinctiveness. On the other, they wished to be accepted as U.S. citizens and to participate fully in U.S. society. They also faced a growing chorus of U.S. citizens who defined a *latina* America as a fundamental threat to U.S. culture.

Latinos in the Twenty-First Century

The tension between transnationalism and assimilation was particularly acute for a Latino population that had expanded so quickly. Up from 4 million in 1950 to 14.6 million in 1980 to 22.4 million in 1990, Latinos in the United States numbered about 40 million by 2005—up to 45 million if illegal immigrants were included. They now surpassed African Americans as the largest minority in the country. These numbers made the United States the fifth largest Latin American country in the world—behind Brazil, Mexico, Colombia, and Argentina.[56] With their birth rates overtaking even their immigration rates as of 2005, Latinos were on their way to becoming one-fourth of the U.S. population by 2050.[57]

The 2000 Census, the first to use the term "Latino" (previously a derogatory term for those who refused to assimilate), revealed other significant immigration trends. First, a Latin American was the typical immigrant, making up 52 percent of the foreign-born population in the United States. Second, of every ten newly immigrated Latin Americans, about seven were from Central America and Mexico, another two were from the Caribbean, and the other one was from South America. Mexicans alone were 30 percent of all the foreign-born in the Census. Third, new Latinos settled in select areas. States with over 70 percent of Latin Americans in their foreign-born population included New Mexico, Florida, and Arizona. More broadly, the West, Southwest, and South were destinations of choice, either because more established populations or families were already there or because they provided low-paying agricultural or service jobs. In small cities such as Hialeah, Florida, and Daly City, California, and most dramatically in Miami, Latinos were the majority.

The Census also revealed—or allowed for—diversity in how Latin Americans identified themselves. Respondents could identify their country of origin or else just check "other Hispanic," and they could write in "Hispanic," "Latino," or "Spanish" as their ethnic group. This allowance for diversity had come a long way from the catch-all term "people of Spanish origin," which appeared on the 1970 Census to cover equally those of European, Indigenous, African, or mixed descent.

The New Cultural Power

With this demographic wind at their back, Latinos sailed into the U.S. mainstream. In 1998 "José" replaced "Michael" as the most common name for newborn boys in California and Texas. Meanwhile, salsa dancing outgrew Latino nightclubs as mainstream clubs offered to teach it along with the faster, easier-to-learn Haitian-Dominican merengue. By 2001–2, the Spanish-language media company Univisión was so powerful that the Justice Department sued it for antitrust law violations. (Univisión won and gobbled up its closest competitor.) Just as Hollywood films and cable television entered almost every consciousness in Latin America, so Latino faces charmed U.S. audiences: Salma Hayek, Enrique Iglesias, Jimmy Smits, Ricky Martin, Christina Saralegui, and stars of *telenovelas* such as Thalia became standard fare at the record store, at the movie house, and on daytime television.[58] While Dominican designer Oscar de la Renta dominated the fashion world, East Los Angeles's Oscar de la Hoya dominated welterweight and middleweight boxing.

Perhaps most dramatically, Major League Baseball (MLB) provided a stage for Latin American sports excellence and inter-American integration. Dozens of academies in Latin America worked for MLB teams to groom talent for the *grandes ligas*. Soon, the best (and highest paid) players had Latin American names: Alex Rodríguez, David Ortiz, Manny Ramírez, Sammy Sosa, and Pedro Martínez. In 2003 over a quarter of MLB players were foreign born, and 86 percent of those were Latin Americans. Certain countries specialized in exporting players. At the end of the 2004 season four out of five finalists for the American League's Most Valuable Player title were not just Latinos, but Dominicans. One of them, Vladimir Guerrero of the Anaheim Angels, took the prize.

Anxieties Over Assimilation

Some U.S. citizens began to articulate fears that this rapidly rising minority was not enhancing cultural interdependence but threatening it. In 1990 one poll revealed that U.S. citizens ranked Latinos as less patriotic than Jews, blacks, Asians, southern whites, and whites.[59] Those who feared a *latina* America argued that "Hispanics" set themselves off from traditional U.S. immigrants by refusing to jump into the so-called melting pot. As one scholar

First Lady Hillary Rodham Clinton stands with Chicago Cubs right fielder Sammy Sosa at the State of the Union Address on January 19, 1999. Sosa became a U.S. celebrity in 1998 when he and Mark McGwire both broke the old single-season home run record in spectacular fashion. President Bill Clinton and the First Lady began inviting Sosa to public events such as this one. This courtship of the photogenic Dominican illustrated the growing importance of Latino support for U.S. political parties. Associating herself with Dominicans, who were concentrated in New York State, may also have been crucial for the First Lady, who won a senatorial seat there in 2000. AP/WideWorld Photos.

expressed it, they threatened to "divide the United States into two peoples, two cultures, and two languages."[60] One of these peoples was not learning English, not converting to Protestantism, and worst of all, "rejecting the Anglo-Protestant values that built the American dream." Furthermore, Latinos were allegedly shutting themselves off from mainstream culture by living in "enclaves" such as Miami (two-thirds Latino in 2000) and Los Angeles (about half Latino by 2010). In areas of heavy Latino concentration, everything was in Spanish—commercial signs, television, radio, magazines. On some streets, one could no longer be served in English in a restaurant or retail store. One Arizona lawmaker, who in 2004 pushed through legislation to limit state services to nonresidents, expressed the concern that "many, many of the people who come here have no intention of assimilating. They come here and they demand: They demand services in their languages, demand that we honor their culture, and that breeds a culture of war."[61]

To reverse these trends, some took matters into their own hands. There were a few dramatic cases of whites gunning down "aliens" crossing the border illegally. In another instance, Southern Californians organized to

"Light Up the Border" by gathering to shine their car headlights across the U.S.-Mexico border and discourage crossings. In 2005 a group of about one thousand vigilantes calling themselves the "Minutemen"—a reference to patriots from the American Revolution—patrolled the Arizona-Mexico line, partly to protest what they saw as the inaction of the U.S. Customs and Border Patrol. Their efforts to take the law into their own hands won the admiration of many politicians, including action film hero and California governor Arnold Schwarzenegger.

Many proponents of Latino rights criticized these fears as "white nativism" and likened its advocates to those of a century before who feared that recent Italian or Irish arrivals would make the white Anglo-Saxon Protestant "disappear." Immigrant-rights activists argued that many who promoted English-as-second-language programs were Latinos who wanted their children to succeed in mainstream culture and that 90 percent of Latinos born in California showed native fluency in English. Moreover, Latin American immigrants had higher labor participation rates than most other immigrant groups, higher even than the U.S. average.[62] And, assimilating or not, Latinos made America younger. Half were under age twenty-seven, a fact that could help the United States dodge the fate of a graying Europe that could not support its oldest citizens.[63]

Attempts at Controlling Immigration

Immigration control became the battleground on which both groups articulated these arguments. At the federal level, in 1986 Congress passed the Immigration Reform and Control Act (IRCA) to, as President Reagan said, "take control of our borders." IRCA was the most sweeping immigration reform since the 1965 amendments to the Immigration and Nationality Act (see chapter 2). It allowed 2.6 million immigrants already in the United States without documents to stay, work, and become U.S. citizens. But it also placed more restrictions on new immigrants, toughened border surveillance, and fined or jailed employers who hired "undocumenteds." As a result, relatively fewer Latin Americans migrated seasonally and more—disproportionately families, women, and children—came over for good. In 1996 President Clinton signed into law the Illegal Immigration Reform and Immigrant Responsibility Act, once again boosting the number of agents at the Border Patrol and the INS and implementing technology to better detect fake crossing cards and speed up the prosecution of those caught sneaking in.

Did these laws reduce illegal immigration? It was hard to say because no one knew the exact numbers before and after. Certainly, U.S. factory owners and landowners continued to need cheap labor, and they kept hiring illegal immigrants. In a clear sign that this kind of law breaking was tolerated, between 1989 and 1994 the INS actually cut by half the number of agents who policed these owners.[64]

In the early 1990s the dream of many anti-immigration proponents began to come true. A wall—of different heights and different materials—

began to rise along the border. By 1998 sixty-two miles were complete. The wall clearly slowed down illegal migrations just south of San Diego, but it also funneled migrants to harsher desert crossings along the rest of the two-thousand-mile border. By 2005 one million illegal immigrants were caught per year, but about the same number were not caught and 350 died attempting to cross. To increase their chances of survival, many used guides, called coyotes, but the price for one of these was around $1,200 a head.[65]

At the state level, in 1994 California voters passed Proposition 187. The law denied most state-provided benefits to illegal aliens, including access to public education, and even forbade automatic citizenship to children of undocumenteds, even if they were born in the United States. "Prop 187" bitterly divided Californians. On one side stood California Governor Pete Wilson, who backed the proposition. He denied any hint of racism or nativism and adopted a law-and-order language attractive to many who believed that only those who paid taxes should obtain government services. (Actually, illegal immigrants *did* pay taxes, although they paid lower taxes than the average U.S. citizen.[66]) On the other side were almost half of Californian voters (and four out of five Latino voters) who saw Prop 187 as permanently identifying Latinos as second-class citizens and targeting innocent children by curbing access to hospitals and schools. "It is not fair to take education away from the kids," explained a tenth grader in Los Angeles. "We could be the future leaders. We could be the ones sitting right where you are someday. You've got to give everyone a chance."[67] Prop 187 led to other anti-immigration bills in other states. In California, however, it immediately hit a wall. Opponents dragged the law through the courts, and it was never enforced.

Transnational Community I: Dominicans

One reality on which anti-immigration arguments were based was the importance of transnational communities in many Latinos' lives. What some called the "new transnationalism" referred to the fact that improved communications and transportation technology brought the world so close together that it was no longer necessary to forego ties to the homeland when migrants moved to a host country. Mexicans who moved from Monterrey to Los Angeles, for instance, could return relatively cheaply over the holidays, wire money to family members at other times, and watch Mexican wrestling and read Mexican magazines throughout the year.

Dominicans presented a particularly urbanized transnational community. They migrated en masse later than Puerto Ricans, Cubans, and Mexicans, but they quickly made up for it. They grew to 765,000 in 2000 with the bulk—455,000—living in New York City (another 103,000 lived close by in New Jersey). In many ways, the new migration meant new prosperity. Dominicans were relatively well educated and, once in New York, launched thousands of bodegas and other stores. The success of their stores helped them feel at home in Manhattan's Washington Heights barrio.[68] It also allowed them to send money home—a cash flow called remittances. By 2002 the ease of wire transfers meant that a typical recipient Dominican household received remittances equal to three-fourths the country's per capita GDP. Partly because of remittances, the Dominican economy became the fastest-growing in Latin America from 1997 to 2001.

Remittances to Latin America and the Caribbean as a whole shot up from $10 billion in 1996 to $32 billion in 2002. In Central America and the Caribbean, they dwarfed foreign direct investment as well as any aid that the World Bank or Inter-American Development Bank could muster.[69]

Migration, however, also caused problems in the Dominican Republic. Many Dominicans who went north, for instance, engaged in criminal behavior, and these were often sent back when caught. Three-quarters of U.S. deportees were criminals, and 90 percent of those had been dealing drugs.[70] Law-abiding Dominicans were none too happy to see these deportees back "home."

Yet Dominicans on the island and on the mainland continued to imagine Nueva York as part of them and themselves as part of it. Political parties in the Dominican Republic typically had bureaus in New York City, and in the 2004 Dominican election Santo Domingo politicians campaigned in New York and U.S.-based Dominicans voted from their consulates. Even movies connected the community. *Nueba Yol* (a colloquial Dominican pronunciation of Nueva York) was a series of comedy films that followed the travails of Dominicans in New York City—avoiding INS agents at work, scrambling to pay the rent, and delving into the world of drugs and crime. The message of this series was not that immigrants were unpatriotic criminals or long-suffering victims; it was that life in New York was perilous but full of possibilities if one worked hard and lived honestly.

Transnational Community II: Guatemalans

The Guatemalans of North Carolina offered a wholly different portrait of Latino struggle. At first glance, North Carolina seemed an odd destination for these migrants. It bordered neither Mexico nor the Caribbean and had a legacy of racial segregation. Yet in the 1990s the state's Latino population increased 449 percent, the highest in the United States. Soon, 40 percent of the state's construction workers were Latinos.[71] By 2000 only about six thousand Guatemalans lived in North Carolina, but they were concentrated in the small community of Morganton, where the Case Farms chicken-processing plant valued their cheap labor so much that it offered free transportation from South Florida to Morganton. More than 85 percent of Case workers were Guatemalans.[72]

Integration into North Carolina rested upon the unique weaknesses and strengths of the past experiences of the Guatemalan migrants. On one hand, many were undocumenteds and did not speak English, and so they could more easily be fooled by corporations and be more fearful of government mediation. More than that, they were overwhelmingly non-Spanish-speaking Highland Mayans. They were thus further weakened by their marginal status among Latin Americans and by linguistic and historical divisions among them.

On the other hand, these Mayans were survivors. One in four of them was displaced because of the violence of the early 1980s in Guatemala. Once in the Tar Heel State, they proved better at organizing a union than did white North Carolinians precisely because they assumed that all factory bosses, like plantation owners back home, aimed to take away their rights and ignore their poor working conditions. Whatever injustice they saw in North Carolina, they had seen worse in Guatemala.

Transnational Community III: Cubans

Perhaps the most politically successful Latino group in the United States was the Cuban American population, about 1.25 million strong in 2000. A particularly prosperous bunch since the middle and upper classes had fled the Cuban Revolution in the early 1960s, Cuban Americans set themselves off from other Latinos by being nearly able to dictate U.S. policy toward their country of origin. Back in Cuba, Castro's regime fell on hard times. After the Cold War, Soviet support evaporated, the economy contracted by 45 percent, and Castro declared a "special period" of belt-tightening coupled with free-market reforms. In 1998 the Department of Defense declared that Cuba no longer posed a military threat to the United States.

Cuban Americans, mostly those around Calle Ocho in Miami, were poised to take advantage of Castro's weakness. Since 1980, when the four-month Mariel boatlift that dropped 125,000 "undesirable" Cubans—disproportionately poor, black, unskilled, and some mentally ill or fresh out of prison—onto the shores of Florida, the longer-established Cubans had founded the Cuban American National Foundation to lobby for a crackdown on Cuba. In 1992 Congress responded positively with the Cuban Democracy Act, which toughened the U.S. embargo on Cuba, in place since the 1960s, by punishing citizens of third countries who did business with both Cuba and the United States.

In 1996 another Cuban American activist group, Brothers to the Rescue, flew small planes over Cuba and dropped propaganda leaflets over Havana. In February, in a clear violation of international law, Cuban MIG jets shot down two of the Brothers' planes over international waters, killing all four people aboard. In response to the incident, Clinton signed the Helms-Burton Law of 1996, which further strengthened the embargo by denying U.S. visas to anyone who held property confiscated from persons who were now U.S. citizens. This, again, applied to third countries that might be doing business with the Castro government, and it drew the ire of Canada, Mexico, and most of Europe. Both the 1992 and 1996 laws had long-term consequences because they placed Cuban policy in the hands of the Congress and out of those of the White House.

Years later, a tug-of-war over a boy named Elián González further illustrated the sharp divisions between Cubans in Cuba and Cubans in Florida.

It also placed the U.S. government in a difficult situation. In late 1999 the six year old was found floating in an inner tube after the makeshift boat that carried him, his mother, and ten others fleeing Cuba for Florida's shores sank and drowned everyone but Elián. Family members in Miami insisted that the boy be allowed to stay in the United States. In Cuba, meanwhile, Elián's father, who was divorced from his mother, demanded that he be returned. U.S. law clearly stated that parents, no matter where they were, could have their children repatriated if they were fit to raise them.

But the Clinton administration's decision was political as much as it was legal. Returning Elián to Cuba might prompt Cuban Americans in Florida to vote Republican in 2000 (they had voted Democratic in 1996), and such a unified voting bloc could swing the entire state—maybe the entire country. In the end, Attorney General Janet Reno saw no way around the law or around the morality of uniting children with their parents. In April 2000 her SWAT team made a dramatic raid into the Miami home where Elián stayed and snatched him from his relatives at gunpoint. Perhaps because of the incident, in 2000 the Democrats faced a nasty recount in Florida that cost them the presidency. One member of Brothers to the Rescue bitterly remarked, "This country doesn't care about Cubans. We're just pawns of politics."[73]

The George W. Bush administration upped the ante on Cuba and actively pursued the fall of the Castro regime. In early 2001, for instance, it jailed five Cubans it accused of spying for Havana. After September 11, despite Castro's denouncement of international terrorism, James Cason, the head of the U.S. Interests Section in Havana, caused a further rift when he offered the homes of U.S. diplomats for dissidents to meet. Castro perceived this as foreign intervention, and in March 2003 he had seventy-five dissidents arrested and jailed for as many as twenty-eight years. It was a harsh penalty, meant to send a message to those whom Castro called the "Miami mafia": as long as Castro was in power, the Cuban Revolution would not be undermined—especially by the United States.

Bush, who again won a close contest in Florida in November 2004, continued to pressure Cuba. "The President is determined to see the end of the Castro régime and the dismantling of the apparatus that has kept him in office so long," declared the head of Latin American diplomacy at the State Department in October 2003. The following January Bush closed all channels for dialogue and appointed a Commission for Assistance for a Free Cuba to recommend "an expeditious end of the dictatorship" and a plan for "a post-dictatorship Cuba."[74] The State and Treasury Departments also continued to reduce visits to and from Cuba for family members, academics, students, and artists.

Opponents of the Bush stranglehold on Cuba included advocacy groups such as the Washington Office on Latin America, who argued that cutting off visits for families and students would do nothing to bring about the end of Castro's rule and that, on the contrary, more exchanges might promote civil society and a freer political system. Even Republican members of Congress from the Midwest now opposed their own president because they wanted Cuba opened up further to U.S. farm goods. But the electoral value of Florida continued to make it too delicate for a loosening of U.S. policy. By 2005 Fidel Castro, now in his mid-seventies, had lost much of the stamina that made him so charismatic. He made shorter speeches, no longer smoked cigars, and often seemed fragile in public. Yet he also seemed on his way to outlasting his tenth U.S. president since Dwight Eisenhower.

Activist Networks Against Dictatorship

Cultural transnationalism did not merely unite communities identified by country of origin. It also helped Latin Americans throughout the world forge alliances behind common interests. In the 1990s and 2000s cosmopolitan Latin Americans were often educated in the United States and called "technopols" or "denationalized elites" because they were increasingly nonideological, believing simply in restoring the rule of law to Latin America. These men—and increasingly, women—built transnational communities of individuals, think tanks, philanthropic foundations, and NGOs to fight injustices. Whether the issue was protesting the Cuban embargo or the School of the Americas, these "advocacy networks" could count on allies around the United States and Latin America to spread the word and raise money.

In 1998 an unprecedented test of these networks took place when a Spanish judge, Balthazar Garzón, filed for the arrest and extradition of former Chilean dictator Augusto Pinochet. Then a senator for life with impunity against prosecution in Chile, Pinochet was in England during the filing. Garzón took advantage of that fact to try the senator for the murder of Spanish citizens in Chile in the 1970s. Garzón eventually lost the right to try Pinochet in Spain, but his efforts sent a chill—the "Garzón effect"—through the dark hearts of former, current, or would-be dictators who might henceforth think twice about violations of human rights lest they be tried one day abroad or at home. The effect finally reached Chile. In October 2004 the Chilean Supreme Court stripped Pinochet of his immunity, and in December he was indicted on charges of kidnapping and murder. Charges of tax evasion and of secretly stowing millions in foreign banks equally hung over the dictator's head.

Pinochet's fate, still undetermined in mid-2005, reflected the broader uncertainties in the future of U.S.–Latin American relations. In some ways, hope reigned as democratic regimes survived myriad challenges and expanded to guarantee political freedoms and to include more diversified groups of citizens following models of rule of law and multiculturalism widely accepted among U.S. citizens. Hope also existed among Latinos within

U.S. borders, whose communities grew in size and influence and who felt more than ever entitled to their full rights as U.S. citizens. Yet the strengthening of U.S.–Latin American ties, to many, also seemed to have worsened economic and social indicators since the end of the Cold War. Poverty, crime, corruption, and environmental devastation were long-standing scourges that new institutions such as NAFTA and the WTO did not seem to begin to eradicate. The old debates between diffusion and dependency continued. And populist authoritarianism again reared its ugly head in the likes of Hugo Chávez. What few could deny was that intimacy and struggle continued unabated and that the future of U.S.–Latin American relations rested greatly on that tension.

CONCLUSION:
FOOD FOR THOUGHT

BY 2005 EVIDENCE THAT THE UNITED STATES and Latin America were fated to be intertwined lay not only in the presidential palaces of Port-au-Prince and Caracas or the School of the Americas in Georgia. It was also served right under our noses—in the foods and drinks we consumed. We are what we eat, the saying goes. This was certainly true in the case of U.S.–Latin American relations. What the citizens of the Western Hemisphere put in their bodies continued to be a compelling illustration of their growing dependence on one another and the increasing intimacy between the two. Food—and soft drinks especially—told a story of growing investment and of Latin American employment by U.S. corporations, of U.S. government intervention to promote cross-border eating and drinking, and perhaps inevitably, of Latin American struggle against whatever culinary intervention turned stomachs south of the border.

Long before 1945 food and drink in the Americas traveled across borders. Prior to the War of 1898, in fact, moving cocoa, coffee, tea, coconuts, rice, pineapples, and especially sugar from south to north was arguably the main reason why the United States was interested in Latin America. In 1900 the Coca-Cola Company, founded in the 1880s, exported the first bottles of its fizzy drink—to Cuba, Puerto Rico, and Mexico. In the 1930s the newly founded Coca-Cola Export Corporation sold its syrup to bottlers in over forty-five countries, and by 1939 Pepsi-Cola had joined the fray with bottling facilities in Great Britain and Cuba.

By World War II bananas best exemplified the successful integration of foodstuffs. First shipped from Havana to New York in 1804, they were originally a fruit fed only to slaves. In 1913 domestic U.S. sales taxes were removed from bananas, and they became a household product soon after. By that date, companies such as Standard Fruit and United Fruit had already created effective chains of distribution to get their quickly rotting products from Central American plantations to mainland supermarkets.

141

United Fruit of Boston operated in Cuba, Jamaica, Honduras, Costa Rica, Panama, Colombia, and Guatemala. It was the largest agricultural business on the globe.[1] The company notably gave birth to "Chiquita Banana," a half-woman, half-banana cartoon shill. Dancing to a calypso rhythm, she instructed customers on how to keep their bananas:

> I'm Chiquita Banana, and I've come to say,
> Bananas have to ripen in a certain way.
> When they are fleck'd with brown and have a golden hue,
> Bananas taste the best and are the best for you.
> You can put them in a salad. You can put them in a pie-aye.
> Any way you want to eat them, it's impossible to beat them.
> But bananas like the climate of the very, very tropical equator.
> So you should never put bananas in the refrigerator. No no no no!

U.S. consumers responded with enthusiasm to bananas, which were cheap, tasty, and high in potassium. By the end of the twentieth century they ate over 2.3 million tons per year, the highest per capita consumption of bananas in the world (along with Canada), making bananas the most-consumed fruit in North America. United Fruit became United Brands, whose subsidiary, Chiquita Brands, kept shipping bananas and other fruits to U.S. supermarkets.[2]

World War II only quickened the interdependence of consumption. The U.S. government and soft drink companies, for instance, formed a partnership during the war to promote one another's goals. Pepsi set up its first syrup processing facility in Mexico during the war. In addition, the army gave preferential treatment to Coca-Cola to provide cheap carbonated drinks to U.S. servicemen and women abroad—namely in Panama, where the United States built about forty military installations. Conversely, Coca-Cola took full advantage of the opportunity to entrench itself; it kept its bottling plants in Latin America once the war was over and grew exponentially in those markets.

Still, at the end of World War II, dinner tables in North, Central, and South America remained quite different from one another. Besides bananas and pineapple, the hundreds, perhaps thousands of other Latin American fruits remained in Latin America. The only U.S. citizens who enjoyed them were the relatively few who traveled there and came back with mouth-watering tales of exotic, juicy flavors.

However, the growth of U.S. "fast food," aggressive investment, and improved distribution networks quickly changed tastes in the hemisphere. By the 1980s McDonald's and similar food chains offered their high-fat hamburgers, sugared drinks, and deep fried potatoes in almost every country in Latin America. Their success south of the border was not so much a product of particularly cheap or fast food; in fact, their goods were more expensive than other food in Latin America. Rather, U.S. fast food offered a clean, well-lit, family-friendly environment that made Latin Americans feel they had reached a state of modern living.

By the end of the twentieth century Latin Americans increasingly purchased their foods not at local farmers' markets but in U.S.-style supermarkets, where goods were more processed, packaged, and expensive. In 1990 supermarkets made up 10 to 20 percent of Latin America's retail food sector; by 2000 they made up 50 to 60 percent. Supermarkets were not only the result of freer trade and better distribution. They were the consequence of urbanization, higher incomes, and the fact that women in the workforce were less able than before to buy food on a daily basis. Supermarkets also signaled foreign control. Of every ten chain stores, six to eight were owned by multinationals that put out of business not only national chains but also small mom and pop stores.[3]

U.S. soft drink companies were especially adept at expanding their markets while holding on to creative power. Executives encouraged the "Americanization" of Latin American tastes, paradoxically, by transferring much of the production abroad. This franchise system, which used water sources, sugar plantations, and bottling plants in Latin America rather than in the United States, increased economies of scale and got the product into the hands of the consumer more easily. U.S. executives also allowed Latin American counterparts to create specific images and campaigns aimed at their own consumers, to modify their products slightly (by adding more sugar, for example), and to allow the appropriation of their corporate identity when it served their purposes (by encouraging the Caribbean to mix rum and Coca-Cola, for instance, thus making a Cuba libre). At the same time, Coca-Cola and Pepsi held onto their image as global yet still U.S. brands. Executives at Coca-Cola's U.S. headquarters in Atlanta, for example, never revealed the "secret formula" behind their syrup, nor did they allow alterations to their trademark logos.[4] The result of both of these strategies was increased consumption of U.S.-style processed drinks. In 2001 Mexico had the second-highest consumption of soft drinks in the world after the United States with 150 liters per person every year. One quarter of Coca-Cola's sales were in Latin America.[5]

While U.S. foods filled shelves in Latin America, Latin American foods, too, tickled the palates of U.S. citizens. In the 1990s mangoes, papayas, and other fruits were still relatively expensive, but now readily available. An array of beans, spices, meats, and tortillas could also be found in specialized Latino markets or in the "ethnic" aisles of mainstream supermarkets. So, too, were Latin American soft drinks such as Peru's yellow Inka Cola now available. Chains such as Taco Bell, Chipotle, and Baja Fresh offered modified Latin American foods to the masses. And in the early 1990s salsa bested ketchup as the most popular condiment in the United States.[6]

Such transnational eating had at least one cultural impact: "de-identifying" food. The enjoyment of food increasingly seemed separate from the production of it, to the point where fewer and fewer consumers, say, in

Illinois had in mind Central America when they purchased bananas.

Nor did they have in mind Central America's workers. One consequence of de-identification was that food producers remained largely forgotten, poorly paid, and often exploited. Central American employers could shirk good working conditions because a great proportion of their workers were women, who, in Latin America, were generally expected to grow, clean, and cook food without pay anyway. The franchise system also helped, allowing local managers to enforce worse working conditions on employees of U.S. affiliates than those workers would have had in the United States. Taking advantage of such distance, in the 1980s and 1990s the Coca-Cola Company—once again a bellwether of integration—pleaded innocent as Guatemalan bottlers allied with local military regimes violently repressed striking workers. Likewise, U.S. banana corporations Standard Fruit (now the Dole Food Corporation) and United Fruit (now Chiquita Brands) moved away from production and toward distribution in the second half of the twentieth century, a decision that shifted risks and labor troubles onto the shoulders of local producers.

Inevitably, the perception that U.S. food consumption patterns were forcing unwelcome change in Latin America met with resistance. Already back in the 1950s journalist E. J. Kahn spoke of foreigners' fears of "Coca-Colonization."[7] After 1959 Fidel Castro's nationalist revolutionaries urged Cubans to "consume Cuban products" such as mangoes and hand-rolled cigars instead of U.S. hamburgers and machine-manufactured cigarettes.

Some saw in food commerce an example of the evils of global capitalism. To explain how "Nicaragua has been an appendage of the United States," for instance, Sandinista Minister of Agrarian Reform Jaime Wheelock said, "Our function was to grow sugar, coca, and coffee for the United States; we served the dessert at the imperialist dinner table." (Interestingly, perhaps not wanting to deprive its supporters of a popular refreshment in Nicaragua, the Sandinistas welcomed the presence of the Coca-Cola Company.)[8]

Others resisted more passively by not consuming the products offered to them. The U.S.-based chain Taco Bell, for instance, found itself forced to pull out of Mexico by 1998 after only six years there. The reasons? Few could afford Taco Bell, of course, but that was the case with all U.S.-style fast food. More important, those who could afford the burritos and tacos overwhelmingly said they could not stomach the imitation-Mexican food compared to the more nutritious, cheaper, and fresher fare their local *taquerias* were serving.[9]

Despite the resistance, food and drink in the South and North continued to bind the continent together. A final look at the soft drink industry reveals the tightness of the bond and how it integrated not just consumers but businesses and governments. In the 1990s the soft drink industry was among the most adamant in support of free trade agreements such as NAFTA. PepsiCo International, for instance, invested heavily in bottling plants in the 1990s and encouraged the U.S. Congress not to delay ratification of the trade pact. In 1995, after NAFTA went into effect, Coca-Cola sold its products to 195 countries, including all of those in the Americas. Even in Cuba, one could find Coca-Cola blended and bottled mostly in Mexico, thus circumventing the U.S. embargo. Ironically, the company's chief executive officer and chairman of the board for most of the 1980s and 1990s was Bob Goizueta, who was born in Cuba. Another Coke executive, Vicente Fox, quit to enter Mexican politics, becoming president in 2000.

Consumption of food and drink is, of course, is not a perfect illustration of U.S.–Latin American relations. But like any act of consumption, eating and drinking involve choice. They are largely acts of pleasure, not of desperation, scheming, or violence. U.S. relations with Latin America since 1945 have touched on all of these themes. But all have equally spoken to the steadily increasing mutual dependence between the northern and southern parts of the Americas. For this reason, some consider the twenty-first century the "American" century, using the word in the broadest sense to include the entire Western Hemisphere. Perhaps this idea is too optimistic, but at the very least, looking back upon the last sixty years of hemispheric relations should make its interdependence stand out from—and above—the temporary event that was the Cold War. Understanding North-South interdependence, however unequal, may now help governments, civic groups, and individuals better tackle the present and future of U.S.–Latin American relations.

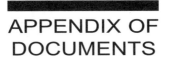

APPENDIX OF
DOCUMENTS

1. Spruille Braden and the State Department:
The Blue Book on Argentina, 1946

Source: U.S. Department of State, *Consultation Among the American Republics With Respect to the Argentine Situation,* memorandum of the U.S. government, February 11, 1946, publication 2473, Inter-American Series 29 (Washington, D.C.: Government Printing Office, 1946).

[T]he Government of the United States at present has information which establishes that:

1. Members of the military government collaborated with enemy agents for important espionage and other purposes damaging to the war effort of the United Nations.

2. Nazi leaders, groups and organizations have combined with Argentine totalitarian groups to create a Nazi-Fascist state.

3. Members of the military regime who have controlled the government since June 1943 conspired with the enemy to undermine governments in neighboring countries in order to destroy their collaboration with the Allies and in an effort to align them in a pro-Axis bloc.

4. Successive Argentine governments protected the enemy in economic matters in order to preserve Axis industrial and commercial power in Argentina.

5. Successive Argentine governments conspired with the enemy to obtain arms from Germany.

This information warrants the following conclusions:

. . . The totalitarian individuals and groups, both military and civilian, who control the present government in Argentina, have, with their Nazi collaborators, pursued a common aim: The creation in this Hemisphere of a totalitarian state. This aim had already been partly accomplished.

. . . It is submitted that the information transmitted to the Governments of the American republics in this memorandum makes abundantly clear a pattern which includes aid to the enemy, deliberate misrepresentation and deception in promises of Hemisphere cooperation, subversive activity against neighboring republics, and a vicious partnership of Nazi and native totalitarian forces. This pattern raises a deeper and more fundamental question than that of the adequacy of decrees and administrative measures allegedly enacted in compliance with Argentina's obligations under Resolution LIX of the Mexico Conference [Act of Chapultepec]. The question is whether the military regime, or any Argentine government controlled by the same elements, can merit the confidence and trust which is expressed in a treaty of mutual military assistance among the American republics.

2. Roy R. Rubottom Jr.: Communism in the Americas, 1958

Source: Address made by the Assistant Secretary for Inter-American Affairs before a joint meeting of the Miami-Dade County Chamber of Commerce and the United Nations Association of Greater Miami at Miami, Florida, on January 14 (press release 10 dated January 13), *Department of State Bulletin,* February 3, 1958.

Today I want to talk to you about the role of communism in the Americas. It is a thoroughly sinister role. It is the same role in North America, Central America, and South America, or elsewhere in the world. It is unchanged. It may have taken on a new coloration, protective to the Communists themselves but always destructive to the rest of us.

This role involves both aspects of the international Communist movement, the ideology of the party line held out by Communists and, even worse, their subversive intervention in the internal affairs of other states and peoples. This, of course, is utterly contrary to our way of life in the Americas and will never succeed.

. . . Nominally, the Communist Party is legal in only five Latin American Republics—Argentina, Bolivia, Ecuador, Mexico, and Uruguay—but in almost all of them Communists are trying to play their kind of subversive game. Party membership apparently varies from a few dozen Communists in several of the Middle American countries to around 50,000 and 80,000 in Brazil and Argentina, respectively. The grand total has been calculated at little more than 200,000, but numbers do not necessarily describe their influence.

The Communists have both immediate and long-range objectives in Latin America, as elsewhere. Ultimately, of course, they would like to seize power and try to set up "popular democratic" regimes in which communism would reign. That being out of the question, they are attempting a gradual approach, minimizing their difference with the non-Communist left, playing down their ties with international communism, and, in general, seeking to gain some degree of respectability and acceptance. In this, they have been notably unsuccessful. The Communists concentrate on trying to infiltrate as best they can into intellectual circles and also into key positions in government, organized labor, student groups, and public-opinion media. They then attempt to sow the seeds of chaos, disunity, and other conditions designed to break down the normal democratic functions.

. . . Communist agents seek to discredit American businessmen, to disparage American products, to stir up criticism of American financial methods, to invite labor difficulties. Even though American industrial concerns abroad are in the vanguard of those who practice modern industrial relations, Communist agents are always trying to promote strikes or violence against them.

. . . [W]e now are confronted by press headlines of a so-called Soviet trade offensive in Latin America. The phrase, of course, is dramatic, but what does it really mean? Undoubtedly, as compared to the situation of previous months, there have been more reports recently of offers being made by Soviet spokesmen and salesmen to exchange Russian manufactured goods for Latin American raw materials. But, of course, as businessmen you know that there is a long way from an offer to a closed deal. We need to keep the facts as we know them in perspective.

In 1957, according to latest estimates, Latin American trade with the Soviet bloc actually decreased around 12 percent, which means that Latin American trade with the Soviet bloc represented a little more than 1 percent of all Latin American trade. This 1 percent in turn was concentrated largely in four Latin American countries—Argentina, Brazil, Cuba, and Uruguay. . . .

. . . I am confident that I echo the sentiments of the leaders and the peoples of the Americas when I leave you with this closing thought—that there is no place in this God-given and God-fearing New World of 360 million souls for anything resembling the materialistic and atheistic concepts of godless communism.

3. Juscelino Kubitschek: Operation Pan-America, 1958

Source: President of Brazil, "Aide Mémoire Sent by the Government of Brazil to Governments of Other American States, August 9, 1958," in Council of the Organization of American States, Special Committee to Study the Formulation of New Measures for Economic Cooperation, *Volume L Report and Documents, First Meeting, Washington, D.C., November 17–December 12, 1958* (Washington, D.C.: 1959), 29–31.

. . . Within the framework of Operation Pan America, the struggle for democracy becomes identified with the struggle against stagnation and underdevelopment. The underdevelopment that prevails in this Hemisphere morally and materially involves the cause that we are defending. Underdeveloped areas are open to the penetration of antidemocratic ideology. From many standpoints and in all of its implications, the battle of the West is the battle for development. Materialist ideologies feed upon the poverty and misery that give rise to them in the first place; to combat these factors is the only sure way to combat those ideologies. Where there is poverty, our cause will always be in danger. It is illusory to expect positive action on behalf of a cause embracing such complex factors from peoples whose isolation in the rigors of extreme poverty prevents them from thinking or feeling anything beyond the narrow limits of their urgent needs for survival.

. . . According to the Brazilian concept, Operation Pan America is a reflection of the need for more active and more vigorous participation and cooperation by the Latin American countries in international policy, and it reveals these countries' full awareness of their moral, political, and demographic importance. Latin America's contribution may become highly significant in the struggle for a balance of power.

III. WESTERN POSTWAR POLICY

A. Inter-American political reorientation: The Brazilian Government believes that the time has come for a revision of inter-American policy, with a view to strengthening hemispheric unity in the face of the increasing common danger. A stronger, more courageous, creative, and dynamic initiative is urgently needed in the Western Hemisphere at this time.

It is imperative that the West become ever more conscious of its mission in the modern world. The principal objective of this mission is to defend and to perfect man's spiritual and moral achievements. Spiritual and moral forces should be the ones to guide and regulate a world expanded and profoundly transformed by technology. This is what is important to the West; this is its own Cause.

. . . The following points might be the basic objectives of the Operation:

1. Reaffirmation of the principles of hemispheric solidarity;

2. Recognition of underdevelopment as a problem of common interest;

3. Adaptation of inter-American organs and agencies, if necessary, to the requirements of more dynamic action to carry on the struggle against underdevelopment;

4. Technical assistance for increased productivity;

5. Measures to stabilize the market for basic commodities;

6. Adaptation to present needs and expansion of the resources of international financial institutions;

7. Reaffirmation of private initiative in the struggle against underdevelopment; and

8. Revision by each country, where necessary, of its fiscal and economic policy, for the purpose of assuring means to promote economic development.

4. John F. Kennedy: Announcing the Alliance for Progress, 1961

Source: Kennedy speech at the White House, March 13, 1961, John F. Kennedy Library, Boston.

As a citizen of the United States let me be the first to admit that we North Americans have not always grasped the significance of this common mission, just as it is also true that many in your own countries have not fully understood the urgency of the need to lift people from poverty and ignorance and despair. But we must turn from these mistakes—from the failures and the misunderstandings of the past to a future full of peril, but bright with hope.

Throughout Latin America, a continent rich in resources and in the spiritual and cultural achievements of its people, millions of men and women suffer the daily degradations of poverty and hunger. They lack decent shelter or protection from disease. Their children are deprived of the education or the jobs which are the gateway to a better life. And each day the problems grow more urgent. Population growth is outpacing economic growth—low living standards are further endangered and discontent—the discontent of a people who know that abundance and the tools of progress are at last within their reach—that discontent is growing. In the words of José Figueres, "once dormant peoples are struggling upward toward the sun, toward a better life."

If we are to meet a problem so staggering in its dimensions, our approach must itself be equally bold—an approach consistent with the majestic concept of Operation Pan America. Therefore I have called on all people of the hemisphere to join in a new Alliance for Progress—*Alianza para Progreso*—a vast cooperative effort, unparalleled in magnitude and nobility of purpose, to satisfy the basic needs of the American people for homes, work and land, health and schools—*techo, trabajo y tierra, salud y escuela.*

. . . [W]e propose to complete the revolution of the Americas, to build a hemisphere where all men can hope for a suitable standard of living, and all can live out their lives in dignity and in freedom.

To achieve this goal political freedom must accompany material progress. Our Alliance for Progress is an alliance of free governments, and it must work to eliminate tyranny from a hemisphere in which it has no rightful place. Therefore let us express our special friendship to the people of Cuba and the Dominican Republic—and the hope they will soon rejoin the society of free men, uniting with us in common effort.

This political freedom must be accompanied by social change. For unless necessary social reforms, including land and tax reform, are freely made—unless we broaden the opportunity for all of our people—unless the great mass of Americans share in increasing prosperity—then our alliance, our revolution, our dream, and our freedom will fail.

. . . The completion of our task will, of course, require the efforts of all governments of our hemisphere. But the efforts of governments alone will never be enough. In the end, the people must choose and the people must help themselves.

And so I say to the men and women of the Americas—to the *campesino* in the fields, to the *obrero* in the cities, to the *estudiante* in the schools—

prepare your mind and heart for the task ahead—call forth your strength and let each devote his energies to the betterment of all, so that your children and our children in this hemisphere can find an ever richer and a freer life.

Let us once again transform the American continent into a vast crucible of revolutionary ideas and efforts—a tribute to the power of the creative energies of free men and women—an example to all the world that liberty and progress walk hand in hand. Let us once again awaken our American revolution until it guides the struggle of people everywhere—not with an imperialism of force or fear—but the rule of courage and freedom and hope for the future of man.

5. Alberto Lleras: Report on the Alliance for Progress, 1963

Source: Alberto Lleras, President of Colombia, *Report on the Alliance for Progress* (Washington, D.C.: Organization of American States, June 15, 1963), v–x.

The reactionary right wing of the American world . . . was and is working against the objectives of Punta del Este. In the United States it was represented by the systematic enemies of all foreign aid, even more exalted now with the apparent initiation of a new program of expenditures; by those who maintain that *loans* and donations to governments only serve to encourage socialization in Latin America and weaken private enterprise; by the adversaries of the type of social-welfare investments recommended in the Charter of Punta del Este. In Latin America, by the system of the *latifundia*, which is always alert to any type of agrarian reform, entrenched in the governments and congresses; by a certain native capitalism, which accepts no restrictions upon its action but which defends itself with the same arguments as United States private enterprise, which is actually subject to strict competition and to anti-monopoly regulations; and, in general, by all the present beneficiaries of the social situation that was boldly denounced in the daring document signed in a moment of inspiration and, why not, of anxiety at the meeting in Uruguay.

In the United States Congress the opposing elements of the Alliance had already found an echo and obtained substantial victories, both in reducing the allocations for aid to Latin America and in introducing conditions for investment that were destined to protect United States capital unnecessarily and excessively, thereby succeeding in giving a displeasing aspect to the generous project. Taking advantage of the terms of the Foreign Trade Act, United States business men were already beginning to threaten the governments of Latin America with a suspension of the aid foreseen in the Alliance, if conditions arose that they considered intolerable and, even worse, the citizens themselves were approaching foreign authorities requesting them to intervene in this respect. The danger of a serious corruption of the spirit of the Alliance, its progressive weakening, and the disappointment of the

people with it, in addition to the continual risk that it might become a bureaucratic operation, was obvious towards the end of 1962, when the enormous rehabilitation enterprise of Latin America began to be talked of as a
new form of imperialism, as a policy on the part of the United States to
soothe Latin American discontent, as a gigantic publicity stunt.

. . . [T]he Alliance cannot achieve its transforming and revolutionary
effectiveness as long as the Latin American countries do not take the full
responsibility that the document appeared to assign them but that unfortu-
nately was not clearly defined in the document and that, finally, the Government of the United States assumed by itself, saving the program from
immediate failure but turning it aside from its original meaning and making
it appear, involuntarily, as a national policy and program of that country
towards its sister nations to the South.

6. Thomas Mann: Against an Invasion of Cuba, 1961

Source: Memorandum by the Assistant Secretary of State for Inter-American Affairs to Secretary of State Dean Rusk, February 15, 1961, U.S. Department of State,
Foreign Relations of the United States, 1961–1963, vol. 10 (Washington, D.C.: Government Printing Office, 1997). Top Secret; Eyes Only.

(1) The military evaluation of this proposal is that "ultimate success will
depend upon political factors, i.e., a sizeable popular uprising or substantial
follow-on forces." It is unlikely that a popular uprising would promptly take
place in Cuba of a scale and kind which would make it impossible for the
Castro regime to oppose the brigade with superior numbers of well armed
troops.

(2) It therefore appears possible, even probable, that we would be faced with
the alternative of a) abandoning the brigade to its fate, which would cost us
dearly in prestige and respect or b) attempting execution of the plan to move
the brigade into the mountains as guerrillas, which would pose a prolonged
problem of air drops or supplies or c) overt U.S. military intervention; a JCS
staff officer has estimated there is at least a 10% chance that U.S. forces would
be required unless alternative (a) were adopted.

(3) Execution of the proposed plan would be in violation of Article 2,
paragraph 4, and Article 51 of the Charter of the United Nations, Articles 18
and 25 of the Charter of the Organization of American States, and Article 1
of the Rio Treaty, which, in general, proscribe the use of armed force with the
sole exception of the right of self-defense "if an armed attack occurs."

The Castro regime could be expected to call on the other American States
(Article 3, paragraph 1 of the Rio Treaty) to assist them in repelling the attack,
and to request the Security Council (Chapter 7 of the UN Charter) to take
action to "maintain and restore international peace and security." The chances
of promptly presenting both international organizations with a fait accom-

pli are, in my opinion, virtually nil. It would therefore be extremely difficult to deal with Castro demarches of this kind. We could not disassociate ourselves from our complicity with Guatemala and Nicaragua; and if we tried to do so, both Ydigoras [of Guatemala] and Somoza [of Nicaragua] are in possession of sufficient information to implicate the United States in the eye of reasonable men.

(4) Since the proposal comes closer to being a military invasion than a covert operation of the Guatemala type, account must be taken of the possibility that the execution of this proposal would attract to Castro additional support within Cuba. More important, a majority of the people of Latin America would oppose the operation, and we would expect that the Communists and Castroites would organize and lead demonstrations designed to bring about the overthrow of governments friendly to us. At best, our moral posture throughout the hemisphere would be impaired. At worst, the effect on our position of hemispheric leadership would be catastrophic.

(5) Time is running against us in Cuba in a military sense since it is probable Castro soon will acquire jet aircraft, since he may acquire missiles and since Castro needs time to train his army and militia. Nevertheless, Defense does not currently consider Cuba to represent a threat to our national security. If later it should become a threat we are able to deal with it. If so, new developments which make Cuba an immediate threat to our national security might increase our chances of obtaining hemispheric support for collective action.

(6) . . . In any case, time is not currently running against us in terms of Latin American public opinion; there has already been a significant decline in Castro's popularity in Latin America, a trend which we have reason to hope will continue, assuming Castro continues to employ the same methods. If one looks at the Castro problem in the context of the struggle between the East and the West for Latin America, if one assumes the success or failure of the Castro policies to achieve a better life for the masses will significantly influence future hemisphere thought and action, and if one assumes that discipline and austerity will be hallmarks of Castroism, the political advantages to us of letting Latin America see for itself the practical results of applying communist theory in a Latin American country could well give us a decisive advantage in the ideological hemisphere struggle ahead of us.

(7) I therefore conclude it would not be in the national interest to proceed unilaterally to put this plan into execution. . . .

7. John F. Kennedy and Advisors: Discussing Options Against Missiles in Cuba, October 16, 1962

Source: Transcript of a Meeting at the White House, October 16, 1962, U.S. Department of State, *Foreign Relations of the United States, 1961–1963,* vol. 11 (Washington, D.C.: Government Printing Office, 1997).

JFK: Secretary Rusk?

[Secretary of State Dean] Rusk: Yes. [Well?], Mr. President, this is a, of course, a [widely?] serious development. It's one that we, all of us, had not really believed the Soviets could, uh, carry this far. . . . I don't think we [can?] sit still. . . . We have to think very hard about two major, uh, courses of action as alternatives. One is the quick strike. . . . I don't think this in itself would require an invasion of Cuba. I think that with or without such an invasion, in other words if we make it clear that, uh, what we're doing is eliminating this particular base or any other such base that is established. . . .

The other would be . . . a combination of things that, uh, we might wish to consider. Um, first, uh, that we, uh, stimulate the OAS procedure immediately for prompt action to make it quite clear that the entire hemisphere considers that the Rio Pact has been violated. . . . The OAS could, I suppose, at any moment, uh, take action to insist to the Cubans that an OAS inspection, uh, team be permitted to come and, itself, look directly at these sites, provide assurance[s?] to the hemisphere. That will undoubtedly be turned down, but it will be another step in building up the, uh, building a position.

I think also that we ought to consider getting some word to Castro, perhaps through the Canadian ambassador in Havana or through, uh, his representative at the U.N. . . .

. . .

[Secretary of Defense Robert] McNamara: . . . if we are to conduct an air strike against these installations, or against any part of Cuba, we must agree now that we will schedule that prior to the time these missile sites become operational. . . . Because, if they become operational before the air strike, I do not believe we can state we can knock them out before they can be launched; and if they're launched there is almost certain to be, uh, chaos in part of the east coast or the area, uh, in a radius of six hundred to a thousand miles from Cuba. . . .

. . .

JFK: What is the, uh, advant- . . . . Must be some major reason for the Russians to, uh, set this up as a . . . . Must be that they're not satisfied with their ICBMs [intercontinental ballistic missiles]. What'd be the reason that they would, uh . . . .

[Chairman of the Joint Chiefs of Staff Maxwell] Taylor: What it'd give 'em is primary, it makes the launching base, uh, for short range missiles against the United States to supplement their rather [deceptive?] ICBM system, for example. There's one reason. . . .

. . .

Rusk: Still, about why the Soviets are doing this, um, Mr. [John] McCone [director of central intelligence] suggested some weeks ago that one thing Mr. Khrushchev may have in mind is that, uh, uh, he knows that we have a substantial nuclear superiority, but he also knows that we don't really live under fear of his nuclear weapons to the extent that, uh, he has to live under fear of ours. Also we have nuclear weapons nearby, in Turkey and places like that. . . .

. . .

JFK: . . . of course, warning them, uh, it seems to me, is warning everybody. And I, I, obviously you can't sort of announce that in four days from now you're going to take them out. They may announce within three days they're going to have warheads on 'em; if we come and attack, they're going to fire them. Then what'll, what'll we do? Then we don't take 'em out. Of course, we then announce, well, if they do that, then we're going to attack with nuclear weapons. . . .

. . .

Taylor?: It'll never be a 100 percent, Mr. President, we know. Uh, we hope to take out a vast majority in the first strike, but this is not just one thing, one strike, one day, but continuous air attack for whenever necessary, whenever we di-, discover a target. . . .

. . .

JFK: . . . We're certainly going to do number one; we're going to take out these, uh, missiles. Uh, the questions will be whether, which, what I would describe as number two, which would be a general air strike. That we're not ready to say, but we should be in preparation for it. The third is the, is the, uh, the general invasion. At least we're going to do number one, so it seems to me that we don't have to wait very long. We, we ought to be making those preparations.

8. Fidel Castro to Nikita Khrushchev: Warning of a U.S. Invasion, October 26, 1962

Source: Prime Minister Fidel Castro's letter to Premier Khrushchev, October 26, 1962, in *The Cuban Missile Crisis, 1962: The 40th Anniversary*, National Security Archive, George Washington University, Washington D.C.

Dear Comrade Khrushchev:

From an analysis of the situation and the reports in our possession, I consider that the aggression is almost imminent within the next 24 to 72 hours.

There are two possible variants: the first and likeliest one is an air attack against certain targets with the limited objective of destroying them; the second, less probably although possible, is invasion. I understand that this variant would call for a large number of forces and it is, in addition, the most repulsive form of aggression, which might inhibit them.

You can rest assured that we will firmly and resolutely resist attack, whatever it may be.

The morale of the Cuban people is extremely high and the aggressor will be confronted heroically.

At this time I want to convey to you briefly my personal opinion.

If the second variant is implemented and the imperialists invade Cuba with the goal of occupying it, the danger that that aggressive policy poses for humanity is so great that following that event the Soviet Union must never allow the circumstances in which the imperialists could launch the first nuclear strike against it.

I tell you this because I believe that the imperialists' aggressiveness is extremely dangerous and if they actually carry out the brutal act of invading Cuba in violation of international law and morality, that would be the moment to eliminate such danger forever through an act of clear legitimate defense, however harsh and terrible the solution would be, for there is no other.

It has influenced my opinion to see how this aggressive policy is developing, how the imperialists, disregarding world public opinion and ignoring principles and the law, are blocking the seas, violating our airspace and preparing an invasion, while at the same time frustrating every possibility for talks, even though they are aware of the seriousness of the problem.

You have been and continue to be a tireless defender of peace and I realize how bitter these hours must be, when the outcome of your superhuman efforts is so seriously threatened. However, up to the last moment we will maintain the hope that peace will be safeguarded and we are willing to contribute to this as much as we can. But at the same time, we are ready to calmly confront a situation which we view as quite real and quite close.

Once more I convey to you the infinite gratitude and recognition of our people to the Soviet people who have been so generous and fraternal with us, as well as our profound gratitude and admiration for you, and wish you success in the huge task and serious responsibilities ahead of you.

Fraternally,

Fidel Castro

9. Nikita Khrushchev to Fidel Castro: Remaining Calm Against U.S. Aggression, October 28, 1962

Source: http://www.gwu.edu/~nsarchiv/nsa/cuba_mis_cri/19621028khrlet.pdf

Dear Comrade Fidel Castro:

Our October 27 message to President Kennedy allows for the question to be settled in your favor, to defend Cuba from an invasion and prevent war from breaking out. Kennedy's reply, which you apparently also know, offers assurances that the United States will not invade Cuba with its own forces, nor will it permit its allies to carry out an invasion. In this way the president of the United States has positively answered my messages of October 26 and 27, 1962.

We have now finished drafting our reply to the president's message. I am not going to convey it here, for you surely know the text, which is now being broadcast, over the radio.

With this motive I would like to recommend to you now, at this moment of change in the crisis, not to be carried away by sentiment and to show firmness. I must say that I understand your feelings of indignation toward the aggressive actions and violations of elementary norms of international law on the part of the United States.

But now, rather than law, what prevails is the senselessness of the militarists at the Pentagon. Now that an agreement is within sight, the Pentagon is searching for a pretext to frustrate this agreement. This is why it is organizing the provocative flights. Yesterday you shot down one of these, while earlier you didn't shoot them down when they overflew your territory. The aggressors will take advantage of such a step for their own purposes.

Therefore, I would like to advise you in a friendly manner to show patience, firmness and even more firmness. Naturally, if there's an invasion it will be necessary to repulse it by every means. But we mustn't allow ourselves to be carried away by provocations, because the Pentagon's unbridled militarists, now that the solution to the conflict is in sight and apparently in your favor, creating a guarantee against the invasion of Cuba, are trying to frustrate the agreement and provoke you into actions that could be used against you. I ask you not to give them the pretext for doing that.

On our part, we will do everything possible to stabilize the situation in Cuba, defend Cuba against invasion and assure you the possibilities for peacefully building a socialist society.

I send you greetings, extensive to all your leadership group.

N. Khrushchev

October 28, 1962

10. Senator William Fulbright: Criticizing the U.S. Intervention in the Dominican Crisis, 1965

Source: *Congressional Record: Proceedings and Debates of the 89th Congress, 1st Session,* vol. 3, no. 170, daily edition (September 15, 1965), 22998–23005.

The Foreign Relations Committee's study of the Dominican crisis leads me to draw certain specific conclusions regarding American policy in the Dominican Republic and also suggests some broader considerations regarding relations between the United States and Latin America. My specific conclusions regarding the crisis in Santo Domingo are as follows:

First. The United States intervened forcibly in the Dominican Republic in the last week of April 1965 not primarily to save American lives, as was then contended, but to prevent the victory of a revolutionary movement which was judged to be Communist-dominated. The decision to land thousands of marines on April 28 was based primarily on the fear of "another Cuba" in Santo Domingo.

Second. This fear was based on fragmentary and inadequate evidence. There is no doubt that Communists participated in the Dominican revolution on the rebel side [the Constitutionalists, opposed by the United States], probably to a greater extent after than before the landing of U.S. marines on April 28, but just as it cannot be proved that the Communists would not have taken over the revolution neither can it be proved that they would have. There is little basis in the evidence offered the committee for the assertion that the rebels were Communist-dominated or certain to become so; on the contrary, the evidence suggests a chaotic situation in which no single faction was dominant at the outset and in which everybody, including the United States, had opportunities to influence the shape and course of the rebellion.

Third. The United States let pass its best opportunities to influence the course of events. The best opportunities were on April 25, when Juan Bosch's party, the PRD, requested a "United States presence," and on April 27, when the rebels, believing themselves defeated, requested United States mediation for a negotiated settlement. . . .

Fourth. U.S. policy toward the Dominican Republic shifted markedly to the right between September 1963 and April 1965. In 1963, the United States strongly supported Bosch and the PRD as enlightened reformers; in 1965 the United States opposed their return to power on the unsubstantiated ground that a Bosch or PRD government would certainly, or almost certainly, become Communist dominated. Thus the United States turned its back on social revolution in Santo Domingo and associated itself with a corrupt and reactionary military oligarchy.

Fifth. U.S. policy was marred by a lack of candor and by misinformation. The former is illustrated by official assertions that U.S. military intervention was primarily for the purpose of saving American lives; the latter is illustrated by exaggerated reports of massacres and atrocities by the rebels—reports which no one has been able to verify. It was officially asserted, for example, by the President in a press conference on June 17 according to an official State Department bulletin—that "some 1,500 innocent people were murdered and shot, and their heads cut off." There is no evidence to support this statement. . . .

Sixth. Responsibility for the failure of American policy in Santo Domingo lies primarily with those who advised the President. In the critical days between April 25 and April 28, these officials sent the President exaggerated reports of the danger of a Communist takeover in Santo Domingo and, on the basis of these, recommended U.S. massive military intervention. . . .

Seventh. Underlying the bad advice and unwise actions of the United States was the fear of another Cuba. The specter of a second Communist state in the Western Hemisphere—and its probable repercussions within the United States and possible effects on the careers of those who might be held responsible—seems to have been the most important single factor in distorting the judgment of otherwise sensible and competent men.

11. Henry Kissinger and César Augusto Guzzetti: Advising the Argentine Military on Dealing With Dissent, 1976

Source: Memorandum of conversation between Secretary of State Henry Kissinger, Argentine Foreign Minister Admiral César Augusto Guzzetti, and others, June 6, 1976 [misdated, actual date June 10], National Security Archive, George Washington University, Washington, D.C. Declassified 2004.

SECRET
Santiago, Chile
June 6, 1976
Secretary's Suite

. . .

[Argentine Foreign Minister Admiral César Augusto] Guzzetti: Our main problem in Argentina is terrorism. It is the first priority of the current government that took office on March 24. There are two aspects to the solution. The first is to ensure the internal security of the country; the second is to solve the most urgent economic problems over the coming 6 to 12 months.

Argentina needs United States understanding and support to overcome problems in these two areas.

The Secretary [of State, Henry Kissinger]: We have followed events in Argentina closely. We wish the new government well. We wish it will succeed. We will do what we can to help it succeed.

We are aware you are in a difficult period. It is a curious time, when political, criminal, and terrorist activities tend to merge without any clear separation. We understand you must establish authority. . . .

. . .

Guzzetti: . . . Chile, when the government changed, resulted in a very large number of leftist exiles. The Peronist Government at the time welcomed them to Argentina in large numbers.

The Secretary: You could always send them back.

Guzzetti: For elemental human rights reasons we cannot send them back to Chile. But we have tried third countries. No one wants to receive them. There are many terrorists.

The Secretary: Have you tried the PLO [Palentine Liberation Organization]? They need more terrorists.

Seriously, we cannot tell you how to handle these people. What are you going to do?

. . .

Guzzetti: We must create disincentives to potential terrorist activities. Specifically, terrorism is becoming extraordinarily virulent. People on the outside don't look for details. They don't see the provocations that we face, or our efforts to resolve them.

The Secretary: Let me say, as a friend, that I have noticed that military governments are not always the most effective in dealing with these problems.

Guzzetti: Of course.

The Secretary: So, after a while, many people who don't understand the situation begin to oppose the military and the problem is compounded. The Chileans, for example, have not succeeded in getting across their initial problem and are increasingly isolated.

You will have to make an international effort to have your problems understood. Otherwise, you, too, will come under increasing attack. If there are things that have to be done, you should do them quickly. But you must get back quickly to normal procedures.

12. Nelson Rockefeller: Reporting on the Americas, 1969

Source: Nelson A. Rockefeller, *The Rockefeller Report on the Americas: The Official Report of a United States Presidential Mission for the Western Hemisphere*, New York Times edition (Chicago: Quadrangle Books, 1969), 57–59.

Throughout the hemisphere, there is growing uncertainty concerning the extent of the United States' commitment to work with the people of the other American republics for their economic and social betterment.

Our neighbors need to be reassured of our conviction that people are, indeed, our basic concern, and that we want to continue to work with them, regardless of the form of their government, to help them raise the level of their lives. In this way we can help strengthen the forces of democracy.

Commitment to representative, responsive democratic government is deeply imbedded in the collective political consciousness of the American people. We would like to see strong representative government develop in the other nations of the hemisphere for both idealistic and practical reasons:

—Our experience convinces us that representative democratic government and free societies offer the best means of organizing man's social, political, and economic life so as to maximize the prospects for improving the individual's dignity and the quality of his life.

—Practically, nations with broadly based political systems of a democratic type are more likely to have outlooks and concepts compatible with the style of the United States and its people, and more willing to cooperate with us in establishing effective world order.

. . . Democracy is a very subtle and difficult problem for most of the other countries in the hemisphere. The authoritarian and hierarchical tradition which has conditioned and formed the cultures of most of these societies does not lend itself to the particular kind of popular government we are used to. Few of these countries, moreover, have achieved the sufficiently advanced economic and social systems required to support a consistently democratic system. For many of these societies, therefore, the question is less one of democracy or a lack of it than it is simply of orderly ways of getting along.

. . . The U.S. should also recognize that political evolution takes time and that, realistically, its long-term interests will be served by maintaining at least minimal diplomatic relationships with other governments of the hemisphere while trying to find ways to assist the people in those countries, and to encourage the governments to move toward democratic processes. Such a policy requires a very difficult balance but is one that must be achieved pragmatically on a case-by-case basis. The U.S. cannot renege on its commitment to a better life for all of the people of the hemisphere because of moral disagreement with regimes which the people themselves did not establish and cannot control.

13. Jimmy Carter: Loosening Tensions With Cuba, 1977

Source: Jimmy Carter, "Presidential Directive/NSC-6," March 15, 1977, National Security Archive, George Washington University, Washington, D.C.

SECRET
THE WHITE HOUSE
WASHINGTON
March 15, 1977
Presidential Directive/NSC-6
Subject: Cuba

After reviewing the results of the meeting of the Policy Review Committee held on Wednesday, March 9, 1977, to discuss U.S. policy to Cuba, I have concluded that we should attempt to achieve normalization of our relations with Cuba.

To this end, we should begin direct and confidential talks in a measured and careful fashion with representatives of the Government of Cuba. Our objective is to set in motion a process which will lead to the reestablishment of diplomatic relations between the United States and Cuba and which will advance the interests of the United States with respect to:

—Combating terrorism;

—Human rights;

—Cuba's foreign intervention;

—Compensation for American expropriated property; and

—Reduction of the Cuban relationship (political and military) with the Soviet Union.

The issues we should raise in the exploratory talks include: fisheries and maritime boundaries; the anti-hijacking agreement; human rights conditions in Cuba (including release of American citizens in Cuban jails, visitation rights, and emigration rights); Cuba's external activities in Angola and elsewhere; Cuba's activities with regard to Puerto Rico; sports, cultural and scientific/technical exchanges; compensation for American property which was expropriated by the Cuban Government; the possibility of trade relations; and the establishment of an American Interests Section in the Swiss Embassy.

To implement this new policy and to negotiate in pursuit of these objectives, the Secretary of States should designate officials to begin exploratory talks with Cuba with the intention that they will lead to appropriate, reciprocal and sequential steps looking toward normalization of relations between our two countries. Following an exploratory round of discussions, the National Security Council should make recommendations to me on how we should proceed.

The Secretary of State should insure that the NATO Governments, Japan and various Latin American Governments are informed of U.S. initiatives toward Cuba, as appropriate.

The Attorney General should take all necessary steps permitted by law to prevent terrorist or any illegal actions launched from within the United States against Cuba and against U.S. citizens and to apprehend and prosecute perpetrators of such actions.

J.C. [signed Jimmy Carter]

14. Gustavo Gutiérrez: Liberation Theology, 1971

Source: Gustavo Gutiérrez, *A Theology of Liberation*, trans. and ed. Sister Caridad Inda and John Eagleson (Maryknoll, N.Y.: Orbis Books, 1973; orig. Spanish, 1971), 133–140. Used with permission.

Although until recently the Church was closely linked to the established order, it is beginning to take a different attitude regarding the exploitation, oppression, and alienation which prevails in Latin America. This has caused concern among the beneficiaries and defenders of capitalist society, who no longer can depend on what used to be—whether consciously or unconsciously—one of their mainstays. This concern is reflected, for example, in the *Rockefeller Report*. . . .

The commitments of Christians in Latin America and the texts which attempt to explicate them are gradually fashioning an authentic "political" option of the Church on this continent. . . .

In this context we must include the Medellín Conference as a major event. At Medellín, the Latin American Church . . . realistically perceived the world in which it was and clearly saw its place in that world. In short, it began to be aware of its own coming of age and to take the reins of its own destiny. Vatican II speaks of the underdevelopment of peoples, of the developed countries and what they can and should do about this underdevelopment; Medellín tries to deal with the problem from the standpoint of the poor countries, characterizing them as subjected to a new kind of colonialism. Vatican II talks about a Church in the world and describes the relationship in a way which tends to neutralize the conflicts; Medellín demonstrates that the world in which the Latin American Church ought to be present is in full revolution. Vatican II sketches a general outline for Church renewal; Medellín provides guidelines for a transformation of the Church in terms of its presence on a continent of misery and injustice.

. . . Here [are] the most important theologico-pastoral questions posed by this new situation. . . .

a) The options which Christians in Latin America are taking have brought forth a fundamental question to the fore: What is the *meaning of the faith* in a life committed to the struggle against injustice and alienation? How do we relate

the work of building a just society to the absolute value of the Kingdom? . . .
b) The problem, however, is not only to find a new theological framework.
The *personal and community prayer* of many Christians committed to the process of liberation is undergoing a serious crisis. This could purify prayer life of childish attitudes, routine, and escapes. But it will not do this if new paths are not broken and new spiritual experiences are not lived. . . .
c) The Latin American reality, *the historical moment* which Latin America is experiencing, is *deeply conflictual.* . . . Because of close contact with those who see historical development from a Marxist viewpoint, we are led to review and revitalize the eschatological values of Christianity. . . . We Christians, however, are not used to thinking in conflictual and historical terms. We prefer peaceful conciliation to antagonism and an evasive eternity to a provisional arrangement. We must learn to live and think of peace in conflict and of what is definitive in what is historical. . . .
d) The Latin American church is sharply *divided* with regard to the process of liberation. . . . The majority of the Church continues to be linked in many different ways to the established order. And what is worse, among Latin American Christians there are not only different political options within a framework of free interplay of ideas; the polarization of these options and the extreme seriousness of the situations have even placed some Christians among the oppressed and persecuted and others among the oppressors and persecutors, some among the tortured and others among the torturers or those who condone torture. . . .
e) In Latin America, the Church must place itself squarely within the process of revolution, amid the violence which is present in different ways. The Church's *mission* is defined practically and theoretically, pastorally and theologically in relation to this revolutionary process. That is, its mission is defined more by the political context than by intraecclesiastical problems. . . .
f) Closely connected with this problem is another very controversial question: Should *the Church put its social weight* behind social transformation in Latin America? . . . Not to exercise this influence in favor of the oppressed of Latin America is really to exercise it against them, and it is difficult to determine beforehand the consequences of this action. . . .
g) The Latin American Church community lives on a poor continent, but the image it projects is not, as a whole, that of a *poor Church.* . . . The majority of the Church has covertly or openly been an accomplice of the external and internal dependency of our peoples. It has sided with the dominant groups, and in the name of "efficacy" has dedicated its best efforts to them. It has identified with these sectors and adopted their style of life. . . .
    . . . Overcoming the colonial mentality is one of the important tasks of the Christian community. In this way, it will be able to make a genuine contribution to the enrichment of the universal Church; it will be able to face its real problems and to sink deep roots into a continent in revolution.

15. Daniel Ortega: The Sandinistas' Relationship With the United States, Interview, 1997

Source: Interview with Daniel Ortega in Episode 18: Backyard, *Cold War Experience*, CNN Perspectives Series, 1998, http://www.cnn.com/SPECIALS/cold.war/episodes/18/interviews/ortega/. Courtesy of CNN.

[We took power] with great enthusiasm and a great desire to transform the country, but also with the worry that we would have to confront the United States, something which we regarded as inevitable. It's not that we fell into a kind of geopolitical fatalism with regard to the United States, but historically speaking the United States has been interfering in our country since the last century, and so we said, "The Yankees will inevitably interfere. If we try to become independent, the United States will intervene."

I would say that we tried to neutralize that confrontation with the United States, and around September of '79 I went to the United Nations, and before that I visited Washington and had a meeting with President Carter. During the meeting with President Carter, we proposed the development of a new kind of relationship with the United States. During our exchange, [he said that] the American government was worried about the implications of the revolution and that the conservative sections of the United States perceived it as a threat. We insisted that this was an opportunity, as I said to Carter, for the United States to make good the historical damage they had inflicted on our country. Our national anthem still includes the words "Yankee, the enemy of humanity," and we said to him that the only way to abolish that line would be for the attitude of the imperialist powers to change throughout the world, and specifically towards Nicaragua. And then, in concrete terms, we asked President Carter for a certain amount of economic help, and for material support to build up a new army, because the old one had been wiped out. We needed weapons, because Nicaragua didn't manufacture any at the time, so we were asking them to help us in this respect. But they couldn't respond, because there was a public debate going on in the United States at that moment, and the conservatives were accusing Carter of opening the door to "communism," which was the word they used for these changes. It was up to the U.S. Congress to make these kinds of decisions, and the Congress did not want to approve such decisions.

[Our relationship with Cuba] was precisely the challenge—that the United States should respect our right to maintain friendly relations with whoever Nicaragua wanted. If the United States wanted to put conditions on Nicaragua's relations [with other countries], then it meant that we were starting off on the wrong foot, that the old imperialist attitude was still the same and there was nothing democratic about it at all, and that they were keeping up their dictatorial attitude throughout the world, supported by their economic and military power. So this meant that we started trying to find weapons in other parts of the world. Of course, the kind of support that Cuba could give us was very limited when it came to building up our army, since they didn't manufacture armaments in the quantities that we required. So we turned to Algeria and the Soviet Union for support. The first weapons that we received came from Algeria. Algeria identified very much with our struggle. We conducted a series of negotiations at the time, and the first reply we received came from Algeria. Then we began to receive support from other countries of the socialist community, and mainly from the Soviet Union. . . .

I remember perfectly well that when we began working in that direction, which we did quite openly, the U.S. government sent us an emissary, Mr. Thomas Enders, and I remember my conversation with him. He came to tell us very clearly that the United States was not going to allow a Soviet-Cuban communist bridgehead to be established in this continent. I said that we had a right to maintain relations with any other country, and that they should respect that right. And then he said that I should understand that they had the power to crush us, to which I replied that we were ready to fight and confront them even though they were a big power—that [Augusto] Sandino had already confronted them in the past and that we were ready to do so again if they tried to crush us.

16. John Negroponte: Soviet Intervention in Central America, Interview, 1997

Source: Interview with John Negroponte, Ambassador to Honduras, in Episode 18: Backyard, *Cold War Experience,* CNN Perspectives Series, 1998, http://www.cnn.com/SPECIALS/cold.war/episodes/18/interviews/negroponte/. Courtesy of CNN.

I certainly think [the Soviets] must have enjoyed our discomfort. Whether they micromanaged this or not, I just don't know. I'd be reluctant to say. My working hypothesis was that they sort of let Cuba have the lead on this, and basically said to them: "Have at it boys, and see what you can accomplish."

. . . I don't think there was any doubt of Cuban involvement. There was evidence of that—of people being trained in Cuba, recruited in those countries, be it Nicaragua, or El Salvador in particular. Trained in Cuban training camps and then reinfiltrated back into their countries. I think there also had been, just before I got to Honduras, a rather spectacular capture of an arms shipment from Nicaragua, [headed] across Honduran territory destined for El Salvador. And I think that some of that equipment had been also to Cuba and the Soviet bloc. But certainly in my own mind I had no doubt that these [Central American] conflicts were being fueled by Cuba, and I think by implication by the Soviet Union. . . .

The experience of the late 1970s was for the United States, I think, a very sobering one. Indeed, as far as the Cold War is concerned, you have in particular two events: the Vietnamese invasion of Cambodia in 1978, and the ensuing Soviet invasion of Afghanistan in 1979. So viewed in that context, what then started to happen in El Salvador and in Nicaragua were I think of considerable concern to Washington: "Well gee, is this all a part of a pattern? And if it is, or if that appears to be the case, then we really have to do something about it."

. . . It was a Central American domino theory if you will: so that if it happened at first in Nicaragua then in El Salvador and if they succeeded in El Salvador, then presumably they would try to finish off the situation in Guatemala, which was rather ripe at the time, you may recall. And then maybe Honduras would have fallen of its own volition, without necessarily even having to make that much effort. That was the theory in any case, and it seemed a plausible hypothesis at the time. . . .

I think it has [always] been recognized that Central America had vulnerability, both politically and economically, because of their social structure, because of their excessive dependence on a very small number of products for export, because of the disparities in wealth between the rich and the poor, and so forth. . . . There is no question that these societies were vulnerable politically and socially. The point was whether just because of these vulnerabilities, should we allow external forces such as the Cubans or the Soviets to come in and try to take advantage of those situations? That was the issue. And that was what we were reacting to and that is why we put so much effort into Central America.

17. The Santa Fe Commission: Renewing the Cold War in Latin America, 1980

Source: "Summary Report," in Committee of Santa Fe, *A New Inter-American Policy for the Eighties* (Washington, D.C.: Council for Inter-American Security, 1980), 52–53.

The Americas are under external and internal attack. Latin America, an integral part of the Western community, is being overrun by Soviet supported and supplied satellites and surrogates. The implosion of the U.S. presence in the Caribbean and Central America—America's maritime crossroad and petroleum refining center—continues. Meanwhile the remaining independent Ibero-American nations, doubting the United States' will and purpose, strive desperately to salvage their own strategic and economic situations.

America's wounds are self inflicted. Decisive action, such as the occupation of the Dominican Republic in 1965, has been replaced by retrograde action, as exemplified by the Carter-Torrijos Treaties in 1978, and by anxious accommodation, as evidenced by the May 1980 cancellation of the sea-air exercise "Solid Shield '80" after a protest by the president of Panama about the provocative presence of U.S. forces in the Caribbean.

The Committee of Santa Fe charges that the U.S. effort to socialize the Soviets and their Hispanic-American puppets is merely a camouflaged cover for accommodation to aggression.

The Committee of Santa Fe, therefore, urges that the United States take the strategic and diplomatic initiative by revitalizing the Rio Treaty and the Organization of American States; reproclaiming the Monroe Doctrine; tightening ties with key countries; and, aiding independent nations to survive subversion.

The Committee of Santa Fe further proposes that the United States initiate an economic and ideological campaign by developing an energy plan for the Americas; easing the Latin American debt burden by encouraging Hispanic-American capital formation; assisting Ibero-American industry and agriculture through trade and technology; and, above all, providing the ideal behind the instrument of foreign policy through educational programs designed to win the minds of mankind. For the belief behind the policy is essential to victory.

Certainly, in war there is no substitute for victory; and the United States is engaged in World War III. The first two phases, containment and détente, have been overtaken by the Soviet scenario of double envelopment; surround the People's Republic of China and strangle the Western industrialized nations by interdicting their oil and ore. Southern Asia and Ibero-America are the actual areas of aggression.

Latin America is vital to the United States: America's global power projection has always rested upon a cooperative Caribbean and a supportive South America. For the United States of America, isolationism is impossible. Containment of the Soviet Union is not enough. Détente is dead.

Only the United States can, as a partner, protect the independent nations of Latin America from Communist conquest and help preserve Hispanic-American culture from sterilization by international Marxist materialism. America must take the lead. For not only are U.S.–Latin American relations endangered, but the very survival of this republic is at stake.

18. CIA: Secret Cable on a Guatemalan Massacre, 1981

Source: CIA, "Guatemalan Soldiers Kill Civilians in Cocob, April 1981," in *The Guatemalan Military: What the U.S. Files Reveal,* vol. 2, National Security Archive, George Washington University, Washington, D.C.

SECRET

1. [Less than one line blacked out] Information that the Guerrilla Army of the Poor (EGPL) unit which attacked an army patrol near Nebaj . . . on 15 April 1981, killing one officer and four soldiers, was operating out of the village of Cocob. . . . On 17 April 1981, a reinforced company of airborne troops entered the village to investigate. A large and unruly crowd of villag-

ers gathered and some pelted the patrol with rocks. Simultaneously, the troops received automatic weapons fire from numerous houses. The troops returned the fire and, in the confusion of the fire fight, opened fire on the villagers. In the ensuing battle many villagers were killed, as were a number of EGP guerrillas. The airborne company suffered one soldier killed and several wounded.

2. Once the village was secured, the airborne troops conducted a house to house search and discovered weapons, a large quantity of ammunition, EGP propaganda, uniforms and other military supplies. Included among the arms were ten M16 automatic rifles, one .30 caliber carbine, and one 9mm Madzen [*sic*] sub-machine gun. Propaganda material found revealed that the EGP unit belonged to the 'Juan Sousa Front,' which has recently become active in the area. In a search of the area surrounding the village, the troops found a series of sophisticated fox holes similar to the 'spider holes' used by the Viet Cong. One soldier almost fell into the entrance of one hole and was killed at point-blank range by a female guerrilla hidden inside. The guerrilla was immediately killed by other troops.

3. [Less than one line blacked out] explained [a few words blacked out] that the village was totally under control of the EGP and that the local population appeared to fully support the guerrillas during the battle. It was impossible to differentiate between the actual guerrillas and innocent civilians, and according to [name blacked out] the soldiers were forced to fire at anything that moved. [name blacked out] comment: The Guatemalan authorities admitted that 'many civilians' were killed in Cocob, many of whom undoubtedly were non-combatants. The repercussions of this incident will reflect negatively against the army throughout the area. The authorities point out, however, that the EGP appeared to completely control the village, and enjoyed the full support of the entire population.

[last page blacked out almost entirely].

19. Iran-Contra Report: Findings, Indictments, and Pardons, 1993

Source: Lawrence E. Walsh, "Executive Summary," *Final Report of the Independent Counsel for Iran/Contra Matters,* vol. 1 (Washington, D.C.: U.S. Court of Appeals for the District of Columbia Circuit, August 4, 1993).

In October and November 1986, two secret U.S. Government operations were publicly exposed, potentially implicating Reagan Administration officials in illegal activities. These operations were the provision of assistance to the military activities of the Nicaraguan contra rebels during an October 1984 to October 1986 prohibition on such aid, and the sale of U.S. arms to Iran in contravention of stated U.S. policy and in possible violation of arms-export controls. In late November 1986, Reagan Administration officials announced that some of the proceeds from the sale of U.S. arms to Iran had been diverted to the contras.

As a result of the exposure of these operations, Attorney General Edwin Meese III sought the appointment of an independent counsel to investigate and, if necessary, prosecute possible crimes arising from them. . . .

Independent Counsel concluded that:

the sales of arms to Iran contravened United States Government policy and may have violated the Arms Export Control Act;

the provision and coordination of support to the contras violated the Boland Amendment ban on aid to military activities in Nicaragua;

the policies behind both the Iran and contra operations were fully reviewed and developed at the highest levels of the Reagan Administration;

although there was little evidence of National Security Council level knowledge of most of the actual contra-support operations, there was no evidence that any NSC member dissented from the underlying policy keeping the contras alive despite congressional limitations on contra support;

the Iran operations were carried out with the knowledge of, among others, President Ronald Reagan, Vice President George Bush, Secretary of State George P. Shultz, Secretary of Defense Caspar W. Weinberger, Director of Central Intelligence William J. Casey, and national security advisers Robert C. McFarlane and John M. Poindexter; of these officials, only Weinberger and Shultz dissented from the policy decision, and Weinberger eventually acquiesced by ordering the Department of Defense to provide the necessary arms; and

large volumes of highly relevant, contemporaneously created documents were systematically and willfully withheld from investigators by several Reagan Administration officials.

Following the revelation of these operations in October and November 1986, Reagan Administration officials deliberately deceived the Congress and the public about the level and extent of official knowledge of and support for these operations.

In addition, Independent Counsel concluded that the off-the-books nature of the Iran and contra operations gave line-level personnel the opportunity to commit money crimes. . . .

COMPLETED TRIALS AND PLEAS

Elliott Abrams—Pleaded guilty October 7, 1991, to two misdemeanor charges of withholding information from Congress about secret government efforts to support the Nicaraguan contra rebels during a ban on such aid. U.S. District Chief Judge Aubrey E. Robinson, Jr., sentenced Abrams November 15, 1991, to two years probation and 100 hours community service. Abrams was pardoned December 24, 1992. . . .

Robert C. McFarlane—Pleaded guilty March 11, 1988, to four misdemeanor counts of withholding information from Congress. U.S. District Chief Judge Aubrey E. Robinson, Jr., sentenced McFarlane on March 3, 1989, to two years probation, $20,000 in fines and 200 hours community service. McFarlane was pardoned December 24, 1992. . . .

Oliver L. North—Indicted March 16, 1988, on 16 felony counts. After standing trial on 12, North was convicted May 4, 1989 of three charges: accepting an illegal gratuity, aiding and abetting in the obstruction of a congressional inquiry, and destruction of documents. He was sentenced by U.S. District Judge Gerhard A. Gesell on July 5, 1989, to a three-year suspended prison term, two years probation, $150,000 in fines and 1,200 hours community service. A three-judge appeals panel on July 20, 1990, vacated North's conviction for further proceedings to determine whether his immunized testimony influenced witnesses in the trial. The Supreme Court declined to review the case. Judge Gesell dismissed the case September 16, 1991, after hearings on the immunity issue, on the motion of Independent Counsel.

John M. Poindexter—Indicted March 16, 1988, on seven felony charges. After standing trial on five charges, Poindexter was found guilty April 7, 1990, on all counts: conspiracy (obstruction of inquiries and proceedings, false statements, falsification, destruction and removal of documents); two counts of obstruction of Congress and two counts of false statements. U.S. District Judge Harold H. Greene sentenced Poindexter June 11, 1990, to six months in prison on each count, to be served concurrently. A three-judge appeals panel on November 15, 1991, reversed the convictions on the ground that Poindexter's immunized testimony may have influenced the trial testimony of witnesses. The Supreme Court on December 7, 1992, declined to review the case. In 1993, the indictment was dismissed on the motion of Independent Counsel. . . .

PRE-TRIAL PARDONS
. . . Caspar W. Weinberger—Indicted June 16, 1992, on five counts of obstruction, perjury and false statements in connection with congressional and Independent Counsel investigations of Iran/contra. On September 29, the obstruction count was dismissed. On October 30, a second indictment was issued, charging one false statement count. The second indictment was dismissed December 11, leaving four counts remaining. The maximum penalty for each count was five years in prison and $250,000 in fines. U.S. District Judge Thomas F. Hogan set a January 5, 1993, trial date. Weinberger was pardoned December 24, 1992.

20. Clinton White House: Answering Critics of NAFTA, 1993

Source: Office of the Press Secretary, "Fact Sheet on NAFTA U.S. Capital Goods Exports," at the William J. Clinton Foundation, http://www.clintonfoundation.org/legacy/092393-fact-sheet-on-nafla-us-capital-goods-exports.htm.

THE WHITE HOUSE
Thursday, September 23, 1993
U.S. Capital Goods Exports—The Real Story
One of the strongest arguments for NAFTA is that it will continue the growth of U.S. exports to the dynamic Mexican market. In the past five

years, the U.S. has gone from a $5.7 billion trade deficit with Mexico to a $5.6 billion surplus. NAFTA critics, however, point out that much of that surplus is made up of capital goods—and claim that this is nothing more than taking apart American factories and sending them south to Mexico. But this claim misses the real story behind U.S. capital goods exports.

In percentage terms, capital goods have been the slowest growing major export category to Mexico in the last five years. While capital goods are still the largest component of U.S. exports to Mexico, they have decreased from 40 percent of total exports to Mexico in 1987 to 33 percent in 1992. In comparison, capital goods make up 40 percent of our exports to developing countries, and 39 percent of our exports to the world.

The flawed logic that assumes that capital goods are merely a one-time export which will produce a flood of cheap imported goods flowing back into the U.S. misses the point. Capital plant equipment exported to factories in Mexico should not be seen in negative terms for the American economy. Production of cutting-edge technology such as robotics, generators, and production machinery supports the highest-paying U.S. manufacturing jobs; just as importantly, a healthy, expanding Mexican economy will continue to need such high-tech U.S. products. Even the U.S., the world's most productive economy, must replace a part of its capital equipment each year.

Additionally, capital goods are some of our most competitive exports and cover many things other than capital plant equipment: Boeing jets, IBM computers, AT&T telephone systems, John Deere tractors. The manufacture of all of these U.S. products support high-paying U.S. jobs, and cannot be construed as a drag on the U.S. economy.

Finally, and perhaps most importantly, without NAFTA Mexico has no incentive not to fill its growing capital goods needs from Japanese and European—rather than U.S.—exports.

NAFTA Fact

83 percent of the growth in U.S. exports to Mexico in the last five years was for Mexican consumption—not re-export. Additionally, in those five years exports to maquiladoras in relation to total U.S. exports to Mexico have fallen. In 1992, U.S. exports to maquiladoras comprised 22 percent of U.S. exports to Mexico, compared to 32 percent in 1987.

21. Rigoberta Menchú: Indigenous Activism and Guatemala, Interview, 1992

Source: Commission for the Defense of Human Rights in Central America, "1992 Interview With Rigoberta Menchu Tum, Mayan," at http://www.indians.org/welker/menchu2.htm. One month after this interview, Menchú received the Nobel Peace Prize.

Q: On the twelfth of October, a great number of countries will celebrate the 500th anniversary of the discovery of America. Do you see this as an insult to the indigenous people?

A: We have seen repeated occupations of our land, long lines of colonists have arrived, and they remain today. For me, to celebrate the twelfth of October is the absolute expression of triumphism, occupation and presumptuousness, and I think that anyone who has mature and responsible politics should not celebrate it. History will remember those that celebrate it.

On the other hand, the 500th anniversary has opened a lot of space in international forums. With respect to this, I am deeply gladdened that 1993 has been declared the International Year of Indigenous Peoples by the United Nations. It is the first year we have had in five hundred years. This is thanks to the struggle of many untitled, unnamed indigenous brothers who, without understanding international law, patiently walked the corridors asking for some time. Thanks to them this international year has been declared.

In addition, I think that the current situation has generated an understanding of the cultural diversity of America. We were the first to talk about cultural diversity, the need to respect the Maya and the environment. . . .

Q: The whole region has seen a pacification process in the last few years. However, in Guatemala the internal war continues. Why has the situation been prolonged in your country?

A: In my opinion, peace has not come to America, to Nicaragua, or to El Salvador. A hungry people is a people without peace. If the demands of the people are not met, what kind of peace are we talking about? . . .

Q: How do you explain the fact that the war in Guatemala has never gotten the same amount of attention as the wars in El Salvador and Nicaragua?

A: One of the reasons is racism itself. We don't have means of communication in our hands. The media and politics have never allowed our people to speak through them. The absolute marginalization of the indigenous peoples is a fact, as is sophisticated militarization. These have been the most significant ingredients in the silent war. . . .

Q: In your opinion, how can the international community contribute to peace in Guatemala?

A: The inaction of the international community towards Guatemala is injustifiable. The community should play an active role with concrete measures and sanctions imposed, as was the case in South Africa, Iraq, Yugoslavia, Cuba and Haiti. Why for us no? Why legalize death in one place and somewhere else no? This is clear in our memories.

Q: Many of your countrymen speak of a culture of violence and death in Guatemala. Do you share this interpretation?

A: The culture of death is imposed by economic and political interests, the arrogance of power, corruption. I blame the first world for having taken our riches for so many years. I am speaking of the superpowers that dominate the life of the world. More concretely, the World Bank, the IMF.

Those that have caused and tolerated the death of our people, those responsible for the plundering of the third world. Silence is also part of repression.

. . . The gap between rich and poor must be eliminated, or we will continue to be the example of conflict in America.

22. Foreign Ministers of the Americas: Diversity and Civil Society in the FTAA, 2003

Source: Ministerial Declaration of the Eight Ministerial Meeting of the Free Trade Area of the Americas, Miami, November 20, 2003, at www.ftaa-alca.org.

INTRODUCTION

1. We, the Ministers Responsible for Trade in the Hemisphere, representing the 34 countries participating in the negotiations of the Free Trade Area of the Americas (FTAA) held our Eighth Ministerial Meeting in Miami, United States of America, on November 20–21, 2003, in order to provide guidance for the final phase of the FTAA negotiations.

2. We recognize the significant contribution that economic integration, including the FTAA, will make to the attainment of the objectives established in the Summit of the Americas process: strengthening democracy, creating prosperity and realizing human potential. We reiterate that the negotiation of the FTAA will continue to take into account the broad social and economic agenda contained in the Miami, Santiago and Quebec City Declarations and Plans of Action with a view to contributing to raising living standards, increasing employment, improving the working conditions of all people in the Americas, strengthening social dialogue and social protection, improving the levels of health and education and better protecting the environment. We reaffirm the need to respect and value cultural diversity as set forth in the 2001 Summit of the Americas Declaration and Plan of Action.

3. We reiterate that the FTAA can co-exist with bilateral and subregional agreements, to the extent that the rights and obligations under these agreements are not covered by or go beyond the rights and obligations of the FTAA. We also reaffirm that the FTAA will be consistent with the rules and disciplines of the World Trade Organization (WTO).

4. Commitments assumed by the countries of the FTAA must be consistent with the principles of the sovereignty of States and the respective constitutional texts.

The Vision of the FTAA

5. We, the Ministers, reaffirm our commitment to the successful conclusion of the FTAA negotiations by January 2005*, [*Venezuela reiterates its reservation expressed in the Quebec City Declaration, with respect to the entry into force of the FTAA in 2005.] with the ultimate goal of achiev-

ing an area of free trade and regional integration. The Ministers reaffirm their commitment to a comprehensive and balanced FTAA that will most effectively foster economic growth, the reduction of poverty, development, and integration through trade liberalization. Ministers also recognize the need for flexibility to take into account the needs and sensitivities of all FTAA partners.

6. We are mindful that negotiations must aim at a balanced agreement that addresses the issue of differences in the levels of development and size of economies of the hemisphere, through various provisions and mechanisms.

7. Taking into account and acknowledging existing mandates, Ministers recognize that countries may assume different levels of commitments. We will seek to develop a common and balanced set of rights and obligations applicable to all countries. In addition, negotiations should allow for countries that so choose, within the FTAA, to agree to additional obligations and benefits. One possible course of action would be for these countries to conduct plurilateral negotiations within the FTAA to define the obligations in the respective individual areas. . . .

14. We acknowledge the differences in the levels of development and size of economies in the hemisphere and the importance of all the countries participating in the FTAA to attain economic growth, improved quality of life for their people, and balanced and sustained social and economic development for all its participants. We therefore reaffirm our commitment to take into account in designing the FTAA, the differences in levels of development and size of economies in the hemisphere to create opportunities for their full participation and increase their level of development. We will establish mechanisms that complement and enhance the measures that address differences in the level of development and size of economies, in particular smaller economies, in order to facilitate the implementation of the Agreement and to maximize the benefits that can be derived from the FTAA. Such measures shall include but not be limited to technical assistance and transitional measures including longer adjustment periods. . . .

26. We appreciate the views that various sectors of civil society have provided us in the last year and a half and especially in parallel to the Mexico and San Salvador Vice Ministerial meetings. We appreciate the recommendations made by the Eighth Americas Business Forum and the First Americas Trade and Sustainable Development Forum, organized with a broad representation of civil society, and with whom we met here in Miami, Florida. We encourage the holding of similar events organized parallel to all Ministerial and Vice Ministerial meetings and recommend that they include broad representation from civil society. We also take note of the regional seminar on the FTAA held by the Andean Community in Lima, Peru. The views expressed at these events constitute a valuable contribution to the

negotiations, and we urge civil society to continue to make contributions in a constructive manner. . . .

23. Jean-Bertrand Aristide: Democracy, Poverty, and Women's Activism, 1996

Source: Address by Jean-Bertrand Aristide, September 19, 1996, from Third World Network Features, Novib Nework, and PeaceNet.

If someone had suggested 15 years ago that by 1996 democracy would be the rule rather than the exception in Latin America, most of us would not have believed him. . . .

Ironically, these transitions towards democracy have coincided with the most severe economic crisis of the century in the countries of the South. . . . The gap between the world's richest and the world's poorest grows every day, with the richest 20% of the world's population now absorbing 85% of global income, while the poorest 20% receive only 1.4%.

What does the triumph of democracy mean to the poorest 20%? . . . Elections may be held once every four or five years, but the day-to-day participation by the population in the decision-making process necessary to focus state policies on poverty alleviation, may never materialize.

. . . Those of us who work alongside the poor, know that even in countries suffering the severest economic crises, like Haiti, people's organizations represent a vibrant and growing force for change. These organizations offer the seeds of hope for the 21st century. Throughout the world, local church communities, peasant organizations, women's groups, grassroots environmental organizations and NGOs are struggling for human and economic rights. Their analysis and convictions are rooted in the day-to-day reality of the poor. These actors are undertaking the task of democratizing democracy: turning formal democracies into living, participatory ones. These actors are holding up alternative economic models, and offering an ethical foundation for debates on economic growth and human development.

The role of civil society has never been more critical. We must be the conscience of our age, articulating a view of development which places the human being at its center, sees economic growth as a means to human development rather than an end in itself, and advocates development which our planet can sustain. As others have remarked, unrestrained growth is the ideology of the cancer cell.

As the state grows weaker, and the price of globalization becomes more apparent, there are growing voices from civil society which testify to these realities. They have an increasing influence on international institutions and, perhaps more importantly, they are making contacts and forming alliances across borders - knowing that in an age when capital needs no visa or passport, so too must solidarity know no borders.

One of the defining characteristics of civil society is the high percentage of women participating. Bearing witness against human rights abuses, organizing cooperatives, creating community health projects—women have long filled the ranks of people's organizations. However, this degree of participation is not at all reflected in the number of women involved in decision-making at all levels. World-wide, women hold only 12% of all the seats in parliament, and 6% of those in national cabinets.

By definition, democratizing democracy means both empowering the large number of women who are already participating through civil organizations, and increasing their representation at the tables of power.

We will all benefit from this. Studies have shown that when the household income is managed by women, it is more likely to be used for human development purposes: health care, education and children's nutrition. I suspect that if national budgets were in the hands of women, or if grassroots women's organizations were to participate in preparing national budgets, the results would be the same. On the economic front, civil groups are taking the lead in addressing inequitable land distribution, giving the poor access to credit, and building cooperative economic structures.

. . . You and I, as citizens of the world committed to fighting poverty, should tend these seeds where we find them, shelter them when hostile and changing conditions threaten their very existence, and plant them in other places where they may take root and bear fruit to nourish the world. As we are nourished today by the fruits of solidarity and hope.

NOTES

Introduction

1. For the 1945 numbers, Norris B. Lyle and Richard Calman, ed. and comp., *Statistical Abstract of Latin America 1965,* 9th ed. (Los Angeles: UCLA Latin American Center, 1966), table 4; for 2005, UN Economic Commission for Latin America and the Caribbean, *Demographic Bulletin,* no. 69, *Latin America and Caribbean: Population Estimates and Projections. 1950–2050,* 37–38.

2. Walter LaFeber, *The American Age: United States Foreign Policy at Home and Abroad Since 1750,* 2nd ed. (New York: W. W. Norton, 1994), 83.

3. Cited in George Kennan, "Latin America as a Problem in United States Foreign Policy," in *Neighborly Adversaries: Readings in U.S.–Latin American Relations,* eds. Michael LaRosa and Frank Mora (Lanham, Md.: Rowman & Littlefield, 1999), 184.

4. Dexter Perkins, "The Monroe Doctrine, 1823–1826," in *Neighborly Adversaries,* eds. LaRosa and Mora, 75.

5. Francis Gregory cited in Frederick Pike, *The United States and Latin America: Myths and Stereotypes of Civilization and Nature* (Austin: University of Texas Press, 1992), 81.

6. Cited in Lars Schoultz, *Beneath the United States: A History of U.S. Policy Toward Latin America* (Cambridge, Mass.: Harvard University Press, 1998), 5.

7. Reverend Jedediah Morse's textbook cited in George Black, *The Good Neighbor: How the United States Wrote the History of Central America and the Caribbean* (New York: Pantheon, 1988), 11.

8. Telésforo de Orea in Judith Ewell, *Venezuela and the United States: From Monroe's Hemisphere to Petroleum's Empire* (Athens: University of Georgia Press, 1996), 20.

9. Simón Bolívar in Ewell, *Venezuela,* 31–32.

10. Simón Bolívar in Piero Gleijeses, "The Limits of Sympathy: The

179

United States and the Independence of Spanish America," *Journal of Latin American Studies* 24 (October 1992): 487.

11. Pike, *Myths and Stereotypes,* 137.

12. Capt. Lemuel Ford, Josiah Royce, anonymous traveler, and Harry Frank cited in ibid., 100, 50, 51, 71.

13. Joel Roberts Poinsett cited in Schoultz, *Beneath the United States,* 19.

14. Edward Hannegan in Thomas Hietala, *Manifest Design: Anxious Aggrandizement in Late Jacksonian America* (Ithaca, N.Y.: Cornell University Press, 1985), 156.

15. Cited in Schoultz, *Beneath the United States,* 64.

16. Ibid., 84.

17. Mira Wilkins, *The Emergence of Multinational Enterprise: American Business Abroad From the Colonial Era to 1914* (Cambridge, Mass.: Harvard University Press, 1970), 113.

18. F. Toscano and James Hiester, *Anti-Yankee Feelings in Latin America: An Anthology of Latin American Writings From Colonial to Modern Times in Their Historical Perspective* (Washington, D.C.: University Press of America, 1982), 17.

19. James G. Blaine, *New York Tribune,* August 30, 1890, 1.

20. U.S. Department of State, *Foreign Relations of the United States, 1893–1897* (Washington, D.C.: USGPO, 1896), vol. 1, 545–562.

21. Cited in Schoultz, *Beneath the United States,* 177.

22. William Jennings Bryan in Black, *Good Neighbor,* 14.

23. Cited in David Schmitz, *Thank God They're on Our Side: The United States and Right-Wing Dictatorships, 1921–1965* (Chapel Hill: University of North Carolina Press, 1999), 52.

24. John Britton, preface to *Radical Journalists, Generalist Intellectuals, and U.S.–Latin American Relations,* by Virginia Williams (Lewiston, N.Y.: Edwin Mellen Press, 2001), i; Thomas O'Brien, *The Revolutionary Mission: American Enterprise in Latin America, 1900–1945* (Cambridge, UK: Cambridge University Press, 1996), 33.

25. Ibid.

26. Theodore Roosevelt in Donald Marquand Dozer, *Are We Good Neighbors?* (Gainesville: University of Florida Press, 1959), 9.

27. Cited in Peter Smith, *Talons of the Eagle: Dynamics of U.S.–Latin American Relations* (New York: Oxford University Press, 1996), 87.

28. Schoultz, *Beneath the United States,* 313.

29. Cited in Black, *Good Neighbor,* 75.

30. Max Paul Friedman, *Nazis and Good Neighbors: The United States' Campaign Against the Germans of Latin America in World War II* (Cambridge, UK: Cambridge University Press, 2003).

31. David Lorey, ed., *United States–Mexico Border Statistics: Since 1990* (Los Angeles: UCLA Latin American Center Publications, 1990), table 717; Roberto Suro, *Strangers Among Us: Latino Lives in a Changing America* (New York: Vintage, 1999), 20.

32. Arthur P. Whitaker, *The Western Hemisphere Idea: Its Rise and Decline* (Ithaca, N.Y.: Cornell University Press, 1954), 5.

33. Cited in Pike, *Myths and Stereotypes,* 273.

Chapter 1

1. Julio Moreno, *Yankee Don't Go Home! Mexican Nationalism, American Business Culture, and the Shaping of Modern Mexico, 1920–1950* (Chapel Hill: University of North Carolina Press, 2003), 172–174.

2. Smith, *Talons,* 123.

3. Kyle Longley, *In the Eagle's Shadow: The United States and Latin America* (Wheeling, Ill.: Harlan-Davidson, 2002), 188.

4. Gaddis Smith, *The Last Years of the Monroe Doctrine, 1945–1993* (New York: Hill and Wang, 1994), 55.

5. Smith, *Talons,* 124.

6. Louis Halle (a.k.a. "Y"), "On a Certain Impatience With Latin America," *Foreign Affairs* 28 (July 1950): 568, 569.

7. Dulles telephone conversation in Schoultz, *Beneath the United States,* 336.

8. Greg Grandin, *The Last Colonial Massacre: Latin America in the Cold War* (Chicago: University of Chicago Press, 2004), especially the introduction and conclusion.

9. Cited in Leslie Bethell and Ian Roxborough, "Introduction: The Postwar Conjuncture in Latin America: Democracy, Labor, and the Left," in *Latin America Between the Second World War and the Cold War, 1944–1948,* eds. Bethell and Roxborough (Cambridge, UK: Cambridge University Press, 1992), 24.

10. Cited in Schoultz, *Beneath the United States,* 332–333.

11. Bethell and Roxborough, "Postwar Conjuncture in Latin America," 22.

12. Article 19 of the UN Charter, http://www.oas.org/juridico/english/charter.html (last visited June 6, 2005).

13. Roger Trask, "The Impact of the Cold War on United States–Latin American Relations, 1945–1949," *Diplomatic History* 1 (Summer 1977): 280; Policy Planning Staff 26 in Schoultz, *Beneath the United States,* 333.

14. Cited in Schmitz, *Thank God They're on Our Side,* 148, 149.

15. Roger Trask, "George F. Kennan's Report on Latin America (1950)," *Diplomatic History* 2 (Summer 1978): 308.

16. Cited in Walter LaFeber, *Inevitable Revolutions: The United States in Central America* (New York: W. W. Norton, 1993), 109.

17. Cited in Schmitz, *Thank God They're on Our Side,* 146.

18. Molly Todd, "Raising the National Conscience: Grassroots Organizing and the Debates Over the U.S. Army School of the Americas," in *The Globalization of U.S.–Latin American Relations: Democracy, Intervention, and Human Rights,* ed. Virginia Bouvier (Westport, Conn.: Praeger, 2002), 121–148.

19. Abraham Lowenthal, "Changing U.S. Interests and Policies in a New World," in *The United States and Latin America in the 1990s: Beyond the*

Cold War, eds. Jonathan Hartlyn, Lars Schoultz, and August Varas (Chapel Hill: University of North Carolina Press, 1992), 69.

20. Lyle and Calman, *Statistical Abstract of Latin America 1965,* table 93.

21. Stephen Rabe, *Eisenhower and Latin America: The Foreign Policy of Anticommunism* (Chapel Hill: University of North Carolina Press, 1988), 5.

22. Roy Rubottom Jr., "Toward Better Understanding Between United States and Latin America," *The Annals of the American Academy of Political and Social Science* 330 (July 1960): 117.

23. Mark Gilderhus, *The Second Century: U.S.–Latin American Relations Since 1889* (Wilmington, Del.: Scholarly Resources, 2000), 153.

24. C. Neale Ronning, "Adolf Berle in Brazil: 1945–46," in *Ambassadors in Foreign Policy: The Influence of Individuals on U.S.–Latin American Policy,* eds. Ronning and Albert Vannucci (Westport, Conn.: Praeger, 1987), 74.

25. Robert H. Swansbrough, *The Embattled Colossus: Economic Nationalism and United States Investors in Latin America* (Gainesville: University Press of Florida, 1976), 57.

26. Ibid., 57, 76.

27. Longley, *Eagle's Shadow,* 194.

28. Spruille Braden in Albert Vannucci, "Elected by Providence: Spruille Braden in Argentina in 1945," in *Ambassadors in Foreign Policy,* eds. Ronning and Vannucci, 58. See also Steven Schwartzberg, *Democracy and U.S. Policy in Latin America During the Truman Years* (Gainesville: University Press of Florida, 2003).

29. Walter LaFeber, "Thomas C. Mann and the Devolution of Latin American Policy: From the Good Neighbor to Military Intervention," in *Behind the Throne: Servants of Power to Imperial Presidents, 1898–1968,* eds. Thomas McCormick and LaFeber (Madison: University of Wisconsin Press, 1993), 169.

30. Juan González, *Harvest of Empire: A History of Latinos in America* (New York: Penguin, 2000), 81.

31. Mariano Picón-Salas in Lester Langley, *America and the Americas: The United States in the Western Hemisphere* (Athens: University of Georgia Press, 1989), 184.

32. Laura Briggs, *Reproducing Empire: Race, Sex, Science, and U.S. Imperialism in Puerto Rico* (Berkeley: University of California Press, 2002).

33. Cited in Guillermo de la Peña, "Rural Mobilizations in Latin America Since 1930," in *Latin America: Politics and Society Since 1930,* eds. Leslie Bethell and Ian Roxborough (Cambridge, UK: Cambridge University Press, 1998), 339.

34. Recorded by Kay Kyser and his orchestra and cited in Black, *Good Neighbor,* 91.

35. Lorey, *Border Statistics,* table 1801.

36. All quotations from Ralph Beals, "The Mexican Student Views the United States," *The Annals of the American Academy of Political and Social Science* 295 (September 1954): 108–109.

37. Lyle and Calman, *Statistical Abstract of Latin America 1965,* table 30.

38. 1956 USIA Barometer Study on Public Opinion cited in Seth Fein, "New Empire Into Old: Making Mexican Newsreels the Cold War Way," *Diplomatic History* 28 (Fall 2004): 712.

39. Cited in Schmitz, *Thank God They're on Our Side*, 194.

40. Fein, "New Empire Into Old," 703–748.

41. John Foster Dulles in Smith, *Talons*, 131.

42. Jules Benjamin, "The Framework of U.S. Relations With Latin America in the Twentieth Century: An Interpretive Essay," *Diplomatic History* 11 (Spring 1987): 106.

43. Cited in Schoultz, *Beneath the United States*, 336.

44. Cited in Smith, Talons, 133.

45. Pan-American Union, *Foreign Trade of Latin America Since 1913;* LaFeber, *Inevitable Revolutions*, 117.

46. Cited in Stephen Schlesinger and Stephen Kinzer, *Bitter Fruit: The Untold Story of the American Coup in Guatemala* (New York: Doubleday, 1983), 52; Schmitz, *Thank God They're on Our Side*, 193.

47. Schoultz, *Beneath the United States*, 337.

48. Schlesinger and Kinzer, *Bitter Fruit*, 75.

49. Cited in ibid., 143.

50. Cited in ibid., 199.

51. John Foster Dulles in Schoultz, *Beneath the United States*, 337; José Manuel Fortuny in Piero Gleijeses, *Shattered Hope: The Guatemalan Revolution and the United States, 1944–1954* (Princeton, N.J.: Princeton University Press, 1991), 4.

52. Alfredo Cucul in Grandin, *Last Colonial Massacre*, 48.

53. John Peurifoy to the State Department, December 17, 1953, from U.S. Department of State, *Foreign Relations of the United States, 1952–1954* (Washington, D.C.: USGPO, 1983), vol. 4, http://www.state.gov/r/pa/ho/frus/ike/iv/20210.htm (last visited June 6, 2005).

54. LaFeber, *Inevitable Revolutions*, 124.

55. Richard M. Bissell Jr., *Reflections of a Cold Warrior*, with Jonathan Lewis and Frances T. Pudlo (New Haven, Conn.: Yale University Press, 1996), 86–87.

56. Cited in Schlesinger and Kinzer, *Bitter Fruit*, 13.

57. Schmitz, *Thank God They're on Our Side*, 196.

58. Longley, *Eagle's Shadow*, 219; González, *Harvest of Empire*, 137.

59. Louis Pérez Jr., *Cuba: Between Reform and Rebellion*, 2nd ed. (New York: Oxford, 1995), 296.

60. Gilderhus, *Second Century*, 165.

61. Arthur M. Schlesinger Jr., *A Thousand Days: John F. Kennedy in the White House* (Boston: Houghton Mifflin, 1965), 173.

62. Cited in Grandin, *Last Colonial Massacre*, 175.

63. Stephen G. Rabe, "The Caribbean Triangle: Betancourt, Castro, and Trujillo and U.S. Foreign Policy, 1958–1963," *Diplomatic History* 20 (Winter 1996): 61.

64. Milton Eisenhower, *The Wine Is Bitter* (Garden City, N.Y.: Doubleday, 1963), xi.

65. Unattributed quotation from William Hines, "The Venezuela Story," *Washington Evening Star*, May 25, 1958, A-1.

66. Richard Nixon, *Six Crises* (orig. 1962; New York: Warner Books, 1979), 256–257.

67. Smith, *Talons*, 148.

68. Cited in Michael Gambone, *Capturing the Revolution: The United States, Central America, and Nicaragua, 1961–1972* (Westport, Conn.: Praeger, 2001), 22.

Chapter 2

1. "Bolivia: The Fanned Spark," *Time,* March 16, 1959, 10. Memorandum of Christian Herter telephone conversation with Allen Grover of Time-Life, folder March 59 (4), box 7, Chron. File, Herter Papers, Eisenhower Library, Abilene, Kans.

2. Stephen Rabe, *The Most Dangerous Area in the World: John F. Kennedy Confronts Communist Revolution in Latin America* (Chapel Hill: University of North Carolina Press, 1999); Khrushchev in LaFeber, *Inevitable Revolutions,* 147.

3. Antonio Nuñez Jiménez, *La liberación de las islas* (Havana: Editorial Lex, 1959), n. p.

4. Pérez, *Cuba,* 319–320.

5. Ibid., 335.

6. *El Mundo* (Havana), April 23, 1959, A-6.

7. Brenda Gayle Plummer, "Castro in Harlem: A Cold War Watershed," in *Rethinking the Cold War,* ed. Allen Hunter (Philadelphia: Temple University Press, 1998), 133–153.

8. Richard Goodwin, *Remembering America: A Voice From the Sixties* (Boston: Little, Brown, and Company, 1988), 147.

9. Rabe, *Most Dangerous Area,* 2.

10. Jules Benjamin, "The Framework of U.S. Relations With Latin America in the Twentieth Century: An Interpretive Essay," *Diplomatic History* 11 (Spring 1987): 91–112.

11. Edwin McCammon Martin, *Kennedy and Latin America* (Lanham, Md.: University Press of America, 1994), 187.

12. Arthur Schlesinger to John F. Kennedy, cited in Schmitz, *Thank God They're on Our Side,* 241.

13. Jerome Levinson and Juan de Onís, *The Alliance That Lost Its Way: A Critical Report on the Alliance for Progress* (Chicago: Quadrangle Books, 1970): 11, 59–73; Rabe, *Most Dangerous Area,* 2.

14. Smith, *Talons,* 151.

15. Langley, *America and the Americas,* 201.

16. Rabe, *Most Dangerous Area,* 155.

17. Smith, *Talons,* 152; LaFeber, *Inevitable Revolutions,* 194; Rabe, *Most Dangerous Area,* 149.

18. Longley, *Eagle's Shadow,* 246.

19. Swansbrough, *Embattled Colossus,* 44.

20. Joseph Tulchin, "The United States and Latin America in the 1960s," *Journal of Inter-American Studies and World Affairs* 30 (Spring 1988): 19.

21. Kennedy speech at the White House, *Public Papers of the President, 1962* (Washington, D.C.: USGPO, 1963), 223.

22. Tulchin, "United States," 20.

23. Bissell, *Reflections of a Cold Warrior,* 153.

24. Langley, *America and the Americas,* 195.

25. Unattributed quotation in Wayne Smith, *The Closest of Enemies: A Personal and Diplomatic Account of U.S.-Cuban Relations Since 1957* (New York: W. W. Norton, 1987), 63.

26. Don Coerver and Linda Hall, *Tangled Destinies: Latin America and the United States* (Albuquerque: University of New Mexico Press, 1999), 125.

27. Bobby Kennedy in Richard Welch Jr., *Response to Revolution: The United States and the Cuban Revolution, 1959–1961* (Chapel Hill: University of North Carolina Press, 1985), 98.

28. Roberto Campos in Samuel Baily, *The United States and the Development of South America, 1945–1975* (New York: New Viewpoints, 1976), 98.

29. McGeorge Bundy in Ernest May and Philip Zelikow, eds., *The Kennedy Tapes: Inside the White House During the Cuban Missile Crisis* (Cambridge, Mass.: Harvard University Press, 1997), 46.

30. Robert F. Kennedy, *Thirteen Days: A Memoir of the Cuban Missile Crisis* (orig. 1968; New York: W. W. Norton, 1999), 25.

31. Arthur Schlesinger Jr., foreword to ibid., 8.

32. Thomas Blanton, director of the National Security Archive, in *Boston Globe,* December 13, 2002; Fidel Castro in James Blight and Philip Brenner, *Sad and Luminous Days: Cuba's Struggle With the Superpowers After the Missile Crisis* (Lanham, Md.: Rowman & Littlefield, 2002), xv.

33. Fidel Castro in ibid., 25.

34. Ibid., 84–85.

35. *Democracy Now!* radio broadcast, June 8, 2004, at www.democracynow.org (last visited June 11, 2004).

36. Longley, *Eagle's Shadow,* 244; Martha Huggins, *Political Policing: The United States and Latin America* (Durham, N.C.: Duke University Press, 1998), 108.

37. Schoultz, *Beneath the United States,* 360.

38. Rabe, *Most Dangerous Area,* 131.

39. Huggins, *Political Policing,* 108.

40. Cited in Robert Dallek, *Flawed Giant: Lyndon Johnson and His Times, 1961–1973* (New York: Oxford University Press, 1998), 91.

41. "Army Guards Canal Zone Border," *Panama American,* November 4, 1959, 10.

42. Recording of telephone conversation between Lyndon Johnson and Georgia Senator Richard Russell, January 10, 1964, tape WH6401.11, Johnson Library, Austin, Tex.

43. Carlos Guevara Mann, *Panamanian Militarism: A Historical Interpre-*

tation (Athens: Ohio University Center for International Studies, 1996), 88.

44. Levinson and De Onís, *Alliance,* 10.

45. William Stokes, "Economic Anti-Americanism in Latin America," *Inter-American Economic Affairs* 11 (Autumn 1957): 14.

46. Rabe, *Most Dangerous Area,* 69.

47. Recording of telephone conversation between Lyndon Johnson and Undersecretary of State George Ball, March 31, 1964, www2.gwu.edu/ ~nsarchiv/NSAEBB/NSAEBB118/index.htm (last visited January 14, 2005).

48. Gilderhus, *Second Century,* 188–189; Langley, *America and the Americas,* 206.

49. Rabe, *Most Dangerous Area,* 35.

50. Rabe, "Caribbean Triangle," 55–78; Rabe, *Most Dangerous Area,* 35–39.

51. Schmitz, *Thank God They're on Our Side,* 229.

52. Recording of telephone conversation between Robert McNamara and Lyndon Johnson, April 30, 1965, WH6504.09, Johnson Library, Austin, Tex.

53. Che Guevara in John Martz, "Doctrine and Dilemmas of the Latin American 'New Left,'" *World Politics* 22 (January 1970): 181.

54. Fidel Castro in ibid., 171.

55. Timothy Wickham-Crowley, *Guerrillas and Revolution in Latin America: A Comparative Study of Insurgents and Regimes Since 1956* (Princeton, N.J.: Princeton University Press, 1992), 86.

56. Ernesto Chávez, *"¡Mi Raza Primero!" Nationalism, Identity, and Insurgency in the Chicano Movement in Los Angeles, 1966–1978* (Berkeley: University of California Press, 2002), 56.

57. Robert Kumamoto, "International Terrorism and American Foreign Relations, 1945–1976" (PhD diss., UCLA, 1984), 1–2.

58. Swansbrough, *Embattled Colossus,* 155–169, 207.

Chapter 3

1. Kevin Middlebrook and Carlos Rico, "The United States and Latin America in the 1980s: Change, Complexity, and Contending Perspectives," in *The United States and Latin America in the 1980s: Contending Perspectives on a Decade of Crisis,* eds. Middlebrook and Rico (Pittsburgh, Penn.: University of Pittsburgh Press, 1986), 8–13.

2. Ibid., 15.

3. Lorey, *Border Statistics,* table 1500.

4. Helson C. Braga, "Prospects for Free Zones Under FTAA," presented at the Integration in the Americas Conference, April 2, 2002, http:/ /laii.unm.edu/conference/braga.php (last visited October 1, 2004).

5. Lorey, *Border Statistics,* table 709.

6. González, *Harvest of Empire,* 238.

7. The exchange is in Seymour Hersh, *The Price of Power: Kissinger in the*

Nixon White House (New York: Summit Books, 1983), 263.

8. Nixon cited in memorandum of conversation, White House, "NSC Meeting—Chile (NSSM 97)," November 6, 1970, reproduced in Peter Kornbluh, *The Pinochet File: A Declassified Dossier on Atrocity and Accountability* (New York: New Press, 2003), chap. 2, doc. 1.

9. Langley, *America and the Americas,* 219.

10. Nelson Rockefeller, The Rockefe*ller Report on the Americas: The Official Report of a United States Presidential Mission for the Western Hemisphere,* New York Times edition (Chicago: Quadrangle Books, 1969), 32–33.

11. Nixon speech, October 31, 1969, in the appendix to Rockefeller, *Rockefeller Report, Latin American Digest* 4 (November 1969): 9.

12. Eduardo Frei, "The Alliance That Lost Its Way," *Foreign Affairs* 45 (April 1967): 428–448.

13. Marc Cooper, "Remembering Allende," *The Nation,* September 29, 2003, 23–24.

14. Charles E. Radford cited in Hersh, *Price of Power,* 259.

15. Roger Morris cited in ibid., 270.

16. Cited in Peter Kornbluh, "Chile, 9/11/73," *The Nation,* September 29, 2003, 22.

17. Henry Kissinger cited in Kornbluh, *Pinochet File,* xiii.

18. CIA, Richard Helms's handwritten notes, "Meeting With the President on Chile at 1525," September 15, 1970, reproduced in ibid., chap. 1, doc. 1.

19. CIA memorandum, September 16, 1970, reproduced in ibid., chap. 1, doc. 2; Nixon cited on 25.

20. Viron Vaky to Henry Kissinger, NSC Action Memo, September 14, 1970, cited in ibid., 13.

21. Peter Kornbluh, "The *El Mercurio* File," *Columbia Journalism Review,* September–October 2003, at www.cjr.org/issues/2003/5/chile-kornbluh.asp (last visited September 5, 2005).

22. Jonathan Goldberg, "Hit Records: The 30th Anniversary of the Chilean Coup, Now-Declassified Documents and the Specter of U.S. Culpability That Won't Go Away," *The American Prospect,* September 2003, at www.prospect.org (last visited December 20, 2004).

23. Kornbluh, *Pinochet File,* 33–34.

24. Paul Sigmund, *The United States and Democracy in Chile* (Baltimore, Md.: Johns Hopkins University, 1993), 61.

25. Nixon cited in memorandum of conversation, White House, "NSC Meeting—Chile (NSSM 97)," November 6, 1970, reproduced in Kornbluh, *Pinochet File,* chap. 2, doc. 1.

26. Smith, *Talons,* 175.

27. Sigmund, *Chile,* 57.

28. William Colby to Henry Kissinger, "CIA's Covert Action Program in Chile Since 1970," September 13, 1973, reproduced in Kornbluh, *Pinochet File,* chap. 2, doc. 18.

29. Ibid., 105–112.

30. Cited in Smith, *Talons,* 201.

31. Cited in Kornbluh, "Chile, 9/11/73," 22.

32. Schoultz, *Beneath the United States,* 360–361.

33. Scott Sherman, "Kissinger's Shadow Over the Council on Foreign Relations," *The Nation,* December 27, 2004, 20–24. Kenneth Maxwell was the editor muscled out, and the book in question was Peter Kornbluh's *Pinochet File.*

34. Kathryn Sikkink, *Mixed Signals: U.S. Human Rights Policy and Latin America* (Ithaca, N.Y.: Cornell University Press, 2004), xiv.

35. Cited in Smith, *Talons,* 203.

36. Tom Harkin in Schoultz, *Beneath the United States,* 363.

37. Sikkink, *Mixed Signals,* 118.

38. Ibid., 130–137.

39. Cited in Gaddis Smith, *Morality, Reason, and Power: American Diplomacy in the Carter Years* (New York: Hill and Wang, 1986), 113.

40. Cited in ibid., 112.

41. Cited in Michael Conniff, *Panama and the United States: The Forced Alliance* (Athens: University of Georgia Press, 1992), 134.

42. John Booth, "Socioeconomic and Political Roots of National Revolts in Central America," *Latin American Research Review* 26 (1991): 38.

43. Ibid., 39.

44. Cited in Clifford Krauss, "Their Bible Is the Bible: Religious Roots of Rebellion in El Salvador," *The Nation,* July 3, 1982, 7.

45. Booth, "Socioeconomic and Political Roots," 43.

46. Karl Bermann, *Under the Big Stick: Nicaragua and the United States Since 1848* (Boston: South End Press, 1986), 267.

47. Bernard Diederich, *Somoza and the Legacy of U.S. Involvement in Central America* (New York: E. P. Dutton, 1981), 93, 100.

48. Bermann, *Under the Big Stick,* 256, 267.

49. Booth, "Socioeconomic and Political Roots," 39; Thomas Walker, "The Sandinist Victory in Nicaragua," *Current History* 78 (February 1980): 59–60.

50. Cited in William LeoGrande, *Our Own Backyard: The United States in Central America, 1977–1992* (Chapel Hill: University of North Carolina Press, 1998), 30, 25.

51. Longley, *Eagle's Shadow,* 281.

52. LaFeber, *Inevitable Revolutions,* 230.

53. Longley, *Eagle's Shadow,* 281.

54. Walter LaFeber, "Inevitable Revolutions," *Atlantic Monthly,* June 1982, 80.

55. Booth, "Socioeconomic and Political Roots," 44.

56. LeoGrande, *Our Own Backyard,* 34; J. Blachman and Kenneth Sharpe, "El Salvador: the Policy That Failed," in *From Gunboats to Diplomacy: New U.S. Policies for Latin America,* ed. Richard Newfarmer (Baltimore, Md.: Johns Hopkins University Press, 1984), 73.

57. John Dear, "Oscar Romero, Presente!" March 24, 2005, Common Dreams NewsCenter, www.commondreams.org. (last visited September 5, 2005).

58. Cited in Krauss, "Their Bible Is the Bible," 10, 8.

59. Longley, *Eagle's Shadow,* 292.

60. Jacobo Timerman cited in Sikkink, *Mixed Signals,* xx.

Chapter 4

1. Citations from Lou Cannon, *President Reagan: The Role of a Lifetime* (New York: Public Affairs, 2000), 405.

2. "National Security Council Document on Central America and Cuba," reproduced in *New York Times,* April 7, 1983, A16.

3. Republican National Convention, "Republican Party Platform of 1980," July 15, 1980, http://www.presidency.ucsb.edu/showplatforms.php?platindex=R1980 (last visited June 3, 2005).

4. LeoGrande, *Our Own Backyard,* 82.

5. Louis A. Pérez Jr., "Armies of the Caribbean: Historical Perspectives, Historiographical Trends," *Latin American Perspectives* 14 (December 1987): 499.

6. Alexander Haig cited in LaFeber, *Inevitable Revolutions,* 280.

7. LeoGrande, *Our Own Backyard,* 201.

8. Cited in Peter Wall, "Negroponte, Honduras, and Iraq," July 9, 2004, http://www.globalpolicy.org/security/issues/iraq/leaders/2004/0709negroponte.htm (last visited June 1, 2005).

9. Cynthia Brown, ed., *With Friends Like These: The Americas Watch Report on Human Rights and U.S. Policy in Latin America* (New York: Pantheon, 1985), 3.

10. Committee of Santa Fe, *A New Inter-American Policy for the Eighties* (Washington, D.C.: Council for Inter-American Security, 1980), 20, 25, 45.

11. "Journalist Allan Nairn: Reagan Was Behind 'One of the Most Intensive Campaigns of Mass Murder in Recent History,'" *Democracy Now!* radio broadcast, June 8, 2004, at www.democracynow.org (last visited June 11, 2004).

12. Title 10 of the U.S. Code, section 4415, in Todd, "Raising the National Conscience," 121.

13. Ibid., 125.

14. John Dinges, *Our Man in Panama: How General Noriega Used the United States—and Made Millions in Drugs and Arms* (New York: Random House, 1990), 148.

15. Todd, "Raising the National Conscience," 125.

16. Ibid., 128.

17. Ronald Reagan, "Address to the Nation on Lebanon and Grenada," White House, October 27, 1983, http://cgi.cnn.com/SPECIALS/2004/reagan/stories/speech.archive/lebgre.html (last visited June 6, 2005).

18. LaFeber, "Inevitable Revolutions," *Atlantic Monthly,* 81; Gilderhus, *Second Century,* 225.

19. Coerver and Hall, *Tangled Destinies,* 154.

20. Alexander Haig and Ronald Reagan in Brown, *With Friends Like These,* 119, 115.

21. Todd, "Raising the National Conscience," 128.

22. Robert Parry and Peter Kornbluh, "Iran-Contra's Untold Story," *Foreign Policy* 72 (Fall 1988): 7.

23. Arian Campo-Flores, "The Most Dangerous Gang in America," *Newsweek*, March 28, 2005, at www.msnbc.msn.com/id/7244879/site/newsweek (last visited September 5, 2005).

24. Coerver and Hall, *Tangled Destinies,* 206–209.

25. All in Mark Danner, *The Massacre at El Mozote: A Parable of the Cold War* (New York: Vintage, 1994), 68, 10.

26. Theodore Draper, *A Very Thin Line: The Iran-Contra Affairs* (New York: Hill and Wang, 1991), 16.

27. Ibid., 17; LaFeber, *Inevitable Revolutions,* 290.

28. Harkin cited in Longley, *Eagle's Shadow,* 298, 300.

29. Parry and Kornbluh, "Iran-Contra's Untold Story," 5–6, 17.

30. Smith, *Talons,* 183; LeoGrande, *Our Own Backyard,* 330.

31. LaFeber, *Inevitable Revolutions,* 301, 333.

32. Draper, *Very Thin Line,* 24.

33. Both in LeoGrande, *Our Own Backyard,* 362.

34. Leslie Gelb, "Pentagon Predicts Big War If Latins Sign Peace Accord," *New York Times,* May 20, 1986.

35. LeoGrande, *Our Own Backyard,* 528.

36. Carlos Fuentes, "Land of Jekyll and Hyde," *The Nation,* March 22, 1986, 337.

37. LaFeber, *Inevitable Revolutions,* 291, 295, 304.

38. Stan Greenberg cited in Eldon Kenworthy, "United States Policy in Central America," *Current History* 86 (December 1987): 402.

39. Brown, *With Friends Like These,* 233–235.

40. Longley, *Eagle's Shadow,* 302.

41. Ronald Reagan cited in Black, *Good Neighbor,* 163.

42. Smith, *Talons,* 186; Forrest D. Colburn, *The Vogue of Revolution in Poor Countries* (Princeton, N.J.: Princeton University Press, 1994), 68.

43. LeoGrande, *Our Own Backyard,* 558.

44. Terry Lynn Karl, "El Salvador's Negotiated Revolution," *Foreign Affairs* 71 (Spring 1992): 147–164.

45. Cited in LeoGrande, *Our Own Backyard,* 399–400.

46. Longley, *Eagle's Shadow,* 307; Gilderhus, *Second Century,* 231.

47. Reagan press conference, June 18, 1985, *Public Papers of the President, 1985* (Washington, D.C.: USGPO, 1986), 779; LeoGrande, *Our Own Backyard,* 402, 407, 410, 462.

48. LeoGrande, *Our Own Backyard,* 478.

49. Ibid., 479; LaFeber, *Inevitable Revolutions,* 334.

50. LeoGrande, *Our Own Backyard,* 482.

51. Longley, *Eagle's Shadow*, 307.

52. Oliver North's paraphrase of President Reagan cited in Draper, *Very Thin Line*, 548.

53. Cited in ibid., 22.

54. Lowenthal, "Changing U.S. Interests," 67; Smith, *Talons*, 241; Gilderhus, *Second Century*, 240.

55. Includes public and private debt and IMF loans. UN Economic Commission for Latin America and the Caribbean, *Statistical Yearbook for Latin America and the Caribbean 2001* (United Nations, 2002), 502; Lowenthal, "Changing U.S. Interests," 67.

56. Smith, *Talons*, 237.

57. Richard O'Brien, "External Debt and Capital Flows in Latin America," in *Contending Perspectives*, eds. Middlebrook and Rico, 201–202.

58. Ernest Duff and John McCamant, "Measuring Social and Political Requirements for System Stability in Latin America," *The American Political Science Review* 62 (December 1968): 1131–1132.

59. R. M. Koster and Guillermo Sánchez, *In the Time of the Tyrants: Panama, 1968–1990* (New York: W. W. Norton, 1990), 275.

60. Dinges, *Our Man in Panama*, 312.

61. Conniff, *Forced Alliance*, 149–152.

62. Ronald Reagan interview with European journalists, May 24, 1988, at http://www.reagan.utexas.edu/archives/speeches/1988/052488g.htm (last visited June 3, 2005).

63. Conniff, *Forced Alliance*, 163.

64. Susan Dudley Gold, *The Panama Canal Transfer: Controversy at the Crossroads* (Austin, Tex.: Raintree Steck-Vaughn, 1999), 103–105.

65. George H. W. Bush, "Iraqi Aggression in the Persian Gulf," September 11, 1990, at http://www.presidentialrhetoric.com/historicspeeches/bush/iraqiaggression.html (last visited June 11, 2005).

66. Smith, *Talons*, 231.

67. Schoultz, *Beneath the United States*, 366.

68. Robert Pastor, *Exiting the Whirlpool: U.S. Foreign Policy Toward Latin America and the Caribbean*, 2nd ed. (Boulder, Colo.: Westview, 2001), 217.

Chapter 5

1. John Williamson claimed "Washington consensus" as his in "Lula's Brazil," *Foreign Affairs* 82 (January–February 2003): 105.

2. Lowenthal, "Changing U.S. Interests," 73.

3. Carlos Lozada, "Latin America," *Foreign Policy* 135 (March–April 2003): 18; Peter Hakim and Tomas Eloy Martinez, "Is Latin America Doomed to Failure?" *Foreign Policy* 117 (Winter 1999/2000): 104–119; Jorge Domínguez, ed., *The Future of Inter-American Relations* (New York: Routledge, 2000), 6.

4. Juan González, "Fifty Years of Empty Promises," *Columbia College*

Today, http://www.college.columbia.edu/cct/dec00/dec00_forum1.html (last visited October 1, 2004).

5. González, *Harvest of Empire,* 234.

6. Moses Naím, "Latin America the Morning After," *Foreign Affairs* 74 (July 1995): 45–52.

7. David E. Lorey, *The U.S.-Mexican Border in the Twentieth Century: A History of Economic and Social Transformation* (Wilmington, Del.: Scholarly Resources, 1999): 169, 176.

8. Bouvier, *Globalization,* 5; Lorey, *U.S.-Mexican Border,* 173; Jaime Serra and J. Enrique Espinosa, "The Proof Is in the Paycheck," *Foreign Policy* 132 (September–October 2002): 58.

9. Alma Guillermoprieto, *Looking for History: Dispatches From Latin America* (New York: Vintage, 2001), 202.

10. Gary Prevost and Robert Weber, "The Prospects for the Free Trade Area of the Americas in the Bush Administration," in *Neoliberalism and Neopanamericanism: The View from Latin America,* eds. Prevost and Carlos Oliva Campos (New York: Palgrave Macmillan, 2002), 76.

11. Naomi Klein, *Fences and Windows: Dispatches From the Front Lines of the Globalization Debate* (New York: Picador USA, 2002), 65.

12. John Cavanaugh and Sarah Anderson, "A Bad Idea That Failed," *Foreign Policy* 132 (September–October 2002): 58.

13. Ralph Folsom, *NAFTA and Free Trade in the Americas in a Nutshell,* 2nd ed. (St. Paul, Minn.: West/Thompson, 2004), 17.

14. Both cited from Matthew Gutmann, "For Whom the Taco Bells Toll: Popular Responses to NAFTA South of the Border," in *Perspectives on Las Américas: A Reader in Culture, History, and Representation,* eds. Gutmann et al. (London: Blackwell Publishing, 2003), 406.

15. Guillermoprieto, *Looking for History,* 293.

16. Beatrice Edwards, "Selling Free Trade in the Americas," *NACLA Report on the Americas* 37 (March/April 2004), 8–9.

17. Cavanaugh and Anderson, "A Bad Idea That Failed," 58.

18. Gary Clyde Hufbauer et al., *NAFTA and the Environment: Seven Years Later* (Washington, D.C.: Institute for International Economics, 2000), viii.

19. In constant 1995 prices. UN ECLAC, *Statistical Yearbook 2001,* 741.

20. Sarah Anderson and John Cavanaugh, "Latin America and the World Economic Crisis," in *Globalization,* ed. Bouvier, 181. See also p. 6.

21. Lozada, "Latin America," 18.

22. Bush in Frank Bruni, "Bush Vows to Put Greater U.S. Focus on Latin America," *New York Times,* August 26, 2000, A1.

23. Naomi Klein, "Reclaiming the Commons," *New Left Review* 9 (May–June 2001): 89.

24. Cited in Tom Hayden, "Bolivia's Indian Revolt," *The Nation,* June 21, 2004, 18–22.

25. Lula in Elizabeth Johnson, "Brazil's Balancing Act," *Foreign Policy*

140 (January–February 2004): 87

26. Hugo Chávez in Christopher Marquis, "A Bitter Chávez Castigates U.S., Saying it Misjudges Him," *New York Times*, March 18, 2004, A1

27. Chávez in Richard Lapper and Andy Webb-Vidal, "As Chávez's Grip Tightens, Oil-rich Venezuela Moves Toward 'Castro Communism,'" *Financial Times,* February 6, 2003, 15.

28. Lydia Gerena Corsino in David González, "Vieques Voters Want the Navy to Leave Now," *New York Times,* July 30, 2001, A1.

29. Bush in Bruni, "Bush Vows," A1.

30. Todd, "Raising the National Conscience," 126.

31. Lorey, *U.S.-Mexican Border,* 161.

32. Julia Sweig, "What Kind of War for Colombia?" *Foreign Affairs* 81 (September–October 2002): 122.

33. Coerver and Hall, *Tangled Destinies,* 226.

34. Guillermoprieto, *Looking for History,* 28; Jaime Preciado Coronado, "The Geopolitics of the Relationship Between Mexico and the United States," with Jorge Hernández, in *Neoliberalism,* eds. Prevost and Campos, 227.

35. Mónica Serrano, "Transnational Crime in the Western Hemisphere," in *Future,* ed. Domínguez, 100; Marshall Beck, "Fear and Loathing in Latin America," *NACLA Report on the Americas* 38 (November–December 2004): 3.

36. Todd, "Raising the National Conscience," 126–127.

37. Douglas Farah, "U.S. Military Engagement in Latin America," in *Globalization,* ed. Bouvier, 150.

38. Adam Isaacson, Lisa Haugaard, and Joy Olson, "Creeping Militarization in the Americas," *NACLA Report on the Americas* 38 (November–December 2004): 4–7.

39. Washington Office on Latin America, "Aerial Spraying Fails to Reduce Coca Cultivation in Colombia," March 31, 2005, http://www.wola.org/ drug_policy/press_release_coca_cultivation_2004.htm (last visited May 25, 2005).

40. Executive Office of the President, Office of National Drug Control Policy, "The Price and Purity of Illicit Drugs: 1981 through the Second Quarter of 2003," November 2004, http://www.whitehousedrugpolicy.gov/ publications/price_purity/ (last visited May 25, 2005).

41. U.S. Gen. James Hill in Hayden, "Bolivia's Indian Revolt," 20.

42. "Bolivians Deal Blow to U.S. Andean Drug Policy," October 24, 2003, at http://stopthedrugwar.org/chronicle/308/bolivia.shtml (last visited May 27, 2005).

43. Irwin Stotzky, "Democracy and International Military Intervention: The Case of Haiti," in *Democracy and Human Rights in Latin America,* eds. Richard Hillman, John Peeler, and Elsa Cardozo Da Silva (Westport, Conn.: Praeger, 2002), 150.

44. Smith, *Talons,* 289.

45. Albright and Clinton cited in Longley, *Eagle's Shadow,* 323, 324.

46. Ibid., 324.

47. Pastor, *Exiting the Whirlpool,* 115.

48. Foley cited in Rafael Lorente, "Bush Administration Refuses Calls for Military Intervention in Haiti," *South Florida Sun Sentinel,* February 27, 2004.

49. "U.S. Plans Military Contingencies for Haiti Crisis," Europe Intelligence Wire, February 27, 2004.

50. Daniel Erikson, "Haiti After Aristide: Still on the Brink," *Current History,* February 2005, 87.

51. "Aristide: US Forced Me to Leave," BBC News World Edition, news.bbc.co.uk/2/hi/americas/3524273.stm (last visited November 26, 2004).

52. About 5 percent of Haitians were infected with HIV and three hundred thousand were living with AIDS. Erikson, "Haiti After Aristide," 83.

53. Bush in Bruni, "Bush Vows," A1.

54. Jorge Castañeda, "The Forgotten Relationship," *Foreign Affairs* 82 (May–June 2003): 67–81.

55. Marta Lagos, "The Image of the United States in Latin America, Latinobarómetro 1995–2004," presented at the Miami Herald's Americas Conference, September 30–October 1, 2004.

56. Rubén Rumbaut, "The Americans: Latin American and Caribbean Peoples in the United States," in *Perspectives,* eds. Gutmann et al., 91.

57. D'Vera Cohn, "Hispanic Growth Surge Fueled by Births in U.S.," *Washington Post,* June 9, 2005, A01.

58. González, *Harvest of Empire,* 215.

59. Rodolfo de la Garza, introduction to *Latinos and U.S. Foreign Policy: Representing the 'Homeland'?* eds. de la Garza and Harry Panchon (Lanham, Md.: Rowman & Littlefield, 2000), 5.

60. Samuel Huntington, "The Hispanic Challenge," *Foreign Policy* (March–April 2004).

61. Russell Pearce, Arizona state representative, cited in Marc Cooper, "High Noon on the Border," *The Nation,* June 6, 2005, 23–24.

62. Lorey, *U.S.-Mexican Border,* 164; González, *Harvest of Empire,* 197.

63. Cohn, "Hispanic Growth."

64. González, *Harvest of Empire,* 195.

65. Cooper, "High Noon on the Border," 21, 22. For different (if older) numbers, see also Sarah Garland, "U.S.-Mexico: Unmanned Aircraft to Patrol Border," *NACLA Report on the Americas* 37 (May–June 2004): 5.

66. González, *Harvest of Empire,* 198.

67. Coerver and Hall, *Tangled Destinies,* 212.

68. Rafael Fernández de Castro and Carlos Rosales, "Migration Issues: Raising the Stakes in U.S.–Latin American Relations," in *Future,* ed. Domínguez, 239.

69. Task Force on Remittances, *All in the Family: Latin America's Most Important Financial Flow* (Washington, D.C.: Inter-American Dialogue, 2004).

70. Fernández de Castro and Rosales, "Migration Issues," 251.

71. Huntington, "Hispanic Challenge"; González, *Harvest of Empire,* 147.

72. Leon Fink, *The Maya of Morgantown: Work and Community in the*

Nuevo New South (Chapel Hill: University of North Carolina Press, 2003); González, *Harvest of Empire,* 146.

73. González, *Harvest of Empire,* 116.

74. Wayne Smith, "Bush and Cuba: Still the Full Moon," *NACLA Report on the Americas* 38 (September–October 2004), 4–5.

Conclusion

1. Black, *Good Neighbor,* 31–32.

2. Cynthia Enloe, *Bananas, Beaches and Bases: Making Feminist Sense of International Politics* (Berkeley: University of California Press, 2000), 127–132; Laura T. Raynolds, "The Global Banana Trade," in *Banana Wars: Power, Production, and History in the Americas,* ed. Steve Striffler and Mark Moberg (Durham, N.C.: Duke University Press, 2003), 39.

3. David Meyer, "What's Eating Latin America?" *Foreign Policy* 135 (March–April 2003): 89–90.

4. Mark Pendergrast, *For God, Country and Coca-Cola: The Definitive History of the World's Most Popular Soft Drink* (London: Orion Business Books, 2000); Frederick Allen, *Secret Formula: How Brilliant Marketing and Relentless Salesmanship Made Coca-Cola the Best-Known Product in the World* (New York: Harper Collins, 1994); S. Bayley, *Coke: Designing a World Brand* (London: Conran Foundation, 1986); Henry Frundt, *Refreshing Pauses: Coca-Cola and Human Rights in Guatemala* (New York: Praeger, 1987).

5. Grupo Continental, "Soft Drink Industry," http://www.contal.com/our_business05.html (last visited January 10, 2005); Niall Ferguson, *Colossus: The Price of America's Empire* (New York: Penguin, 2004), 19.

6. Domínguez, ed., *Future,* 7.

7. E. J. Kahn Jr., *The Big Drink: The Story of Coca-Cola* (New York: Random House, 1960), 4.

8. Longley, *Eagle's Shadow,* 280.

9. Gutmann, "Taco Bell," 405.

INDEX

197

ABOUT THE AUTHOR

Alan McPherson is originally from Montreal, Canada, and obtained his Ph.D. at the University of North Carolina at Chapel Hill in 2001. He is associate professor of history at Howard University, where he specializes in U.S. foreign relations. He is the author of *Yankee No! Anti-Americanism in U.S.–Latin American Relations* (Harvard Press, 2003), named an Outstanding Academic Title by *Choice* magazine and winner of the A. B. Thomas book award from the Southeastern Council on Latin American Studies. He is also editor of *Anti-Americanism in Latin America and the Caribbean* (Berghahn Press, 2006). His articles have appeared in *The Americas, The Latin American Research Review,* and *Diplomatic History.* He lives in Washington, D.C.